D0150204

Crisis in the Commons
# THE ALASKA SOLUTION

# CRISIS IN THE COMMONS

## The Alaska Solution

WALTER J. HICKEL

**ICS PRESS**

INSTITUTE FOR CONTEMPORARY STUDIES
OAKLAND, CALIFORNIA

ALASKA PACIFIC UNIVERSITY
ANCHORAGE, ALASKA

This book is a publication of the Institute for Contemporary Studies, a nonpartisan,
nonprofit, public policy research organization. The analyses, conclusions, and opinions expressed in ICS Press publications are those of the authors and not necessarily
those of the institute or of its officers, its directors, or others associated with, or funding, its work.

Inquiries, book orders, and catalog requests should be addressed to ICS Press, 1611
Telegraph Avenue, Suite 406, Oakland, California, 94612. (510) 238-5010. Fax
(510) 238-8440. To order, call toll-free (800) 326-0263.

Crisis in the Commons: THE ALASKA SOLUTION is set in 11 point Goudy type by
Rohani Design.

Library of Congress Cataloging-in-Publication Data

Hickel, Walter J., 1919–
    Crisis in the commons : the Alaska solution / Walter J. Hickel.
        p. cm.
    Includes bibliographical references and index.
        ISBN 1-55815-521-X (pbk. : alk. paper)
        1. Commons—Alaska. 2. Natural resources, Communal—Alaska.
    I. Title.
    HD1289.U62 A44 2002

                                                          2002003322

# Dedication

*This book is dedicated to my wife Ermalee, our six sons, their wives, children, and grandchildren. It is also dedicated to the thousands of Alaskans who have helped pioneer the creation of our Owner State; and for people around the world looking for hope.*

# Acknowledgements

I would like to thank those who helped make this book possible: writer/researchers Charles Wohlforth, Malcolm Roberts, and Tom Kizzia; Mead Treadwell, the managing director of the Institute of the North; and Yvonne Lindblom, my secretary for 37 years. A special thanks to Bob Hawkins, the president of the Institute for Contemporary Studies, Perenna Fleming, ICS executive publisher, and editor Kathleen Erickson, for their enthusiasm for this book and its message.

# Contents

**PART FIVE: THE FUTURE**

**TABLES AND MAPS**

# Note from the Publisher

The implications of September 11th are far reaching and force a number of important questions about human development on the table of public discussion. Long before September 11th, increasing numbers of intrastate conflicts as well as regional conflicts, such as those besetting the great lakes region of Africa, suggested that all was not well in developing countries. Increasing numbers of individuals and groups now feel that conflict is the only way to remedy problems facing their societies. A recent study by the British Department of Foreign and International Development found that "pathologies of the state" account for a good deal of the conflict in today's world. In other words, a great deal of conflict is constitutional: we have built institutions that create pathology rather than wealth.

This raises the question of how do we create productive forms of human association to produce social, political, and economic wealth? This is a very practical question. For example, does the United States government, especially the U.S. Department of State and its Agency for International Development, know how to spend the estimated three hundred million dollars allocated to Afghanistan in ways that significantly reduce the likelihood of a repeat performance in ten years? Do these agencies know how to build deeply rooted democracies rather than democratic caricatures? Or will they support more grafting of western notions of democracy on Afghanistan rather than building on the foundations of hundreds of common resource-governing structures that have operated for thousands of years?

These are not idle questions, given the failures of western aid to advance human welfare and reduce poverty around the world. *Crisis in the Commons: The Alaska Solution* provides us with alternatives to the sterile choices between government and market. It lays out a theory of governing the commons that makes room for both governance and markets. Nor is this just theory. Through its founding and constitution Governor Hickel shows how Alaska, in its fight for statehood, went through a deep constitutional discussion to come up with new ways of governing its common resources. As one reads the history of the struggle for statehood by Governor Hickel, one can see this same political drama being played out in most developing countries around the world today.

One can ask a rather simple question to see the importance of what Governor Hickel is recommending. How would citizens have benefited in oil rich states in the Middle East if those resources had been treated as a common resource? Would the level of both individual and community wealth be higher? *The Alaska Solution* is the solution of choice of many communities around the world, going back hundreds of years. What Hickel has helped develop in Alaska, Elinor Ostrom and her colleagues at the Workshop in Political Theory and Policy have documented on irrigation systems in Nepal, fisheries governing in Turkey, and forestry governance in Uganda. In fact, common resource governance, through self-governing institutions, may well be the natural tendency of communities, suggesting that the "modern" forms of governance are not natural.

As Hickel wisely points out, the Owner State must also be the enabling state, creating the opportunities and assisting local citizens and community to govern their commons for the benefit of their communities. I would answer in the negative the question of whether our State Department and aid agency know what to do in Afghanistan. The probabilities are high that they will try to apply the same old remedies, with the same depressing results, and then put the blame squarely on the backs of the Afghans. I would also recommend to them that they read Governor Hickel's book, to provide them with the key ideas on which to build a new society. The Governor's ideas are fresh, and their greatest attribute is: they work.

— Robert Hawkins, Jr., President and CEO
Institute for Contemporary Studies

# PART ONE

## Introduction
## to the Commons

# 1

# The Alaska Solution

**N**ot many people are fortunate enough to attend at the birth of a great idea. In the decade of the 1950s, in a new land called Alaska, there were many believers that anything was possible, and the future was full of hope. Around us lay a vast realm of natural beauty and extraordinary wealth in oil, gas, fish, timber, and minerals. Within us lay a shared spirit to explore and build, to invent a great civilization, and to do it together, as one people.

The new idea was this: we, the people of the world, own most of this planet in common. Our future depends on learning to use and develop this *commons* for the good of the total, and not just for the few. Here in the Far North we built a new state based on that concept. It's the only place like it. The Alaskan people, through our state government, won ownership of much of our land and our natural resources. Using neither classic capitalism nor socialism, we have developed a new way to prosperity, based on common ownership and rooted in constitutional democracy. Since then, after more than forty years of striving, stumbling, and regaining our balance, falling flat and standing tall, this new way is now a remarkable success. Alaska today is a diamond, a brilliant star, a state with an outstanding quality of life, celebrating a glorious natural environment and a robust, healthy economy. We are ready now to share what we have learned with the world.

We Alaskans over this period have often disagreed among ourselves. We have fought over our personal visions, ambitions, and interests, but our land came first. It was so much bigger than any one

3

person, and we knew it could do anything for us if only we could win the right to use it. This was the necessity and the opportunity that welded us into one people and brought a new kind of state into the world, a state powered, democratically, by its commonly owned natural resources.

If you or I were to travel the world's great, open resource regions, too often we would see poor people living on rich land, and many of these lands are commons. They include immense swaths of Africa and Asia, the Middle East, the Arctic, the Antarctic, vast lands in Canada and the rest of the Americas. The United States of America owns 600 million acres of publicly owned lands and 3.5 billion acres of commonly owned continental shelf. In a larger sense, all of us own the seas in common. We own the air and space. If we could learn to use these God-given resources productively for the benefit of all—not just for one leader, one family, one business, or a handful of corporations—the world would stand today on the threshold of wealth and social advancement we cannot yet imagine. There would be no legitimate reason for poverty.

*There is no legitimate reason for poverty.*

It is in this context that America should address its role in determining the management of more than 217 million acres of land in Alaska owned by all Americans. For instance, at this writing, the U.S. Congress is deciding whether to allow oil and gas exploration on the Coastal Plain of the Arctic National Wildlife Refuge (ANWR) on Alaska's North Slope. Chapter 12 is dedicated to an in-depth look at ANWR in the context of larger energy and environmental issues, to help the American people understand their choices and obligations as owners of the commons in Alaska.

In 1952, I put down my hammer and took off my carpenter's overalls to make the first of dozens of trips to Washington, D.C., to fight for Alaska to receive a sufficient land entitlement. Seventeen years later, after our state was a magnificent success, I traveled to Washington again, this time as Secretary of the Interior under President Richard Nixon. The Alaskan people elected me governor twice, with two decades separating my terms. When not in public office, my battles continued to be those facing Alaska—for control of our land, for Alaska Native land claims, for a pipeline to carry our oil, for another to carry our gas, for a national and global environmental awakening, and for cooperation among the Arctic regions of the world.

This book is the biography of an idea. The bold thinking and actions of many people in Alaska can guide and change other parts of the world that have been left out of the global economy and face poverty, hunger, and hopelessness. The Alaska approach may become the solution for many others to learn to use and share the commons, far beyond Alaska.

We've proven here that a local, democratic government can harness the natural resources it owns and the efficiency of the private sector to provide its citizens opportunity and an enviable quality of life. This form of government might aptly be called an Owner State, for the majority of Alaska's lands and resources are owned by the people through two remarkable documents—our State Constitution and the Alaska Statehood Act.

Since these documents were created and adopted, Alaskans, through trial and error, have learned how to make an Owner State work for the benefit of the people. Similar to underdeveloped countries, Alaska appeared at birth too poor to sustain the basic services expected of self-government. Our message to our critics in Congress was that if they would give us a sufficient land entitlement and the subsurface minerals beneath those lands, we would not only support ourselves but contribute to the economic health of the nation. Congress eventually agreed and signed a Compact overwhelmingly approved by our people at the ballot box, both in our relatively small urban centers and in our even smaller rural villages.

In that Compact, Alaska won the right to select a land grant the size of California, comprising nearly one third of Alaska's land mass. We chose a desolate section of land, north of the Brooks Range, and bordering the Beaufort Sea. There, on flat, cold, unpopulated acreage, we discovered the largest oil reservoir in the history of North America. We confounded our detractors by developing that oil in a fashion that protected the resident wildlife and the natural environment, as no other oil field that has been developed before or since. In the process, we transformed our stepchild of a territory into a robust, healthy new state able to meet our needs, without levying state income taxes on our citizens.

This is the Alaska solution—a citizen-controlled democracy governing and managing the commons for the good of all. It's a model that, on a smaller scale, has been used in parts of the South 48, where innovators have discovered how to care for and draw upon the commons to benefit their communities. But it is not necessarily an easy concept to grasp, and there are pitfalls that await the creators and shapers of an Owner State. It can easily lose its bearings. This book, therefore, describes our challenges as the owners of our Owner State. It reports both the remarkable victories we've enjoyed and the lessons we have learned.

First, local people must acquire constitutional control of the local commons—resources managed from afar, by a colonial or distant master, are usually mismanaged and exploited for the interests of those far away. The people who live on the commons have the knowledge and the interest in using their pieces of the earth responsibly and sustainably for the long term. Without doubt, it takes a struggle to win local control, but with the end of the era of colonialism and the disintegration of the Soviet Union, it appears to be possible worldwide. We must take advantage of this unique moment to help local peoples win control of the world's resources close to them.

Second, the Owner State works best as a constitutional democracy. The state acts as the custodian of the commons on the people's behalf. It must have both a strong, accountable leader and citizens who are involved and informed. The culture must inspire each citizen to take responsibility. In Alaska, the governor works for the owners—here, the public—and while on the job he or she has both the authority and the obligation to manage the land and its resources. It's the responsibility of the citizens to decide if their leader is doing his job and, if not, speak up and, if necessary, vote him out. They, and their knowledge about how their assets are performing, are the essential check on his power or weakness.

Next, the private sector plays a crucial role. No government can match the initiative and efficiency of the free market system. The Owner State uses the incentives of the market to develop the wealth of the commons. The role of the state is to decide resource policies, to provide access and infrastructure, and to get things started. On a competitive basis, private industry leases the right to extract the common resources and employs the citizens to do the work. The state then uses the revenues it receives from the development of its resources, instead of taxation, to meet common needs and enhance the lives of the people it serves. In fact, most taxes can be eliminated.

A successful Owner State must then grapple with the issue of the wealth it creates. Some oil provinces, including Alberta, Canada, and Alaska, have sometimes dispersed their surpluses by giving away some of their land and resources or the money those resources earned. In Alaska's case, this policy reflected a basic misunderstanding of our carefully crafted Statehood Compact. The U.S. Congress deeded to us our mineral-rich lands so that our state government could afford to provide basic services. The intent was not to generate cash payments to the people. Government-generated payments or dividends create an insatiable appetite, and the intoxicated electorate will ignore the basic needs of their communities, including the vital ongoing maintenance of the economic and social infrastructure. An Owner State demands that its citizens "seek not what your country can do for you . . . ." and understand their obligations of ownership. If these obligations are ignored, and everyone focuses solely on what's best for him, the commons will lie fallow or be abused.

Historically, the alternative strategy for Alaska was to dispose of the commons from the start, which was the traditional pattern of growth of the United States. We could have opened up the commons and let the first to arrive grab their share, putting it to use or selling it off to the highest bidder. Advocates of that Wild West approach did not understand the North. Unlike the South 48, most of Alaska is designed differently. In the northern half of the state, an area larger than Texas, the growing season can be as short as 45 days. Permafrost eliminates trees in vast areas or allows only shallow-rooted, scrub growth, muskeg, and tundra. Living off the land involves hunting and fishing rather than planting and harvesting. And Alaska's wild game population, contemporary images notwithstanding, can be sparse in some seasons and nearly impossible to find in many areas of the state.

Alaska was designed by the hand of God to *be* commons. Therefore, only the steady hands of custodian/owners can successfully manage the Alaska commons. And those authentic owners must be the local people, because they suffer if policies go wrong, and they benefit if they work. To be successful, citizens must be inspired with a unifying vision, because if fragmented into individual or regional interest groups, they, too, can become exploiters, each ravaging the commons to get his share.

Does this mean there is no place for private property? Not at all. Many Alaskans, including myself, have made good livings developing private property. But some parts of the earth don't lend themselves to deeds of trust and property lines—for instance, the Arctic and the oceans. We must learn to care for these commons collectively—as a common responsibility and as a common source of wealth, quality of life, and the wonders of nature. We need commitment as citizens that goes beyond "enlightened self interest" to "enlightened community interest."

There is urgency to this discussion and this model for the world. Wherever we go worldwide, these are the times for the discovery of new and better ways. In caring for the earth, we know what it looks like when we mishandle natural resources. We understand the damage when raw sewage or spilled crude oil chokes beaches and clutters stream banks. We have seen fished-out waters, polluted air, damaged wildlife habitats, and eroded hillsides. We know what happens when no one cares. We've seen grinding poverty, hopelessness, and political turmoil that result when colonial powers or homegrown despots plunder a land of its wealth and pocket the profits.

In Alaska, we have experienced the helplessness of having our hopes dashed and our opportunities strangled as distant forces have locked up our economic lives. We've seen our raw materials for life and progress set aside, either as someone's playground or as a shield for powerful interests from their competition. After all the mistakes mankind has made, we need to look for a better way.

The Owner State we have created in Alaska works, and the philosophy behind it has the potential to solve these problems—to be that better way. We are far from perfect, and we do not presume to tell any country how to set its course or use its resources. What we offer is our solution that others may use to safeguard their own lands and resources, to solve their own problems, and to build an economy that benefits all.

The idea was born 50 years ago. It's still young, but it is thriving here in our corner of the North. And we're eager to share what we've learned with the world.

# PART TWO

## Crisis in
## the Commons

# 2

# Assault on the Commons

Steve Shropshire phoned me at the governor's Anchorage office early on the morning of October 26, 1994. He had just seen the news of one of the largest oil spills in history; an oil pipeline had ruptured in the northern Russian republic of Komi. Steve was Executive Director of the Northern Forum, of which Komi was a member, and I was Secretary General. The Forum, a United Nations chartered nongovernmental organization, links regional leaders around the top of the globe. Through four years of meetings and other exchanges, we had become colleagues and friends with Komi's president and the governor of the Nenets Okrug, a northern coastal subdivision of Komi downstream from the oil spill on the great Pechora River. I told Steve to contact them immediately and to offer our help.

Officials from the U.S. State Department also called my office asking for information. But it wasn't easy to discover what was going on, as Komi lies on the other side of the world from Alaska. Steve used the Northern Forum's Russian office in Yakutsk to relay our message, and the next day he put letters in my hand from Komi and Nenets leaders describing the situation and asking for our help. A letter from the president of the Komi Republic pleaded with us for equipment to clean up oil from the broken pipeline that had fouled lakes, streams, swamps, and the Pechora River drainage, on which thousands of Arctic people depend. Estimates of the spill ranged up to eight times the size of Alaska's *Exxon Valdez* disaster in 1989, five years earlier.

Alaska knew a lot about oil, and how to clean it up. Our friends in Komi knew that. Alaska's development of the Prudhoe Bay oil fields was a model for Arctic development. Much of the debate over the construction of the Alaska Pipeline in the early 1970s concerned oil spill prevention and response. The completed system had been free of environmental harm for nearly two decades. Then the tanker *Exxon Valdez* hit the rocks in 1989, and Alaska mounted the largest environmental cleanup in world history. In the process, we learned more about removing oil from the northern environment than anyone else on earth. As soon as Steve briefed me on the situation in Komi, I decided to visit the spill, and we planned out how to put the trip together. We wanted to help our Arctic colleagues cope with the emerging catastrophe.

*Moscow was denying it. Washington, D.C., was accepting it. And we, as Alaskans, couldn't believe it.*

Vice-President Al Gore was in charge of Washington's handling of the emergency. I soon found myself in a heated argument with him on the phone, and he told me not to go. His information, flowing to Washington from Moscow, suggested that the situation wasn't as bad as the media was making out. Besides, they told him, nothing could be done until spring. I also received word from those same higher levels in Russia downplaying the crisis, but the regional authorities—who were on the ground—were telling me a different and disturbing story. We in Alaska understood that winter, not spring, is the best time to deal with an oil spill, because when the ground is frozen hard crude oil can be more easily contained. I ended the conversation, "Mr. Vice-President, I'm going. I'll call you when I get back."

Gore was in a tough position. He couldn't force aid on the Russians when they were refusing it, although he must have sensed the situation was worse than they were admitting. Helping Russian oil development had been a key part of U.S. policy—the fastest way to help the new Russia gain solvency in world financial markets. The spill was an embarrassment. Gore and President Bill Clinton may have feared that if the world learned the true nature and extent of the spill, Russian President Boris Yeltsin might be toppled by his opponents in the Duma, the Russian parliament. I saw it differently. Local authorities, bypassing Moscow, had requested our assistance. Our mission presented an opportunity to help our friends and the

Arctic environment on a region-to-region basis. Perhaps seeing this advantage, Gore changed his mind and, in a second conversation, offered diplomatic resources to help clear my way to Komi.

The conflicting reports and lack of clear information was no surprise to me. As U.S. Secretary of the Interior, I had discovered how to deal with the 1969 Santa Barbara oil spill only after reaching the scene. When elected governor of Alaska for the second time, in 1990, I inherited the lingering *Exxon Valdez* oil spill cleanup and had to cut through a tangle of agencies and interests to resolve outstanding litigation and restore Prince William Sound.

The information coming from Komi was chaotic. Confusion and high emotions spread from oil spills as fast as crude on water, and this was no exception. While Moscow played it down, officials closest to the disaster called it a "developing catastrophe," blown out of control by rains that had breached dams of spilled oil. The international press reported a clampdown on information, and wildly diverging assessments of the size of the spill ranged from 4–84 million gallons. Part of the confusion arose from the fact that the spill was not a discrete incident but was a sudden worsening of a chronic problem. We were to learn later that oil had been leaking from the Komi pipeline for months.

It was the autumn of 1994, three years after the fall of the Soviet Union, and the first instinct of the Russians remained to hide the mess, just as their Soviet predecessors had attempted to cover up the Chernobyl disaster. But the problem of denial, I believed, wasn't only a hangover from communism. It was simply the way governments act when they are too far from their people. For Moscow bureaucrats, the easiest way to deal with an expensive environmental mess was to pretend it didn't exist.

Steve Shropshire was struggling with a more immediate problem: no airplane. The Governor of Alaska has no airplane, and although I had the prestigious title of Secretary General, the Northern Forum lacked a budget for a trip like this. As he called around Anchorage, he couldn't find an aircraft capable of a swift journey half way around the globe. Finally, at the end of the workday, John Ellsworth of Alaska Interstate Construction, an oil field service company, called from the airport. He had just arrived from Viet Nam on his way to

Seattle in his company's Westwind II executive jet. "I heard the governor needs my plane," he said. "Where does he want to go, and when does he want to leave?"

Next, Steve worked through the night on the visas and flight clearances to cross Russia and to land for refueling along the way, and to arrange for a required Russian navigator. From Alaska, we would fly west across the International Dateline, then continue west across all of Asia, beyond China, with our destination a remote region on the longitude of Tehran, Iran, and the latitude of Reykjavik, Iceland. By 4 A.M., he had received the clearances. Our team would include six: Bill Allen, whose company, VECO, led the *Exxon Valdez* oil spill cleanup, and two other Alaskan oil spill cleanup executives, a spill response expert from the Alaska Department of Environmental Conservation, Steve, and myself. Steve and I would handle the diplomacy, work to get the facts on the spill out to the world, and assemble the information needed to rally financial assistance. Alan Walker, director of Alaska's spill response team, had the technical knowledge to evaluate the spill and its impacts. The executives contributed the cleanup know-how, as well as the desire to sell their Alaskan company services in Russia.

The Vice-President's office wanted us to take one more person: Ray Kreig, an Alaskan member of a Central Intelligence Agency environmental team called Medea. I refused. The Russian officials we were visiting were friends, as a result of relationships developed over several years. They were asking for help, and that was why we were going. The newly formed team of intelligence personnel and con- sulting scientists was chartered to help the environment, but our hosts would interpret Kreig's presence as spying and a betrayal of our friendship. Besides, the plane only had room for six.

Kreig showed up at my front door. He was an engineer and Arctic geotechnical expert based in Anchorage. He didn't want to come inside, so, like characters in a spy novel, we talked while walking around in the October cold outside, down my driveway, among the birch and spruce trees around my home, and along Anchorage's Coastal Trail. I didn't plan to give in, no matter how far we walked. Kreig briefed me on what the CIA knew about the spill. We agreed that his team could debrief us on our return.

In fact, there was so little room on the plane that a supply of fruit and water we carried fit only in the head and had to be moved for anyone to use the toilet. During the 68-hour trip, crossing 12 time zones and back again, we spent about half that time in this small aircraft, with only six hours of sleep while on the ground.

Four years earlier, in September 1990, when outgoing Alaska Governor Steve Cowper convened the world's Arctic leaders in Anchorage, we began talking about founding the Northern Forum. The opportunity presented itself for Alaska to share its experience of managing the commons with our neighbors around the top of the globe and to learn from them. Now, we would get to do so in a crisis situation.

## ONE HUGE MESS

We stopped for clearance and fuel as we flew across the Russian Far East and Arctic regions. At each stop, our hosts greeted us like returning family—perhaps distant cousins—on our way to help another branch of the family. In Kamchatka, Russia's extreme eastern peninsula, the president served us a feast, with toasts to our work. When a storm forced us to divert from Magadan to Yakutsk, President Mikhail Nikolayev also feted us, and provided a substitute Russian navigator for the man we had planned to pick up in Magadan.

These generous Russians made us feel at home. It was no surprise to me. In the early 1940s, my first Russian friends were the pilots and mechanics who regularly stopped in Anchorage on their way home to Russia with planes built in the U.S. as part of the Lend Lease Program. These aircraft and some of their crews were headed to fight Hitler on the eastern front. As an aircraft inspector at Ft. Richardson (now Elmendorf Air Force Base), I enjoyed their wit and hearty laughter. They were real people locked in a fight for survival, as were we all.

After the war, Alaska's next-door neighbors to the west intrigued many of us. Not subscribing to the fears of the anti-Communist era, I believed that people-to-people initiatives were needed, approaching the Russians from the frontier or Arctic side instead of the more jaded European side. We have much in common—our geography, our history, and part of our cultural and religious heritage. In the late

1940s, several of us talked and dreamed about a friendship delegation from Alaska crossing the Bering Strait and taking along a Catholic priest and other dignitaries. We were 40 years too early. FBI Director J. Edgar Hoover shut down our border with Russia in 1950, creating an Ice Curtain that proved more impenetrable than the Iron Curtain. But I continued to read and think about the eastern regions, what we used to call Siberia. The region we now know as the Russian Far East never seemed half a world away to me, as it did to many who live in the rest of the United States. The Russian coast was always within sight of Alaska's St. Lawrence Island. We could see each other, even if we couldn't communicate.

In 1988, the Ice Curtain between Alaska and the Russian Far East began to melt. A joyful planeload of emissaries from Nome, Alaska—the sort of flight we had hoped for in the 1940s—landed on the other side of the Bering Strait in Providenya. This was more than the "Friendship Flight" it was billed to be. I will never forget the scene as Alaskan families were reunited with their Russian cousins after decades of separation. Native Alaskans from our side of the border conversed in their own languages with Natives from the other side. The fall of the Berlin Wall the next year raised our hopes even higher. But during frequent trips to Moscow in the early 1990s, we watched with concern when the gray, somber pallor of Soviet culture was not brightening as rapidly as we expected.

For the Russian Arctic and Far East, too little had changed, and we in Alaska readily identified with many of their problems. Before we gained statehood, we had witnessed how our resources could be stolen when distant federal authorities were in league with unethical, private businessmen. Now the same pattern was developing in Russia. I warned my Russian friends to beware of those from the West who preach against all government, and I stressed that control of natural resources under regional democracies was their best hope. But, too often, individual Russians chose to play the game, not change it. The abuses of the old communist system, including old boy networks and under-the-table deals, became features of the newer, so-called market economy. Those willing to pervert the public interest kept winning, only now with higher stakes. Organized crime enterprises were among the most successful. A cynical public shrugged at seeing the old become the new. With the Komi oil spill, these problems came to a head in one huge, symbolic mess.

When our jet arrived in the Komi capital of Syktyvkar, the mood bore little resemblance to the warm cordiality we had encountered on our journey across the wide expanse of Russia. A frenzied crowd of international journalists swarmed us at the airport, desperate to find out what was going on in a confused situation. Since we had just arrived, we had nothing new to tell them.

The scene went from frustrating to surreal when we met with Komi President Yuri Spiridonov. His letter of a few days before described a "dire" situation and asked for emergency aid, drawing us there from the other side of the world. But now, Spiridonov behaved as if he didn't have a problem. It seemed the emergency was over, and the oil mostly cleaned up. He wanted to know why we had come—what exactly was the purpose of our visit?

*For Moscow bureaucrats, the easiest way to deal with an expensive environmental mess was to pretend it didn't exist.*

We sat in the president's wood paneled conference room, plied with coffee and cookies, and listened to a parade of bureaucrats present upbeat reports. They assured us the oil spill had been grossly exaggerated. I was surprised when Spiridonov asked us for money. He emphasized that the area needed investment in its infrastructure. This was obviously true, but one had to wonder why a region exporting millions of barrels of oil didn't have enough cash to patch a leaky pipeline. As for this spill, it was old news as far as our hosts were concerned.

I guessed that Spiridonov was saying only what he was allowed to say. Years later, speaking at a Northern Forum assembly of governors, he thanked us graciously and emotionally for our intervention. But when we arrived in Komi, Spiridonov reflected the official line from Moscow. Cleaning up an oil spill costs a lot of money. Moscow's goal was to extract the resources of this far-away region as cheaply as possible. The bureaucrats in the Kremlin had no intention of paying for the cost of cleaning up the environmental damage.

As our meeting dragged on, we insisted on an overflight of the spill area. Since Spiridonov had invited us across the world, he couldn't very well refuse. He assigned Vice-President Alexander Mikhailovich Okatov to take us by helicopter from the town of Usinsk the following day.

We flew our borrowed jet 400 miles north to Usinsk, ground zero for the spill, and were mobbed again by the international media, this time with even greater ferocity. They had been allowed this far but had been kept from seeing the spill. They didn't believe the official line, but couldn't get even the most basic information about the size of the spill or what was being done. The frustration in the air was palpable. Now I bore the brunt of that frustration as some 20 reporters and cameramen crowded around me and demanded to know why I was there, what I knew about the spill, and what I would do to solve the problem. I didn't know much yet, and I didn't want to give answers that would embarrass my hosts, so my comments were noncommittal—perhaps much like the noncommittal answers the Russians had been giving. The less I said, the angrier the reporters became. Finally, a Finnish reporter became so aggressive, my temper flared. Having been a Golden Gloves boxer as a youth has its downside. Fearing I would deck the guy, another journalist held me back.

The chaos of the situation was written in the faces of the people in Usinsk. The spill was much worse than anything they had dealt with before, yet at the same time the onslaught of world media attention added to their stress and confusion. Vice-President Okatov and a Russian general escorted us on a helicopter tour of the spill area. Okatov's eyes told of his dismay over the devastation, even as his words downplayed it. Nor could the helicopter's circuitous route hide the mess. A fresh snow conspired to cover up pools of congealed oil we would later learn were the size of football fields. But nothing could fully conceal a catastrophe of this magnitude. The scene looked like a war zone. Smoke from burning oil rose in columns into the sky—workers had scooped globs of crude into barrels to burn. In some places, the pipeline lay exposed and unsupported on the ground. Where it crossed a river, it sagged like a rope. As we flew over smooth, snow-covered tundra, we could see steaming black oil boiling up through the snow and ice—the broken pipeline was still pumping oil!

The general landscape reminded me of interior Alaska, where scrubby spruce and occasional groves of upland trees break broad, desolate plains of treeless ground. Under snow, the Pechora River valley was smooth and white, but our party of Alaskans recognized this was largely muskeg, the northern wetland of hummocks, damp ground, and standing water. The hard winter freeze would allow crews to take in equipment to remove the spilled crude oil far easier here than summer's mud and water, but our hosts kept talking about waiting for spring to start the cleanup.

At our insistence, the helicopter landed near a bridge on a small tributary to the Pechora River. Our hosts tried to contain our group, but Alan Walker, head of our State of Alaska spill response division, was determined to get a sample of the oil. With a sample, we could chemically "fingerprint" the oil in our lab in Alaska. One of our major worries was that the oil would flow downriver, north into the Arctic Ocean. With a chemical fingerprint, we would be able to prove whether or not any oil found in the ocean came from Komi. Our hosts hadn't planned on providing such a souvenir, but as I engaged the General in lively conversation to divert his attention, Alan scurried down under the bridge. Single-mindedly ignoring the Russians, Alan scooped up a sample of thick, foul-smelling crude and returned.

Nearby we saw the only evidence of an ongoing cleanup we encountered that day. A small bulldozer had pushed up a dike of earth and tundra as a dam to contain a pool of leaking oil. One Russian cleanup technique was to dam up the oil and set it on fire. As the oil grew deeper, the bulldozer operator would simply push the dam higher to contain it. Not surprisingly, dams like this one all along the pipeline had burst when filled by heavy rains. At the same time, increased internal pressure from the new, larger volumes of oil being added to the corroded sieve of a pipeline forced larger leaks. Oil spread on the tundra and into the wetlands and rivers. Yet there was little sense of urgency here. Indeed, the bulldozer operator had a hut where he was living near this source of steady employment. No one was working today. The bulldozer operator was in his hut.

As the helicopter took off, we flew over the Pechora River, a broad, north-flowing lifeline for the region. We could see a sheen of oil in the water and a line of oil on the bank. The spill was horrendous—far worse than we had imagined. Yet while it surely was a disaster, it clearly was no accident. Instead, this devastation was the predictable result of a policy of neglect, expedience, and decisions made in ignorance as far away as Washington, D.C. The Clinton Administration was pushing hard to increase Russian oil production without understanding the reality of the conditions or the environmental impact. We saw black bathtub rings on the higher banks of the rivers and riverbank trees. Locals told us these stains were the high-water marks of the spring floods. The load of crude oil on top of the water painted the shore each year. Apparently, large oil spills were standard operating procedure here.

In Komi, a distant bureaucracy and multinational oil companies had chosen to use a pipeline they knew was riddled with holes, for the simple reason that it was cheaper in the short run than maintaining the line. At the same time, the local people who depended on this Arctic commons for hunting, fishing, grazing, and gathering saw their birthright being wasted and destroyed. They were powerless to prevent a spill and lacked the resources or authority to clean up the mess.

This state of affairs drew no world attention until Russian and western oil companies brought on new production and tried to force additional oil through the same failing pipeline. Predictably, the increased pressure made the chronic spills much worse. And as the disaster was unfolding, these oil companies knew of the environmental damage and did nothing to stop it. In Usinsk, an environmental official saw the pipeline leaking badly on August 23, 1994. Within the next two days, he demanded that the eight oil companies using the pipeline meet him at the town hall where he asked them to shut it down. They refused.[1] The evidence shows a joint venture involving Conoco began feeding additional oil into the line September 2, *after* the disaster was already evident.[2] Still, the devastation remained unknown to the outside world for another seven weeks, when, on October 25, *The New York Times* finally broke news of the spill, after being tipped off by the U.S. Department of Energy.[3] As we stood there in the middle of the mess on November 2, oil was still flowing through the pipeline and out onto the ground.

From Usinsk we flew north, across the Arctic Circle, to Naryan Mar, capital of the Nenets Okrug, an autonomous region of the Komi Republic downstream on the Pechora River. Here, people who lived from the land viewed the spill with terror. Some already were suffering because of the pollution of their fishing grounds. Here, there was no attempt to hide the danger. Governor Yuri Komarovsky's pleas from across the world had brought us to Nenets, and now, amid great hospitality, he and his people laid out their fears with moving openness.

At this local level, the people and their leaders, including dynamic young Governor Komarovsky, cared about the environment and refused to follow the Moscow line to downplay the disaster. These were the people who should be controlling the area's resources, but instead they were powerless to stop the devastation that would flow in the spring melt if nothing was done about the spill over the winter. Before we left, one of the locals slipped a videocassette to a member of our team. It showed the extent of the spill before the snows had covered the oil. Determined to carry their message, we pledged to get the tape to the outside world.

The remainder of the trip was uneventful until our last stop, Magadan, the former Gulag capital of the Russian Far East. There, our plane was detained for more than six hours and repeatedly searched. We were all nervous. Was it the videotape they were looking for? Magadan Governor Victor Grigovievich Mikhailov came to the airport to intercede with the authorities on our behalf, but after we taxied the plane to the runway and were ready to take off, we were recalled again for another search. Dave Thomas, of Alaska Interstate Construction, the firm that owned the plane, went to an office with Alan Walker, where the official in charge of airport security said we were free to go at any time—but no one would be able take off safely until the snow was cleared from the runway. Out the window, they could see the runway didn't have a flake of snow on it. Thomas asked how much it would cost to bring in some snow removal equipment, pulling hundreds from his billfold. After a certain number of bills had landed on his desk, the official glanced outside and announced that the runway was now cleared of snow.

## TRUTH TO THE RESCUE

We headed home, back across the time zones in our little jet. The flight allowed ample time to think about the purpose of this extraordinary trip and what we might yet accomplish. We could offer advice and technical expertise, we had the people who knew how to mount a cleanup, and, perhaps most important, our unique access to the scene and voice in the media would allow us to rally help to deal with the disaster. Upon reflection, it was clear that we couldn't solve the fundamental problem Komi faced. That was up to the Russian people, and now, in the post-Soviet era, it would be their chance to do it.

In Alaska, the public's elected representatives controlled the resources. If I, as governor, learned of a leaking pipeline, it would be shut down. If industry failed to clean up a spill to our satisfaction, the state or federal government could force them to do so. Nothing remotely like Komi's chronic pipeline leakage was tolerated. The difference: in Alaska, a democratically elected government, close to the local people, managed the resource commons for the benefit of all Alaskans, while protecting the environment they lived in and subsisted from. In Komi, international businessmen and distant bureaucrats were calling the shots. Whether under the flag of communism or capitalism, their abysmal environmental record in Komi and elsewhere in the Russian Arctic proved they cared first and foremost for their financial interests and their public image.

As soon as we landed in Anchorage, we plunged into the task of getting help to the people of Komi and Nenets. We were exhausted after the many hours on the small plane and the few, stressful hours on the ground. But we had a message to broadcast to the world, and we were determined to find the money needed to start a cleanup operation before spring. I briefed Vice-President Gore and U.N. Secretary General Boutros Boutros-Ghali, as well as a CIA-led team of nine that met us in Anchorage on our return. Their mission was to apply Cold War spy technology to the benefit of the environment. Piecing together our experience on the ground with maps they had compiled using high-tech, intelligence-gathering equipment from outer space, we were able to create a comprehensive view of the situation. Later, we showed the videotape from Nenets at a press conference.

Our next job was to find the money to pay for a cleanup. To help with that task, Mead Treadwell, Deputy Commissioner of the Alaska Department of Environmental Conservation, met with the U.S. State Department and contacted officials in other Arctic nations to explain the extent of the problem and the need for aid. The message reached the World Bank, which agreed to consider loans for the cleanup and for replacement of the pipeline. We were amazed, however, and extremely frustrated, when we learned that the Russian government would not request the money. Even on reasonable terms, they still did not see the benefit of incurring debt to clean up spilled oil. So, we helped plan a meeting in Moscow with Bill White, the Deputy Secretary of the U.S. Department of Energy, the U.S. official on site dealing with the Komi spill, and with the World Bank, top Russian officials, and the regional leaders we had contacted on our trip.

Since my days in Washington as Secretary of the Interior, Punch Sulzberger, long-time publisher of *The New York Times*, and I had maintained a friendship. When we returned from Komi, I called his son, Arthur Ochs Sulzberger Jr., the *Times'* current publisher, and told him what we'd seen. The world needed to learn that the spill was continuing—oil was still leaking—because multinational oil companies and their partners in the Russian government were putting profit above all else. In the short run, Komi needed international support to clean up the mess. In the long run, they needed a new economic and political system in which local people had an interest in the earnings from resource development so they could invest it back in the local infrastructure.

Sulzberger agreed to publish my views on the *Times'* Op-Ed page. The piece hit the paper just as Mead flew into Moscow. Arriving late in the evening at Deputy Secretary White's suite of offices on the second floor of the Radisson Slavjanskaya Hotel, Mead learned the article had been published that morning in *The International Herald Tribune*, the widely read overseas newspaper published by the *Times* and *The Washington Post*.

"I just want you to know that all hell broke loose when the governor's Op-Ed piece was published. It made a lot of people mad," White told him. Mead's face fell, and he began to detail the facts when White interrupted. "Don't get me wrong. I'm sure glad he did it," he said. The article had finally motivated the Russians at the meeting to move forward, and now it looked like the money would go through.

In fact, the Russians did not accept the $124 million loan from the World Bank and the European Bank for Reconstruction and Development for another two months, and cleanup work by an international joint venture, including an Alaskan firm, didn't begin until

March, an additional two months later. Therefore, the cleanup was not complete when spring thaws revealed the true enormity of the spill, a monster of more than 30 million gallons, nearly three times the size of the *Exxon Valdez* spill. Even more oil may have flowed down river, never to be counted in spill estimates. Marshes were dead, creeks choked with oil, rivers coated. Fish and even the milk from cows in the region were tainted. Oil had gushed from leaks and holes along the pipeline, continuing to flow even after the catastrophe was evident. The cleanup gathered much of the oil, a success by the accounts of the foreigners involved and local environmentalists in the region, but it fell far short of the zero tolerance standard we require in Alaska, the most stringent in the world. We require 100% cleanup and the payment of fines.

More important, it left a big question. For Russians admitted this spill was not the only one like it, or even the worst. It was only the best known. Other spills simply had never come to world attention. Incredibly, the Soviet-built oil production and transportation system in western Siberia routinely spills great quantities of oil even to this day. Fixing this infrastructure would do much to correct the region's chronic economic problems and would help with its social problems as well by giving the ruined land a chance to heal, land that formerly supported the indigenous people and other residents. But we saw no sign of a change then. Indeed, the new pipeline that replaced the broken pipeline in Komi was built using the same shoddy methods. It was simply laid down under the dirt, where it once again would be vulnerable to corrosion.[4]

## THE CONSCIENCE OF THE COMMONS

What became evident was that the problems in the Russian Arctic were not unique. They were universal problems of the world's commonly owned lands and resources. Only a basic change in the people's relationship to their government and their land can protect the environment in the long run.

The dark memories of Komi, and the knowledge that the basic problems in Russia's Arctic industry remain unsolved, might tempt some people to see the situation as hopeless. Such views are understandable. Those attitudes belong to a long tradition of pessimism about natural resources that emphasizes the finite nature of the earth rather than the infinite nature of our imagination.

In his famous 1968 essay, *The Tragedy of the Commons*,[5] Garrett Hardin explained well the conflict of freedom and the common ownership of a resource. He described a traditional commons on which each villager has freedom to graze his cattle, knowing that any additional animals he adds will bring him greater benefit in spite of the degradation of the range. Hardin wrote, "Each man is locked into a system that compels him to increase his herd without limit—in a world that is limited. Ruin is the destination toward which all men rush, each pursuing his own best interest in a society that believes in the freedom of the commons. Freedom in a commons brings ruin to all."[6] Hardin concluded that the solution to save the world from a ruinous overuse of our planet—the ultimate commons—was to take away the freedom of mankind to reproduce. Other scholars have followed his work, often drawing similar conclusions, by studying the commons in the context of agricultural and fishing societies that destroyed their very livelihood through overuse of their resources.

*Commonly owned resources will be destroyed if individual interests have free rein to exploit them.*

The truth is much brighter. Undeniably, commonly owned resources will be destroyed if individual interests have free rein to exploit them. That is part of the lesson of Komi. But Elinor Ostrom, a political scientist, and others have discovered that Hardin's "villager" has survived through a multitude of ingenious strategies using local governing systems. These community-based approaches have shown that it is possible to share the fruits of the commons without destroying them.[7]

The difference between the situation in Komi and most academic work on the commons in other areas is that Komi is not poor in resources, it is rich. Nor is it overrun with an excessive population, like the tragic commons Hardin imagines. Remarkably, in our modern world, the kind of rich commons found in northern Russia may be more important than the poor herdsmen's range, and yet it is mostly ignored by academia. The problem is not one of scarcity, but of management and distribution of the benefits of the wealth. There is nothing inevitable about destructive systems, and pessimism would be justified only if we believed ourselves incapable of change. I believe in the capacity of the human race to find solutions. With so much at stake, humanity must consciously choose a path different from the one we saw in Komi.

Unfortunately, most of the world's commons are controlled under poorly integrated systems or are barely controlled at all. Colonialism, or federal systems that are colonial in all but name, continue to extract wealth from regions in the Arctic with little benefit for the local people. Competitive fishing fleets plunder the oceans on their way to fishing themselves out of existence. Some leaders of resource-rich nations in Africa, Latin America, and elsewhere enrich themselves, pouring the people's wealth into secret foreign bank accounts, while the population suffers in poverty.

*When it came to space exploration, the Soviets excelled. But they couldn't get their potatoes across town.*

The Democratic Republic of Congo (the former Zaire) was once the property of a single man, Belgium's King Leopold II. After independence, the country became the virtual property of another individual—Mobutu Sese Seko. Although the Congo is rich in diamonds, oil, and other minerals, its people are poor because Mobutu looted its resources,[8] not unlike the Belgians before him. Corruption led to instability and war, and now the Congo's mineral wealth is being plundered by its neighbors.

Likewise, in Nigeria, military strongman Sani Abacha controlled some of the world's richest oil reserves, yet his people were among the world's poorest.[9] In each case, one man or a narrow elite essentially claimed the commons as their own. Political independence and local control of resources are the first steps to guarantee proper development of the commons. Equally important, a constitutional democracy, built on a foundation of law upheld by a separate and incorruptible court system, is essential to make a government's interest one with its people's.

In addition to a democratic, regional government, a strong economy, based on the efficient development of the commons, depends on a competitive, regulated, free enterprise system. In the largest economic experiment of all time, the Soviet Union demonstrated, for all to see, the total failure of communism. In their economic system, there were no incentives for success and no accountability or responsibility for failure. Cumbersome projects were built with inherent economic flaws. When it came to great national enterprises, such as space exploration, they excelled. But they couldn't get their potatoes across town.

While the flaws of the former Soviet system are clear to all, the pendulum is swinging in the other direction with awesome momentum. The current generation of Russian leadership faces the dangers inherent in unregulated capitalism. This is not a new phenomenon. The United States confronted a similar danger in the late nineteenth and early twentieth centuries. When the market alone dictates how resources are used or exploited, those riches are often wasted, the environment ravaged, and employees abused. A free market offers no incentive for conservation to a coal company that will leave town as soon as the resource is exhausted or to a fisherman competing to catch the last fish. The market incentive calls for extraction of the resource in the fastest, cheapest way possible. Such practices cut costs in the short run, but the long-run results can be ugly, abusive, and expensive for both the workforce and the common owners of the resource.

The chapters to come will explore how the commons has been abused in the world's fisheries and in whaling, oil, gas, coal, and timber, and in preservationist and economic lock-ups of the land. And we'll offer a solution.

In Alaska, a locally elected democratic government manages private sector development of collectively owned resources, and the citizens share the benefits. The land and water are used productively with sensitivity to the environment, and living resources are harvested, by order of Article VIII of the state constitution, only at the level of a sustainable yield.

Revenues from these resources are used by the state to provide services that improve the lives and economic opportunity of all people in the region, while development, in most cases, provides wages sufficient for a decent living for most Alaskans. Survival in the Arctic has always been a challenge and is so even today. This concept of ensuring basic services paid for from the proceeds of wide resource development can work in many parts of the world.

*The great wealth of the Arctic, and its history as a commons, make it a perfect place to learn.*

The Arctic is the test. The great wealth of the northern regions, and their history as a commons, make this a perfect place to learn, and a place where these lessons are especially needed. Many parts of the Northland—the glaciers, mountaintops, and vast expanse of tundra—simply are not suitable for human habitation as we know it. The severe northern climate leaves these regions sparsely populated, with the indigenous people dominant in many places. The Inuit, Inupiat, and Yup'ik in the Arctic still treat the land as commons, which is the only practical way of living here. Throughout history, they always shared resources with the community in order to survive. The Inupiat in Alaska still harvest the whale, not to sell, but as a necessity of life, and a successful hunt is shared by all members of the community. In their tradition, it is unthinkable for an individual to own a whale.

## OPENING UP THE COMMONS

We invite all true pioneers to share the Arctic in the same way. There is only one condition. We ask for those who come north that they come to stay, dedicating themselves to building a society that lasts. The Arctic has traditionally been exploited by those who come, take, and leave.

The challenge is how to tap into, manage, and sustain the staggering wealth God gave us. Some look at the commons as a problem of how to limit human endeavor. The conscience of the commons implores us to use our common ownership to provide for people's needs and to protect the natural environment. In every part of the world, wise, knowledgeable stewards of our commons wait, ready to take over responsibility for our neglected world heritage. They are the local people in each region, in Komi, in Nigeria, and in Alaska, the ordinary people who know the land, air, and water because they live there twelve months a year. Give them the opportunity to care for what they rightfully own, and they will create the greatest societies of the world.

# 3

# Alaska Fights
# for Its Land

## A REVELATION

**O**ne conversation determined the goals I worked toward for fifty years. In that discussion, a friend of mine explained the concept of the resource commons and the need to create a state that could manage them for the good of all Alaskans. That thought guided me through the battle for Alaska statehood, through two terms as governor, through multiple projects in the private sector, and through two exciting and tumultuous years as U.S. Secretary of the Interior.

The person who explained the commons was Paul F. Robison, an Anchorage land attorney, and the year was 1949. I was a young builder in the small town of Anchorage, population 30,000, interested in politics mostly because politicians kept getting in the way of the projects we were trying to build. An older group of downtown businessmen had the town sewn up, and the city government was holding back development on their behalf by refusing to extend utilities. Some of the young go-getters who wanted to move the community and state forward met frequently.

Robison was an attorney for the federal Bureau of Land Management and had arrived in the territory a few years earlier. He attended those bull sessions in the office of physician Harold Sogn in downtown Anchorage. Bob Atwood, publisher of *The Anchorage Times*, rarely missed a meeting. Banker Elmer Rasmuson attended, as did miner Harold Strandberg, and attorney Harold Stringer, to name just a few. In the coming years, we would all hold positions of responsibility in government or business, but back then we were just talking and looking for direction. We talked about local politics, and also where Alaska should be heading and how to get there.[1]

Alaska was a territory in those days, without a vote in Congress, and we knew it needed to become a state. But that wasn't all. Somehow, we had to free up land and resources for Alaskans. The federal government owned virtually 100 per cent of the land, with property coming into private ownership primarily through home-steading, the process that encouraged pioneers to file on 160 acres of public land and then "prove them up," receiving ownership by living on the land for five years. Homesteading made sense. It seemed obvious that as private owners came to own more land, they would naturally develop the resources necessary to build the kind of state we dreamed of.

> *Somehow we had to free up land and resources.*

That was fundamentally how the American West was settled. My perspective grew out of my childhood in Kansas, where my father, Robert Hickel, was not fortunate enough to own a homestead and lived the majority of his adult life as a tenant farmer. Our large, German-Catholic family (we were 10 kids in all) worked together to plant and harvest wheat on 360 acres near Claflin. But it wasn't our farm. We lived in a big frame house. But it wasn't our house. When storms swept over the plains, my mother, Emma, used to pray to pro-tect the crop, but it wasn't even our crop. A third of the harvest went to the owners of the farm, the Grizell family. During the Dust Bowl years of the Depression, when we could see the topsoil blowing over our heads, land out west fell to a dollar or two an acre. I urged my father, "Dad, we could buy a whole section for $600." He agreed, but he never had $600 to spend.

Uncle Emil Potsner, married to my father's sister, owned his 360 acres. Oil wells sprung up around his farm, but when oil companies approached him, offering him a standard 12 per cent royalty, he turned them down. The land was only worth $5 an acre for farming, but he held out for two or three years in the depths of the Depression, to discover the value of the oil underground. Meanwhile, wildcatters were drilling all around him, and his neighbors were getting rich.

Finally, my uncle accepted an offer from an independent company. The rumor around town was that he received $250,000 and a 25 per cent royalty.

As teenagers, my cousins Martin and Willie Miller and I were hired to dig a cellar for an oil platform on a neighboring farm where the drillers could set up their equipment. We got $10 among us for digging a hole in the hard clay ten feet square and nine feet deep, with steps going down. The drilling crew brought in a cable rig, a machine that lifted a weight and dropped it, pounding its way down into the earth.

The very first hole they drilled on Uncle Emil's land blew the bit from the cable rig apparatus right out of the well, and oil gushed for two days before they could shut it down. That oil landed on Highway 4, a quarter mile away, and closed it to traffic until the roughnecks got the well under control. That was a huge well, producing hundreds, perhaps thousands, of barrels a day. There was no question in my mind about the benefit of owning your own land.

A few years later, I left Kansas. Farming probably would have been my life if I could have owned the land, but that wasn't an option. Instead I started selling insurance and traveling as an amateur boxer, looking for opportunities far away. Eventually, in 1940, the steamer S.S. Yukon carried me safely to Alaska, with just a few cents in my pocket. Climbing out of steerage class to get some air as we approached Prince William Sound in late October, I saw Mt. St. Elias and the Wrangell Range towering above us in the sky beyond. From the rail of that steamer, a promise came out of my lips, a promise to this new, great land. "You take care of me," I pledged. "And I'll take care of you."

After World War II, financial independence became my goal, the key to freedom and the ability to be true to everything important to me. I set out to finish a house for my family, teaching myself the fundamentals of the building trades. At times it seemed like my greatest talent was profanity, but that first house gave us a base for our young family and became an asset to invest. Borrowing against it, we started our first housing project. Then we borrowed against the housing project—leveraging our assets once again—to build a bigger project. The idea of selling those homes was counter to my intuition, but finally a few were sold when banker Dan Cuddy suggested that it would be helpful in gaining financing for larger projects.

By the time we started meeting in Dr. Sogn's office late in the 1940s, it was firmly engrained in my brain that wealth comes from the land, and the land's wealth could be leveraged into greater wealth. Like so many before and since, I assumed that the way to a bright future was to get the land into the hands of individual Alaskans who could develop it privately. Lucky or astute Alaskans, like my Uncle Emil in Kansas, would then start bringing in gushers on their homesteads and investing that money to build a better Alaska.

Paul Robison pulled me up short, but in a gentle way. He said, quietly, "Wally, it doesn't work that way in Alaska."

Paul explained that since Teddy Roosevelt's presidency, the federal government maintained ownership of the subsurface mineral rights of the public land conveyed to homesteaders. This policy, established under TR, eventually became the law of the land soon after Roosevelt's death. President Woodrow Wilson, in 1920, signed the Mineral Leasing Act that established that the subsurface of all federal lands and all future homesteads would be classified as commons and forever remain with the federal government to be managed for the good of all American citizens. In other words, even if all of Alaska were carved up in homesteads, oil, gas, and other minerals would belong to everyone through government, not just to the homesteaders, pioneers, speculators, or farmers like Uncle Emil.

*"Wally, it doesn't work that way in Alaska."*

It hit me like a thunderbolt. To my great dismay, it became obvious that the Mineral Leasing Act of 1920 had virtually eliminated private ownership of natural resources in Alaska. My vision of Alaska developing the way the Lower 48 had developed evaporated before my eyes.

For a year, hammering nails and mixing cement, Paul Robison's words turned over and over in my mind. It just didn't seem right.

There's a little voice inside that tells me what's right to do. I call him "my little guy," and I was born with him. He has always been there. Every day I like to spend some time alone, to go for a quiet walk and gather my thoughts. Other people may see me as decisive or even impulsive in business or politics, but that's only because I've spent time alone in quiet hours thinking through problems, listening to what that voice inside has to say. I can see myself as a boy growing up on the farm, walking in the pastures. That little guy was always there helping sort out problems that, from my perspective as a child, loomed as large as the national issues that boy would handle later as an adult.

*I began to wonder if we could accomplish even more together than if we owned the resources individually.*

When Paul explained what we would later call the commons—lands and waters owned in common, as in Alaska, or owned by no one, as on the high seas—it took a year thinking on those walks alone before the answer eventually broke through. It hit me like a heavy thump on my chest, the kind that makes you catch your breath.

"We can make this work," I said aloud.

Alaskans could still develop our resources like an owner, and we could do it responsibly and profitably. Like Uncle Emil, we could be tough with those who prospect for and develop natural resources. We could demand top dollar for our assets and lay down the terms and conditions for responsible development. But instead of operating as individuals, we would act as a community. The future would be as bright as ever—brighter—if we could learn to develop these assets in common. Possibly, if we thought it through, we could accomplish even more together than if we owned the resources individually.

## AMERICA'S UNDERGROUND COMMONS

On the eve of statehood, Alaska faced an opportunity unique in world history. Being a territory in a nation of states was frustrating, but Alaska's late development also meant that by the time statehood became a possibility, we had the opportunity to become a new kind of state. In the late 1940s, the implications of this opportunity were difficult to understand. Since then, I have pieced together some of the history that led us to that point. The evolution of U.S. land law assured that the mistakes made in the previous 100 years of westward settlement did not have to be repeated in Alaska.

Early in our nation's life, the American West stood as a wide-open invitation to the landless poor and to struggling farmers seeking a better life for their families. "The West" meant anything beyond the developed eastern seaboard, and, from the perspective of the non-indigenous people, the seemingly endless land and resources on the western frontier appeared open for the taking by anyone with energy and daring.

The question of who would own the great mass of North America, the public domain, became an issue as early as the fall of 1776. That year the Maryland legislature declared that lands that the British crown had owned, "if secured by the blood and treasure of all, ought, in reason and justice . . . be considered as common stock." The idea highlighted a conflict for the Thirteen Colonies, for seven of them had claims to lands west of the Appalachian Mountains, rights granted by the British monarch or by Indian treaty. In a series of agreements, the last of which was concluded in 1802, one year before the Louisiana Purchase, each state ceded its western land claims to the central government. But each kept control of lands within its own borders.

The federal government's massive holdings continued to expand, and in 1867 Secretary of State William Seward successfully negotiated the purchase of Alaska from Russia for $7.2 million. In all, through conquest, purchase, and treaty, the federal government acquired 1.8 billion acres. The moral and legal rights of that ownership would be challenged and fought by Native Americans who, in many cases, had never ceded their ownership rights, but under federal and international law, the U.S. government owned the land. These unreserved lands were called the public domain, and they were essentially free for the using. Other than the original thirteen states, only the Republic of Texas became a state already owning all the public land within its boundaries.[2]

Early on, the United States privatized its holdings by selling land at auction. Homesteading evolved gradually, as people built farms on western acreage. In 1830, Congress passed a law allowing those who had already built farms to legalize their ownership by buying up to 160 acres at the minimum price set in land auctions. In 1841, that law was extended to anyone who wished to claim and farm public land. The authors of the new law recognized that for the American West to be settled, it needed pioneers who could own private property.

The Homestead Act of 1862 allowed any citizen to claim 160 acres—including the mineral resources under that land.[3] By 1900, 1.3 million homestead claims were filed, with about half of those patented, as settlers acquired legal title to the land and the subsurface estate. Towns also received land, and the West grew, the public domain dwindled, and the general outlines of the nation we know today were drawn.

*The mistakes made in the previous 100 years of westward settlement did not have to be repeated in Alaska.*

Abuses also occurred. Even by the 1870s, government investigators learned that corporate interests were manipulating the laws to gain large swaths of rich timber for next to nothing.[4] The fast disappearance of forests raised the concern that there would be none left, and in 1891, under new authority from Congress, President Benjamin Harrison began the process of withdrawing forest reserves, later called National Forests, from disposal to private parties.

We privatized the underground commons, too. The federal system of mineral allocation evolved from the way prospectors in the gold fields of 1848 recorded their mining claims, essentially on the basis of "finders keepers." Mining laws championed by a Nevada prospector turned U.S. Senator, William M. Stewart, eventually took final shape as the Mining Location Law of 1872. That law, which is still in use today, essentially followed the miners' practices, giving ownership of relatively small pieces of land to the first person who found valuable minerals, filed the proper claim, and paid a nominal fee. No real return from the mineral assets went to the public.

The oil business was born in Titusville, Pennsylvania, when the first oil well came in on August 28, 1859.[5] This new industry expanded rapidly and was regulated under the 1872 mining act, but it didn't fit. The 1872 law, designed for hard rock and placer mining, permitted small claims only, and gave them to the first person to find something of value. The oil industry, however, required expensive drilling equipment, and drillers had to cope with flowing underground oil reserves that covered large areas. This arrangement was a prescription for chaos and waste. Under the mining laws, no one could own the right to prospect in the public domain until he or she found valuable minerals and filed a claim. That meant oil derricks were drilled side by side in a frantic race. A single pool of oil might be "discovered" by tens of locators with valid claims, each of whom withdrew oil as fast as possible to beat the competition. Drilling oil too fast damaged the reservoirs by allowing water to invade the formations and by releasing the gas pressure that lifted the oil.[6]

The homesteading laws were abused, too, by those seeking coal and oil underneath the ground rather than agricultural land on the surface. When President Teddy Roosevelt came to office in 1901, he assigned Gifford Pinchot, first head of the U.S. Forest Service, to investigate the waste of public lands. As a result, in 1906, Roosevelt withdrew 66 million acres of the west from homesteading or other disposal until government geologists could locate lands with coal potential. The action outraged westerners, including Alaskans. Cordova residents revolted, dumping coal from the South 48 off their dock, frustrated that they were forbidden from mining their own cheaper, more immediate resources. Critics charged that Roosevelt had no legislative authority for the withdrawals. Roosevelt responded, essentially, "The President always has authority to protect the public interest," and he ultimately was upheld in court.[7]

With authority granted under the Pickett Act of 1909, President William Howard Taft withdrew 61 million acres of potential oil lands to protect them from rampant waste by drillers competing under the 1872 mining law. With oil being exhausted so quickly—and so much of it being left behind in the ground—Taft feared for the defense and economic life of the nation. Government analysts predicted the oil might run out, and the Navy was alarmed at the prospect of lacking a secure supply for its new oil-powered battleships.

Out of the controversies over Roosevelt's coal withdrawals and Taft's oil withdrawals came an almost haphazard decision to divide the ownership of the surface of the land from the minerals below. On his last day in office, in March 1909, Roosevelt signed a bill conveying homestead patents to those who had valid claims on the withdrawn coal lands if the settlers agreed their patents would not include the coal underneath. A series of laws, passed over the next five years, completed the separation of the minerals underground from the land on the surface of new home-steads—the laws that so shocked me when Robison told me about them thirty-five years later.

*The decision to sever the land from the resources would ultimately affect Alaska more than any other part of the country.*

The decision to sever the land from the resources would ultimately affect Alaska more than any other part of the country, because so little Alaska land had passed into private own-ership by that time. In 1914, when President Woodrow Wilson signed the law that finally reserved the subsurface rights from all future homesteads, fewer than 200 homestead applica-tions had been filed in Alaska. Many homesteads would later be patented by future waves of modern Alaska pioneers, but *without* the mineral rights attached. Only with the passage of the Alaska Native Land Claims Settlement Act in 1971 did any significant amount of Alaska mineral rights pass to private hands, and those 44 million acres went to all Alaska Native people then living, not to any one individual.

Not until 1920 did the U.S. resolve the problem of how to develop oil and coal from the commons. The fight lasted ten years in Congress while presidential withdrawals continued on oil and coal lands across the west. Western senators and representatives vehe-mently opposed a scheme to require payment of petroleum royalties to the federal government but ultimately gave in to restart resource development in their states.

## A LANDMARK ACT OF CONGRESS

The Mineral Leasing Act of 1920 for the first time recognized that the commons belonged to the public and required that income from development of the commons must be paid to the public's govern-ment. On lands where the government expected oil to be found, oilmen had to compete, bidding against each other, with bonus payments and a standard royalty percentage on oil they produced. On lands not classified as oil lands, a non-competitive leasing system allowed individuals and companies to acquire exclusive rights to explore in an area for a nominal payment. If they found oil, they still had to pay royalties to the government. All oil leases would cover larger areas, reducing the incentive for oil rigs to compete side by side, draining the same reservoir as fast as possible.

Under the 1872 mining law, a prospector had little practical chance of making a discovery on a homesteader's land unless the homesteader let him look.[8] That's still the case for hard rock minerals, which fall under the 1872 law to this day. But under the 1920 Mineral Leasing Act, anyone could drill for oil on either public or private land, because the government retained the subsurface rights. An oil developer was required to pay for any damages on the surface, but property owners could not block access to the public's underground wealth. (My Uncle Emil, and most other Kansas farmers, owned the oil under their land because their land title predated the changes made by Roosevelt.)

The oil leasing system has served the nation well since 1920, but it didn't shield the commons from theft and abuse. That depended then, and still does today, on the integrity of the public officials charged with managing the commons, a point proved soon after the passage of the landmark leasing bill.

President Warren Harding named New Mexico Senator Albert Fall as his Secretary of the Interior. Fall had been involved in committee work on the Mineral Leasing Act, and was now charged with implementing the law. Soon after taking office, he accepted some $400,000 in bribes from two men in return for leases worth hundreds of millions of dollars in Naval Petroleum Reserves Number 1 and 3, otherwise known as Elk Hills, California, and Teapot Dome, Wyoming. The Constitution's self-correcting system of checks and balances worked, however, and Albert Fall ultimately spent more than a year in prison, and the leases were recovered for the government.[9]

Alaskans watched these events closely, because Fall and other occupants of the Secretary of the Interior's office held the power of monarchs over our territory. Congress passed Alaska's Second Organic Act in 1912, giving the Alaska territory a weak legislature and retaining all power over natural resources with the U.S. Interior Department. Whether the Interior Secretary was conscientious, or neglectful, or even corrupt like Albert Fall, each held the power of a distant czar over Alaska. The President or the Secretary of the Interior appointed our governor and all our significant government officials. The Interior Department ruled our land and subsurface oil and minerals, the wildlife we hunted, and the fish in our waters. The Agriculture Department controlled our forests through the U.S. Forest Service.

Uniquely, history had decreed that the commons of Alaska would not pass into private ownership as they had in many other places. But, the flip side of that coin was that the commons was of little benefit to the local population while they lived under the territorial system of government.

The next step was to bring the commons home.

## 100 MILLION ACRES

Until we achieved statehood, Alaska's citizens were entirely at the mercy of an often-invisible political process motivated by interests other than our own. We could not vote for the President or any other federal official (with real power). Members of Congress from all other parts of the nation stood up for their constituents—constituents that included economic interests who wanted to exploit Alaska's resources and take the profits back home. Alaskans elected only a non-voting delegate to the House of Representatives, who had no power, no vote, no authority.

Leaving aside the pivotal issues of resource ownership and development, Alaskans lacked even the minimal voice needed to demand a normal level of government services. In Anchorage in 1950, a fast-growing town of 30,000, we had no mail delivery. Everyone had to drive or trek through the snow to the post office to receive letters and packages. A small issue, but it illustrated our political weakness. U.S. Post Office officials knew we had no clout and paid us no heed.

With such powerlessness, it was understandable that many Alaskans who campaigned for statehood were willing to accept it on any terms. These well-intentioned campaigners were confronted with opposition within the territory and faced major economic and political powers on the national scene. When a statehood bill finally passed the U.S. House of Representatives in 1950, most statehood advocates viewed it as a victory, even though the bill was fatally flawed. It allowed the federal government to continue its disastrous management of Alaska's fisheries and gave the new state little share in resource revenues. Worst of all, the bill kept the federal government as our all-powerful landlord. Only 23 million acres of Alaska's 365 million

*The 1952 statehood bill was fatally flawed.*

would be owned by the new state, and of that 23 million, 20 million would be designated for the University of Alaska and 3 million for Southeast Alaska communities surrounded by the Tongass National Forest.

I was barely 30, too young to know what couldn't be done, but it was obvious to me that Alaska needed more land.

After three years in business, I was still swinging a hammer on my own projects. I was owner or part owner of 48 duplexes, and I was clearing a modest $1,000 a month. Meeting with my friends at Dr. Sogn's office, we talked about practical politics—how to get the streets paved and utilities extended in a town with a political establishment that stood in the way of any project that wasn't blessed by the "in" crowd. In the fall of 1950, Mayor Z. J. Loussac, a member of that establishment crowd, ran for a seat in the territorial Senate. I gained some visibility on the local political scene when I campaigned on the radio against Loussac, and he lost the race.

That winter, the Anchorage Republican Club asked me to arrange for a speaker for the annual Lincoln Day Dinner. Without thinking about what a small town in our remote, heavily Democratic territory could expect, I went after Herbert Hoover, the nation's most recent Republican president. Guy Gabrielson, chairman of the National Republican Committee, told me it couldn't be done, but I wouldn't take no for an answer, so the party bought me a plane ticket to Seattle to talk to Washington Governor Arthur Langlie. After an hour, he convinced me that the senior Mr. Hoover couldn't be expected to travel to Alaska in February. People still thought Alaska was on the dark side of the moon. It was as if we were asking the former president to fly to Antarctica.

The next time Gabrielson called, Langlie had already contacted him on our behalf, and the party chief offered a choice of two names, both young, western U.S. Senators elected that fall: Herman Welker of Idaho and Richard Nixon of California. I'd never heard of either one of them, but Welker was on the Senate Interior and the Post Office committees, so he was an obvious choice.

Such was our isolation that the visit of a freshman Senator from Idaho made major front-page headlines for several days in February 1951. Welker was a hit in Alaska and became an instant friend. At 44, he was only a dozen years my senior and relatively new to politics. We developed a warm friendship that lasted until his untimely death six years later. He gave a rousing speech to the Lincoln Day Dinner, and upon his return to Washington, soon delivered mail service to Anchorage as well. More important, he committed to support the fight for statehood for Alaska on the right terms.

Welker caught on quickly to Alaska's special problems and why we needed a special kind of statehood. Our tiny population was spread across a vast, rugged region where providing services and building transportation and economic infrastructure was costly and difficult. State government could not sustain itself by taxing our small population. Our remoteness and severe climate meant our economy must depend on extracting our natural resources from the ground, the rivers, and the forests for export from Alaska.

The pro-statehood forces in Alaska targeted our admission to the Union as the end in itself. They weren't thinking about how we would survive after we sewed our star on the flag. On the other hand, I believed adamantly that becoming a state while leaving more than ninety per cent of the land and resources in federal hands would be statehood in name only, disappointing and discouraging. Our dreams would be dashed. We knew all too well the shoddy job the federal government did from Washington, D.C., in handling our resources. To perpetuate that system by incorporating it in our statehood compact would lock us into permanent colonial status.

Almost a year after Welker's visit, in January 1952, *The Anchorage Times* reported that another statehood bill had passed the House and was due to come up in the Senate, with the Truman Administration's support. It had a good chance of passing. This bill was similar to the 1950 bill and had virtually nothing in it for Alaska. The news shocked me as I stood reading it on the construction site. I decided right then to fly to Washington to try to stop it. I set aside my tools, and my wife Ermalee and I boarded a plane for the long journey east. My plan was simple: to take my case to President Harry Truman and the top Republicans in the Senate and persuade them to grant the new state more land and resources.

Neither Ermalee nor I had ever set foot in Washington, or even in the eastern U.S. We felt slightly lost when we arrived at the airport, all alone in that great city. Crowds of strangers rushed around us. Suddenly, Senator Welker stepped out from behind a column where he had been hiding. Not only was he there to meet us, but he had brought a huge, chauffeur-driven black limousine, borrowed from Senator Styles Bridges, the Senate president *pro tempore*. They whisked us into the city. It certainly seemed like a promising start.

We tried repeatedly, but I couldn't get in to see the President. Senator Welker did arrange for me to meet Vice-President Alben Barkley, but I made little headway. The meeting was brief, and the point I wanted to make wasn't simple. Besides, Truman's Administration was committed to the statehood bill as written. I remember insisting with Barkley, "It won't work, Mr. Vice-President. It just isn't enough land. It simply won't work." He patted me on the shoulder. "Young man, it's going to be okay. The other states make it work."

Welker also arranged a meeting with Ohio Senator Robert A. Taft, the son of former President Taft. Known for his brilliance and agile mind, Senator Taft commanded the Republican majority in the Senate and was the dominant figure in both Congress and in the Republican Party at that time. The courteous, distinguished Senator sat across the desk from us. Welker and a Taft staffer were at my side. Welker told me to do the talking, and I spoke with all the intensity I could muster on why Alaska must not become a state without a sufficient land base. Taft quickly understood the problem.

Conservative Congressional Republicans had various reasons for opposing statehood. The Republican Party in Alaska at that time was controlled by the Seattle-based canned salmon industry and other economic interests who benefited from the status quo, with light taxes and heavy Outside control of Alaska's natural resources. The

Republicans also anticipated losing the two new seats in the U.S. Senate with Alaska statehood, as twenty years of Democratic patronage had built a powerful political base within the state. To counter that concern, I argued that Alaskans were by nature more aligned with the independent, stand-on-your-own-two-feet Republican philosophy. Finally, and perhaps most important, conservatives opposed statehood because they were afraid Alaska could never support itself. Taxes paid by the relatively small Alaskan population would never replace the sustained federal revenues we enjoyed. That was true, and remains true to this day. The State of Alaska relies primarily on revenues from our natural resources, not taxes paid by individuals.

The beauty of our position, to base Alaska statehood on the resource commons, rested on the fact that it addressed the concerns of those statehood opponents. We might not have the tax base to support state government, but we had a rich storehouse of natural resources, which, if developed under state government, could more than pay the bills. From a political point of view, cutting the ties of patronage with Washington, D.C., would let Alaska find its own political balance. And by putting lands in Alaska's hands, the development of our natural resources could take place more rapidly and responsibly than under the faraway federal government. The point was, I wanted Taft's support for statehood, but not unless they amended the bill before the Senate, with its pitifully small land allocation.

Taft asked, "Well, how much land do you need?"

Being a carpenter and still pretty young, I frankly didn't know how much land it would take. I didn't even know how much land there was in Alaska.

"One hundred million acres," I blurted out.

The meeting went on, and it seemed clear Senator Taft was won over. He assigned staff members to put my ideas into legislative language that could be brought forth as amendments to the statehood bill.

Leaving the office, I turned to Senator Welker and asked, "Herman, how much land do we have?"

He didn't know, either, so he called the Interior Department. They told us that Alaska contains 365 million acres.

"Oh my God, I should have asked for at least half," I said with a laugh.

That week Taft's staff attorneys enlisted my help as they tried to amend the statehood bill. The best solution would have been immediate statehood, with the addition of the land we needed. Unfortunately, the job of rewriting the bill and improving it by amendment proved too difficult. It would have to be sent back to committee, or recommitted, which meant that it was dead for that Congress and would have to be reintroduced, starting all over again, when the next Congress convened. I preferred to wait for statehood on the right terms rather than have Alaska become a state without land.

That week at the Capitol gave me a quick immersion in the highest levels of national politics, and my new friends served us well in the statehood fight for years to come. I was with Welker in the Senate cloakroom when Taft came in and, unaware I was present, started talking. Three Senators rose as if to block me from his view when I heard him say, "We should listen to that young man from Alaska," before he walked onto the Senate floor.

*"Now you've got your work cut out for you."*

On Taft's recommendation, Ermalee and I left for home before the vote on recommitting the statehood bill came up in the Senate. This was the critical vote that would kill this potentially disastrous version of the bill, and Taft assured me he had it under control. The vote was far from easy, however. Two senators had to return from campaigning for re-election to cast their votes, and one, Senator Thomas Hennings, Jr., of Missouri, left his sickbed, coming to the Senate accompanied by his doctor. In the end, after three tie votes, the bill was sent back to committee by a tally of 45 to 44. It was a close call. Southern Democrats opposed Alaska statehood because they saw us as a vote for civil rights. Enough of them combined with the conservative Republicans led by Taft to kill it.[10]

We were in the Los Angeles Airport on the long trip home when my name came booming over the public address system. Who could be paging me here? Jack Martin, Taft's chief of staff, was on the line, and relayed the good news. "We just recommitted the bill by one vote," he said. Speaking for the Senator, he said, "Now you've got your work cut out for you."

Not surprisingly, those who wanted statehood right away, regardless of the terms, were disappointed with the death of the bill in the

Senate, and I would feel their wrath. Alaska's Congressional Delegate, E. L. "Bob" Bartlett, said, "Anyone would like to have 100 million acres, but we're not going to get it."

Bob Atwood questioned the sincerity of my support for statehood. We exchanged a series of hard-hitting newspaper opinion articles. Atwood led off with a blistering, unsigned editorial in *The Anchorage Times* charging Taft with opposing the bill because he had made a deal with Alaska Republicans to support his presidential bid with their three delegates to the national convention later that year. "Senator Taft opposed the bill because of his understanding that Alaska Republicans wanted him to," Atwood wrote. "Had the Senator favored it, the vote would have been quite different because so many other Republicans follow his lead."[11]

I fired back in defense of Taft the next week in the *Anchorage Daily News*, calling Atwood's charge against the Senator, "a barefaced lie . . . I went back to Washington of my own volition and talked with Senator Taft. I explained the Statehood Bill to him as I saw it. I have reason to believe that he agreed with me."[12]

More important, I explained what was wrong with the bill and how Alaska's advocates on the Statehood Committee had come close to leading us into a colossal disaster. We nearly had created a state crippled from birth, without adequate resources or control of its own destiny.

The very next day, Atwood responded with a second editorial, this one more than 2,500 words, titled "Hickel's Heckles." He angrily accused me of following "the salmon packer's line." His argument showed that he had not thought through the pivotal importance of a state-owned land and resource base for our future.

"The 23 million acres that would be available for the new state are almost equal to the total area of the great state of Indiana. We have never heard Indiana complain that it does not have enough land to operate a state successfully," the editorial said. "Land in the public domain would still be available for settlement and development under the same land laws that exist today. They would not be 'closed' because of statehood."[13]

Atwood wrote about the land of Alaska as if it should remain with the federal government, and that we should be grateful for any gift we received from Uncle Sam. But I believed, then as now, that the commons in any country is best managed by the people who live there. We needed local control so we could control our own destiny. Putting another star on the American flag was not the end in itself, but a way to a new kind of government that no one had yet tried: a resource commons controlled by a local, democratically elected government.

Two days later, my response to "Hickel's Heckles" in the *Anchorage Daily News* included a youthful promise: "I am but a young man who was leaving the tasks of government to you older people. You have failed miserably. From here on out, you can count me in."[14] This was 1952.

*Alaska's leaders came to recognize that a large land grant would be fundamental to the new state's success.*

Soon I was fighting for statehood side by side with Bob Atwood, who became my steadfast friend. But the most important issue was settled. No longer did we talk about getting statehood as soon as possible, regardless of the terms. Alaska's leaders came to recognize that a large land grant would be fundamental to the new state's success. When Alaska's constitution was written four years later, it was based on the premise that our state would own a large portion of its land mass and that its government would need a special structure to take care of the resource commons.

As for the figure of 100 million acres blurted out to Taft in our meeting in January 1952, it set the bar. There's no way of knowing for sure what effect that had through the long statehood battle, but no statehood bill that followed was less than 100 million acres. In the ensuing years, statehood bills in Congress contained various amounts of land for Alaska, ranging up to 180 million acres. But the version that finally passed six years later granted us 103 million acres of land, almost a third of the land mass, containing more than enough subsurface wealth to build a great civilization.[15] We would become a self-sustaining state, and one with special opportunities and responsibilities rarely given to a people.

# 4

# Winning
# Local Control

## ENTRENCHED COLONIALISM

**A** half-century later, it's easy to forget the outrage and frustration Alaskans felt in the 1950s over our status as a colony of the United States of America. We weren't just unhappy that we couldn't vote for the President or elect members of Congress. We were struggling under a system of exploitation that placed some of our resources under lock and key and allowed others to be destroyed by Outsiders. Either way, this system robbed Alaskans of the ability to develop a self-sustaining economy.

In a powerful address to the Alaska Constitutional Convention in 1955, former territorial Governor Ernest Gruening compared Alaska's grievances to those of the original Thirteen Colonies. With eloquent yet biting words and sentences, he showed how the words of the Declaration of Independence applied as well to our relationship with the federal government as they had to the colonies' relationship to King George III. In a postwar world in which nations were giving up their colonies, Gruening made the case that the U.S. relationship with Alaska even violated the United Nations Charter. Gruening declared:

> It would be impossible in any one address, even one that assumed the length of a Senate filibuster, to list all the wrongs, disadvantages and lack of immunities that Alaska has endured in its 88 years as a territory.

They constitute an incredible story. Even for those who know it, it is hard to believe. It is hard for us as Americans who long ago established our faith in American intelligence, competence, good sense, and above all in American fair play, to contemplate the story of American colonialism in Alaska.[1]

The moral argument was on our side, as the American public recognized: national public opinion polls overwhelmingly approved statehood for Alaska. But, as Gruening understood, our territorial status was fundamentally an economic issue. Business interests used the federal political process to hold Alaska in a colonial stranglehold for their own advantage. And it was only through winning political power of our own that Alaska could escape economic oppression.

Seattle-based interests bled the territory, and our history contains an abundance of examples. One of the most blatant instruments of oppression was the Maritime Law of 1920, better known as the Jones Act after its sponsor Senator Wesley Jones of Washington. The act forced (and continues to force today) all cargo sailing between Alaska and other U.S. ports to travel on U.S.-built ships. In the closest port, Seattle, a single family, the Skinners, owned the U.S.-built Alaska steamship lines and an Alaska fish brokerage, and, upon the act's passage, gained a near monopoly on shipping to the territory. The Skinners gave a fifty per cent break to their fishing interests over the prices Alaskans paid to send cargo on the same vessels. Cargo rates doubled for some shippers who were compelled to use U.S. ships and ports rather than the competing Canadian ports and railroads they had used prior to the Jones Act. Even for cargo traveling across the country by rail, if it was destined to be loaded on a ship to Alaska, federal rules allowed the railroad to charge a special, higher Alaska rate than other cargo traveling the same distance on the same train on the same rails.[2]

In addition to shipping, Alaska's abundant salmon harvest motivated Seattle interests to resist Alaskan statehood and to manipulate the weak political institutions within the territory. Until the wide-scale development of Alaska oil in the 1960s and 1970s, the salmon fishery was our richest resource. Alaska's salmon fisheries ranked among the world's most abundant and profitable from the beginning, and remain so today.

These Outsiders cared little about conserving our fisheries. Even more than other natural resources, salmon survive only if conserved. They spawn in the streams of their birth, leaving fragile eggs in the stream gravel to hatch in the spring. Given the right conditions—which are easily disturbed by pollution, sedimentation, or loss of shade—the young fish swim out to sea to grow and mature, returning, depending on the species, up to five years later. The run of returning fish up river lasts but a few weeks, as a mad profusion of salmon surges against the current, then spawns, and dies. The process brings protein from the oceans into Alaska's coastal and interior regions, feeding both wildlife and people who have relied for millennia on the salmon's return for their sustenance. But the cycle continues only as long as fishermen allow enough salmon to survive the struggle up river to spawn each year.

*Bloodshed was the predictable result.*

The salmon industry in Alaska started years before the Klondike gold rush of 1898. West Coast fish packing companies came north to harvest a seemingly limitless food resource. In those early days, companies set up fish traps that amounted to floating blockades across the rivers to catch the returning fish, canning as many as they could and leaving the rest to waste. If the run was destroyed, it mattered little to them, as there were plenty more streams full of salmon. In the complete absence of government oversight, companies set up their traps in front of one another, preferring to destroy fish rather than allow a competitor to catch them. Armed guards protected the traps, and bloodshed was the predictable result. As is often the case in an arena of completely free competition, the strong dominated the rest, concentrating Alaska's salmon industry in the hands of a few companies located in the South 48.[3]

Stream barricades were outlawed by Congress in 1889, but the law was not enforced, and the industry continued to grow according to the pattern set early on. Canneries still could legally set up fish traps in the rivers. The traps, like the barricades, could easily catch too many fish and damage the runs. Before the arrival of the fish companies, Southeast Alaska Natives consumed an annual average of 500 pounds of salmon each, and all Alaska Natives averaged over 400 pounds of salmon a year.[4]

When streams were blocked or overfished, the Natives lost their most important food source. Episcopal Missionary Hudson Stuck lobbied Congress in the early 1920s when canners blocked Yukon River salmon, which brought famine to Natives across thousands of miles of the territory.[5] Non-Native commercial fishermen suffered, too, because they could not compete with a fish-catching machine that worked without human intervention. By 1947, Alaska had 434 fish traps, and only 38 belonged to Alaska residents. In that same year, more than seventy per cent of the payroll expended by the fishing companies went to workers brought in from outside the territory. These workers received a single paycheck, sent to them after they returned home, keeping that money out of the Alaska economy.[6]

*Skilled and cynical use of the political process.*

The canned salmon industry maintained its control through skillful and cynical use of the political process—a process to which Alaskans didn't have access. West Coast members of Congress chaired key committees with control over Alaska salmon. Bills seeking conservation of Alaska salmon lost their momentum in committees chaired by Congressmen supporting the Seattle-based interests. Those Northwest Congressmen also kept a leash on the federal agencies that managed the fishery, underfunding their enforcement and research and beating back regulations that would respond to Alaska concerns. Although Alaska was allowed limited self-determination in the Organic Act of 1912, Congress made it the *only* territory or state without control of its own fish and game. The same act provided apportionment of the new Territorial Senate by area rather than population, making it relatively easy for the canned salmon industry to block legislation and keep fish taxes low. They had only to control a few seats from sparsely populated districts.

Overfishing and weak markets hit the salmon industry in the early 1920s, and for the first time Seattle interests were confronted with the undeniable need for conservation. Self-interest, however, always played a role in their thinking, as conservation would mean less fish to the market and higher prices. Congress passed the White

Act in 1924, named for Representative Wallace White, of Maine, who chaired the House Merchant Marine and Fisheries Committee. The Act gave the Bureau of Fisheries more power to conserve and for the first time recognized the need for sufficient salmon to be allowed to escape the fish traps to ensure sustained runs, although it failed to assure adequate escapement.

Alaskans won one important battle in the law. The Outside canned salmon industry had sought exclusive rights to fish and can salmon in certain areas. Their public argument was based on conservation—a limited-entry system would reduce the competition for fish, allowing companies to operate their traps for sustained yield rather than maximum short-term catch. But giving the fish trap owners exclusive permits would, in essence, take the publicly owned salmon resource and give it to these private firms as private property. Limited entry sometimes is necessary to protect the commons from overuse, but the motive behind this bill was to export ownership of Alaska's fish permanently to those who lived outside the territory. It was an outrageous proposition.

Debate in the U.S. House of Representatives revealed that the committees that had drafted the bill were doing the bidding of the Seattle-based industry. Alaska's one, non-voting delegate, Dan Sutherland, stood in opposition to the bill, and other Congressmen who had toured Alaska came to his defense. One of those who had made the trip noted that in British Columbia local fishermen with small boats were on the water, but in Alaska they were absent because the fish traps captured all the salmon. In the end, the canned salmon industry prevailed on most issues, except for one key point. The final compromise version stated that ". . . no exclusive or several right of fishery shall be granted therein, nor shall any citizen of the United States be denied the right to take, cure, or preserve fish or shellfish in any area of the waters of Alaska where fishing is permitted . . . "[7]

The commons were so important to Alaskans that words similar to those in the White Act would later be adopted in the Alaska Constitution, stating, "No exclusive right or special privilege of fishery shall be created or authorized."[8]

Ultimately, however, once Alaska controlled its own commons, we recognized that limited entry to fisheries was a critical means to conserve them. In 1972, we amended our constitution to allow the state to give limited-entry salmon permits to long-time fishermen, the great majority of whom were Alaskans.[9] Later, we also brought similar regulation to bottom fish in federal waters.

The White Act preserved the common ownership of the salmon fisheries, but accomplished little for conservation. When salmon prices increased—in part due to the expectation that the White Act would reduce supply—the canned salmon industry returned to its former ways, with an ever-increasing catch. The industry's political power assured that federal management of Alaska fisheries presented no real barrier to taking as many fish from the fish traps as canneries pleased. Even the regulations implementing the White Act itself were diluted so that they had little impact. As prices rose, fishing effort increased. As runs were destroyed, canneries turned to new streams. The salmon industry finally crashed in the late 1930s. Runs fell dramatically across the state. The decline continued through the years as we fought for statehood, until, on the eve of admission to the union, the catch had diminished to only one quarter of the number of fish caught at the peak.

Gruening gripped his audience at the Constitutional Convention with the seriousness and the source of the problem:

> Nowhere, as in the Alaska fisheries fiasco, is the lesson clearer for the superiority, in purely material terms, of self-government to colonialism. In the neighboring British Columbia and Washington State, where the fisheries are under home rule, and where fish traps have been abolished, the identical resource has not only been conserved but augmented.
>
> In a clear-cut issue between the few, profiting, non-colonial Americans and the many, seriously damaged, colonial Alaskans, the stateside interest wins hand-down. And it wins because the government, which is also supposed to be *our* government, throws its full weight on their side against us. *That's* colonialism.[10]

## REACHING FOR THE REINS

In the early 1950s, the canned salmon industry held the Alaska Republican Party firmly in its nets. That meant the Republicans opposed statehood. The boss was Al White of Juneau, a lawyer who also owned a dry goods business. He had been U.S. Marshall and held various other federal posts before the Republicans lost the White House in 1932. His rotund figure perfectly fit the role of power broker. After 20 years of Democratic rule under Presidents Franklin Roosevelt and Harry Truman, the territorial Republican Party was small and weak. The President or his Secretary of the Interior would appoint all government jobs, from the governor on down to employees of the Alaska Railroad. It didn't pay to be a Republican in Alaska in those days. White and his cronies in the Party had a brief agenda—to block any bill in the Territorial Senate that would tax canned salmon at a reasonable rate, and in that they succeeded for many years.

The statehood fight drew me into Alaska politics, so one might imagine that I would join the pro-statehood Democratic Party. But having grown up as a Republican in Kansas, I set out to try to change the Alaska Republican Party into a pro-statehood party. For Alaska to enter the Union, we would need both parties supporting the cause. Besides, on a practical level, the Republicans offered my best chance of getting to a position to make a difference. After so many years in power, the Democratic Party had little room for a young man who wanted to be involved. The Alaska Republican Party, on the other hand, existed as a front for the canned salmon interests. It lay vulnerable to takeover by people with energy and new ideas.

As the national party conventions of 1952 approached, most pro-statehood Republicans backed Dwight D. Eisenhower for president. He announced his support for statehood for both Alaska and Hawaii in a speech in 1950. When Eisenhower was elected, the political landscape in Alaska changed overnight. Republicans captured the territorial legislature and, far more important, the new President and his Secretary of the Interior appointed our governor and all other positions of real power.

Eisenhower appointed Oregon Governor Douglas McKay, an opponent of Alaska statehood, as his Interior Secretary. As we would learn over the years to come, the President's support for Alaska state-hood, mentioned in a speech in 1950, did not last. McKay's appoint-ment was the first signal of the trouble we would have with the Administration.

The President no longer mentioned Alaska in his statements in favor of statehood for Hawaii, later explaining that his new position was based on national security concerns. He appeared to believe that keeping Alaska in territorial status would enhance the military's abil-ity to use its land for defense, but no adequate explanation of his reasoning surfaced. The federal government still owned virtually the entire Alaska land mass, and even after statehood the President had the power to reserve military lands.[11]

Politics provided a better explanation for the Administration's opposition to statehood. Alaska traditionally fell in the Democratic column, meaning its admission would cut into the narrow Republi-can majority in the Senate. Hawaii was Republican, and the Eisen-hower White House supported its admission.

Not only was Interior Secretary McKay against statehood, so was our newly appointed Republican governor, B. Frank Heintzleman, and Senator Hugh Butler of Nebraska, the chairman of the all-important Interior and Insular Affairs Committee. Democratic patronage during the Roosevelt and Truman Administrations had helped keep Alaska in the Democratic camp. Now, to our dismay, McKay and Heintzleman's Republican patronage appointments for Alaska went mostly to Out-siders. Not only did this undercut our efforts to build the Republican Party in Alaska, it was wrong for the territory to have the officials who would govern us, such as U.S. Marshals and judges, sent from the South 48. What's more, the national Republican leadership did it without even checking with us, adding to our frustration over our colonial status.

Pro-statehood Republicans faced problems at home, too. It was difficult to build support for the Party in the territory so long as it was controlled by the hated canned salmon industry and opposed to statehood. More important, before we could make progress in gaining control over Alaska's resources, we would have to take over the Alaska Republican Party. Only then could we get the Eisenhower Administration's attention for our aspirations. Once again, politics, colonialism, and economics were completely intertwined.

The White House had no desire to see an Alaska statehood bill go through Congress in 1953, but since it wanted a Hawaii bill, both were allowed to advance at least to committee hearings. Senator Butler, perhaps thinking that he would gather anti-statehood ammunition, announced that he would hold hearings in Alaska that summer to hear "the reaction of the little people—not just a few aspiring politicians who want to be Senators and Representatives."[12]

It was true that Congress had heard mostly from official Alaska representatives up until that time. But, far from bringing out a different point of view from the "little people," Butler's hearings unleashed a flood of new popular support for statehood. Alaskans demonstrated as "Little Men For Statehood" when Butler's committee arrived in Anchorage by train from Fairbanks. Organizers included attorneys Roger Cremo and Cliff Groh, entrepreneur Barrie White, and town planner Vic Fischer in Anchorage. Out of this activity grew Operation Statehood, a new, more energetic lobbying group, which generated hours of testimony to the committee and demanded immediate statehood.[13]

A crowd packed the committee hearing at Anchorage's Carpenters Hall where several of us testified as "little men." We wanted to counter the Administration's argument that Alaska wasn't ready for statehood because we didn't have an economic base to support a state. Of course it would be impossible for Alaska to develop an economic base as long as the federal government tied up our lands and resources. I raised the idea of the state of Alaska owning its own lands as the built-in economic base we needed:

> "No, we cannot support ourselves when everything is taken away, such as the control of our seals, fisheries, and minerals. I wonder if the great state of Nebraska could economically support itself with two per cent of its lands, if its vast agricultural richness were under federal control such as our fisheries are . . . I could go on for hours, but we only ask that you give us what we have . . . (and) we will develop not only a great state of the union, but a great nation of the world."

The pro-statehood audience erupted in applause, and the newspaper excerpted my comments the next day. When the hearing ended, I

returned to work and shortly thereafter Senator Butler appeared at
the door of the Hickel Company on Gambell Street. "Young man,
that was a great speech," he said. "I was impressed." Of course, I was
even more impressed to have the chairman of the Senate Interior
Committee in my modest office. We developed a friendship and
eventually the powerful senator threw his support behind statehood.
He didn't go that far in my office that day, but he did commit to work
to free up Alaska's land. He made me give him a commitment, too.

Butler said, "Now I'm going to work hard for
this, but when I ask you to be with me, will you
be there? Whenever I speak on this issue, I want
you standing behind me." I agreed to help
whenever possible.

> *Give us what we
> have, and we will
> develop not only
> a great state of
> the union, but a
> great nation of
> the world.*

Winds of change were blowing in Anchorage in 1953. The younger Republicans in town
were energized by the Butler hearings, and we
set out to take over the party from the canned
salmon interests. Toward that end, I ran for
president of the Anchorage Republican Club,
winning the position from E. Wells Ervin, who was a member of Al
White's crowd and a supporter of Governor Heintzleman. A group of
Republicans from our part of the state signed a letter demanding a
meeting with Heintzleman to discuss our grievances. After a series of
false starts, weathered-in planes, and telegrams—all prominently
reported in the papers—our meeting with the governor never came
about, so we released our list of demands to the press. We wanted him
to support statehood and to end special interest control of the territorial government, among other issues. The demands made it clear
that the anti-statehood governor did not represent all Republicans.
They also provided our cause with needed publicity, a first step to
taking over the party.

The territorial legislature in its 1953 session had passed a bill requiring that the national committeemen and committeewomen of both
parties be elected by popular vote rather than chosen at party conventions. This was a dramatic change in favor of a more democratic system
of representation. Each party had two national committee members
from each state and territory, including Alaska. These party leaders

were our only representatives to the national political system with any voice and power. Selecting them by popular vote would give us at least one way for the territory as a whole to express itself nationally and be heard. This also was our opportunity to wrest the party from the control of Al White and his crowd.

In the spring of 1954, I campaigned aggressively for the position of Republican National Committeeman, traveling throughout the territory with plenty of help from our group of Young Turks. Although I won by a solid margin in the April 1954 election, the old guard didn't give up, and they still had influence at the national level. As a result, Republican National Party Chairman Leonard Hall would not accept the resignation of the outgoing Alaska national committeeman, Robert McKanna of Fairbanks. Back home, however, our younger group simply took over and carried on the fight for statehood.

An Alaska-Hawaii statehood bill passed the U.S. Senate and was stuck in a House committee, so in May 1954, the pro-statehood forces in both parties joined together to charter an Alaska Airlines plane and took a delegation of fifty Alaskans to Washington, D.C. At the time, apparently at the urging of Interior Secretary McKay, Eisenhower demanded a new condition for his support of Alaska statehood: The territory must be partitioned, with only the populated, southern portion entering the union and all the land north of the Yukon and Kuskokwim rivers, in western Alaska and the Aleutians, remaining a territory or becoming an immense military reserve. Various reasons were given for "the McKay line," none making much sense. The president had suggested it was for national security—the massive Distant Early Warning line of radar installations was then under construction—but Bob Atwood confirmed that military officials supported full statehood. Heintzleman said the purpose was to make the new state smaller and less expensive to administer. But the lands to be left out of the new state included some of Alaska's richest mineral deposits and fishing grounds, including Bristol Bay, taking away the wealth we would need to support ourselves. This certainly would help appease the canned salmon industry and would maintain Interior Department rule over the greater part of the territory, perhaps two reasons for the support of McKay.

Alaskans had come to agree by now that our new state must join the union with a land grant of at least 100 million acres to sustain it. The Alaska-Hawaii statehood bill that passed the Senate had included the land grant, but President Eisenhower's partition would have eliminated that concept, taking away our richest assets, including one we didn't know about yet: the oil fields at the North Slope.

The phone rang in my room at the Washington Sheraton Park Hotel. It was Alaska's Congressional Delegate, Bob Bartlett, a Democrat. Bartlett and Operation Statehood Director Barrie White had set up a meeting with Eisenhower through White House Chief of Staff Sherman Adams. Bartlett said, "Wally, they won't clear anything unless they clear it through you. You have to call Sherman Adams. You are going to have to clear this thing so we can get in." Adams told me to send a list of no more than 16 names. As the Republican National Committee still had not recognized me as a member, it was surprising that the White House put me in charge of the meeting.

We had fifty in our delegation, both Republicans and Democrats. Bartlett and I met and pared the list down to 16, including representatives of both parties, with future Governor Bill Egan and future Congressman Ralph Rivers, as well as the secretary of the Alaska Statehood commission Helen Fischer, and Miles Brandon, a Yup'ik student working and studying in D.C. We based the list on commitment, not party.

Adams told me to stand with him by the President's desk and speak for the group, and only one other person would be allowed to address the President. I chose Johnny Butrovich over better-known politicians Bartlett and Egan. Even though Butrovich had never even been to Washington, D.C., before, Johnny wouldn't be intimidated by being in the Oval Office with the President. Born in Fairbanks within a decade of its founding as a gold mining camp, he lived the self-reliant, libertarian philosophy of the Alaska frontier every day of his life. He would get the point across. When Butrovich learned that he had been selected, he said, "You talk. Then I'll get the goddamn story straight."

The meeting began with introductions, and we presented the President with Alaskan gifts. Eisenhower came around his desk and leaned back against it with his arms folded. We had only half an hour, so I went right to the point. We needed all of Alaska to become a state. We didn't want Alaska divided by an arbitrary line. I spoke adamantly, my voice rising. The President was bald, and when he set his jaw the blood began rising in his face and forehead. He obviously wasn't used to being addressed this way. Growing a little nervous at his reaction, I tossed it to Johnny.

Butrovich was good to his word. He was so tough; he made my comments appear mild. "Mr. President, we feel that you are a great American," he began, "but we are shocked to come down here and find that a bill which concerns the rights of American citizens is bottled up in a committee when you have the power to bring it out on the floor." As Butrovich went on in this vein, Eisenhower grew angrier and redder by the moment, and Adams began pulling on my coat sleeve, whispering, "Shut him up, shut him up, shut him up." I let him go on, because he was saying what we all felt. Adams yanked on my sleeve a second time and said, "Hickel, shut him up or you'll never get back in here again." I didn't make a move, saying to myself, "We're in here now. Let's get it said." Johnny finished his remarks with forcefulness and volume. Eisenhower turned to me and said, "Well, at least I'm glad you think I'm an American."

We might have made Eisenhower mad, but we also made our point. He offered no commitments at the meeting, but the bill didn't make it out of committee, and the partition idea faded away. The final Statehood Act included the whole territory, with a provision allowing future military reservations—a provision that has never been used.

As poor as Alaska's prospects seemed, an all-important shift had occurred. No longer were we asking for statehood. Now we were demanding it, right to the President's face, and demanding it on our terms. We knew we weren't going to create the kind of state we wanted without a fight. The days of Alaska as a subservient colony were coming to an end.

## THE BIRTH OF A DISTANT STAR

The Territorial Legislature took a bold and historic decision in the 1955 session: they called a Constitutional Convention for later that year, whether Alaska received statehood first or not. The National Municipal League would later hail the Alaska Constitution as among the best of all the states. But at the time, the writing of the document wasn't only an attempt to frame Alaska's future as a state. It was also a way of forcing the statehood issue nationally.

As national committeeman and in the midst of some of my busiest years in building my business, I did not run as a candidate for delegate to the Constitutional Convention. My younger brother, Vern, held together our growing holdings and development projects while statehood and party business kept me in Washington, D.C., a large portion of each year.

The fight for statehood was a team effort, and one of the most effective members of the team literally came out of the blue. His name was George Lehleitner, and his credentials raised eyebrows. He was a floor-covering wholesaler from New Orleans, but there was more to this man than just his history as commander of a troop ship in World War II. Lehleitner had observed the military control of the territory of Hawaii. Through his research, he became a principled opponent of colonialism. With no other interest in the matter, and at his own great expense, he dedicated himself to support both Hawaii and Alaska in their battles for statehood.[14] It was Lehleitner who offered one of the most decisive ideas in Alaska's crusade.

Lehleitner studied earlier statehood movements in American history and found an obscure precedent used by prospective states as they won their way into the union. In 1796, people living in the area that was to become Tennessee became impatient after three Congresses failed to approve their request for statehood, so they went ahead and elected Senators without the prior approval of Congress. Tennessee's "Senators" went to Washington, D.C., and four months later they achieved their goal. Over the next 65 years, six other states were successful using the same "Tennessee Plan."

Lehleitner recommended the strategy to Hawaii, but leaders there thought the idea too aggressive. Hawaii had adopted a constitution in 1950, and they had the support of President Eisenhower and House Speaker Joseph Martin and feared they would alienate these important allies if they became too outspoken. So Lehleitner came to Alaska in 1955 to sell his idea, aiming to change the history of the territory the very first time he visited. Here he fared better, for we were already taking the aggressive route.

When Lehleitner showed up at my office and presented his idea, I had never heard of him. Small of stature and retiring in demeanor, he was an unexpected advocate for such a bold proposal, but his idea was appealing. He had done his homework, getting support from various congressmen and lobbying many well-known Alaskans. Lehleitner's persistence and steadiness made him persuasive. To show the bipartisan nature of our support for his plan, Alex Miller, Alaska's Democratic National Committeeman at the time, and I traveled to Fairbanks to introduce him to the Constitutional Convention. Lehleitner gave a convincing speech conveying his almost religious belief that the Tennessee Plan would work for Alaska. The fifty-five convention delegates, all duly elected by the Alaska people, jumped to their feet and gave the floor-covering salesman a standing ovation. The convention not only adopted the plan but also made Lehleitner an honorary member of the convention and an "Alaskan ambassador of good will."

The freshly drafted Constitution went to the voters for ratification that spring of 1956 along with two attached ordinances, one endorsing the Tennessee Plan and the other outlawing fish traps as soon as statehood was granted. All three votes passed by large majorities.

By the time of the state convention that summer, we had consolidated party control behind the new, pro-statehood Republicans. We then nominated our choices for Tennessee Plan Congressmen—John Butrovich, Juneau forester Charles Burdick, and publisher Bob Atwood, the latter only agreeing to run after my strenuous lobbying. That fall, however, the Democratic slate carried the Tennessee Plan election, sending Ernest Gruening, Bill Egan, and Ralph Rivers to Washington.

Congress refused to seat our delegation, but these outstanding Alaskans were effective nonetheless. For us, the sessions of 1957 and 1958 were the homestretch, with our elected representatives working together every day in Washington to make the case for statehood. It was among Alaska's brightest moments, when, as a people, we worked together for an idealistic, well-defined goal—Alaska, a state in its own right, endowed with a sufficient land base and resources under the law of our new Constitution.

Good luck came to our aid, as well. Oil was discovered along the Kenai Peninsula's Swanson River, south of Anchorage, and the argument disappeared that Alaska would be too poor to support itself. It was assumed by now that our state would live on its resource bounty, and here was proof that we had the resources to make it work. Also, Douglas McKay left the office of Secretary of the Interior and was replaced by Nebraska Senator Fred Seaton. In this shift, one of our greatest adversaries departed from the scene, and in his place Eisenhower appointed a statehood advocate of long standing.

The day after Seaton took office, he received a call from his friend C. W. Snedden, publisher of the *Fairbanks Daily News-Miner*, recommending an Alaskan for his solicitor's office. Ted Stevens, a pilot in the famous Flying Tigers unit in Asia in World War II, had earned his reputation as U.S. attorney in Fairbanks, wearing cowboy boots and carrying a gun on his hip. Seaton hired him, and Stevens became an invaluable ally in Washington, using Interior's vast power in support of our cause. Finally, Governor Heintzleman resigned in 1956, and Seaton replaced him with Fairbanks attorney Mike Stepovich, who avidly favored statehood.[15]

Capitol Hill was crawling with Alaskans. Several of us worked the Republican side of the aisle while our all-Democrat delegation lobbied every Congressman. The national media picked up on the issue, and strong public support built behind it. Still, when a statehood bill came to the floor of the House, the outcome was in real doubt. A series of floor amendments made major and historic changes to the bill, including reducing our land grant from a proposed 180 million to 103 million acres. The Land would be selected over a 25-year period after passage. Finally, the bill passed on May 28, 1958, by a 44-vote margin, surprising even our strongest supporters.

The House had amended the bill to require that the Alaskan people approve the terms of statehood in a plebiscite. This was an historic change. With that public vote, Alaska's admission would become an agreement, or compact, between the U.S. Government and the people of Alaska. When the bill came up in the Senate, unchanged from the House version, statehood opponent Senator John Marshall Butler of Maryland warned, "You colleagues must understand this is unusual legislation and will not be able to be changed by this body alone." For the first time, many of us realized that statehood would be more than a chance for Alaska to determine its own destiny and to own and develop its commonly owned lands. The people of Alaska, through casting a favorable vote, would also be entering into a solemn agreement with the U.S. Government on the terms of entry to the union. These terms would become known as our Statehood Compact.

The terms in that Compact included our land grant of 103 million acres—the state commons upon which we would build our future—and they also guaranteed that Alaska would receive 90 per cent of the revenues from oil, gas, and coal development on federal lands within the state. This revenue provision originally had been set at 100 per cent—essentially, transferring all subsurface wealth to the state—but 10 per cent was retained to justify federal expenditures needed to manage the federal lands and resources on Alaska's behalf. This has become known in Alaska as "the 90/10 split." It was understood that both the state and federal government would contribute to Alaska's viability by developing the resources they controlled. It made sense that before this new, cooperative form of government came into existence, both sides would have to agree—Alaska by a public vote, and the federal government by the approval of Congress and the President. For later amendments to this Compact, once again both sides would have to be consulted and both would have to agree.

*We had no business groveling at the feet of Congress. We were equals, and we should demand our due.*

This concept of using the commons to support Alaska government fundamentally shaped the Statehood Act. The immense land grant we received was not a gift, but a necessity. Congress realized that our size, Arctic climate, and sparse population meant we could never support a state government through taxation of our citizens. But, given the chance to develop what lay in our land, we could become self-sufficient and contribute to the national public good. That was the hopeful and revolutionary idea that underlay Alaska's founding.

As we shall see, a clear understanding of the Compact between Alaska and the federal government faded with the next generation. As governor in the early 1990s, I sought to reawaken that understanding and enforce the Compact. By then, the federal government had set aside important lands and closed off access across vast regions of Alaska, foreclosing the state's right to select them or receive revenues from their development. We had a deal, and Congress broke it over the vehement opposition of Alaska. Our people and even some of our own politicians came to forget that. After Congressional passage and Alaskan ratification of the terms of the Compact, we had no business groveling at the feet of the President and Congress. We were equals, and we should demand our due.

As the final Senate vote on statehood approached, our team of Alaskans lobbied the senators we'd come to know during the years of battle. Our targets were conservative Republicans and those southern Democrats who opposed admission of a new, pro-civil-rights state. As our Tennessee Plan delegation was entirely Democratic, I took on the other side of the aisle, telling Secretary Seaton, "Let me take on the tough ones. Let me speak to the opposition." Many of these Republican Senators who opposed us had become my friends, some of whom I'd brought to Alaska and hosted at my home. My argument was a familiar one that I had been making for almost a decade: Alaska's resources must be developed right, and only with local control would that occur.

As the final vote approached, we knew we would win, and we could have had an even larger margin. Senator Andrew Schoeppel of Kansas called me and said, "Wally, I have two more votes, Styles Bridges' and mine, if you want them, if you need them. But we'd like to stay on the other side." It was unknown to me why a "no" vote would be advantageous for the two Senators, and I didn't ask. Our count had only seven Republicans and thirteen Democrats against us. Schoeppel had been to my home, and Bridges, of New Hampshire, was the minority leader and both were my friends. "Go ahead and vote the other side if you want," I said. All we needed was a win— the tally didn't matter.

The Senate gallery was jammed on June 30, 1958, as the vote count progressed. As I sat there, the adrenalin in my system reminded me of my Golden Gloves days. When the yea votes finally went over the top, New Hampshire's Senator Lamar Cotton looked up at me, clasped his hands over his head in victory, and began jumping up and down on the Senate floor. All of us in the gallery cheered. Back home, Alaska exploded in celebration.

We had won our land and resources. Now we would control the Alaska commons to use, save, or waste. With our destiny finally in our own hands, the exciting work of building Alaska could begin.

# PART THREE

## The Owner State

# 5

# The Creation of an Owner State

A remarkable thing happened in Alaska in the late 1950s. After a decade of struggle for statehood, an exceptional group of leaders emerged, men and women who shared a clear and revolutionary vision of the new kind of state we were creating. These common people were our Jefferson, Washington, Franklin, and Adams. America's founding fathers were intellectual giants who changed the world; Alaska's founders were fishermen, miners, business owners, and newspapermen. But, like America's first leaders, they emerged from across the political spectrum, sharing a new idea and a common commitment to bring it to reality. Later, leading the new state through the 1960s, this group, including Bill Egan, Bob Atwood, Bob Bartlett, Ernest Gruening, and others, would often split on the smaller issues typical of day-to-day politics. But amid the great events and ideas that shaped the state at its birth, all worked together with one accord.

## A STATE CONSTITUTION BEFORE STATEHOOD

Alaska's founding fathers and mothers met in the classrooms of the University of Alaska in Fairbanks' dark, frigid winter of 1955 and 1956. These ordinary people, chosen for their experience and wisdom rather than their party, joined in earnest and thoughtful discussions about how their new state should be shaped. During the day they sat on metal chairs and debated across student desks, drafting constitutional provisions and meeting in plenary sessions in the student union. With temperatures outside dropping as low as −40°F., delegates sometimes had to recess to go outside and start their cars to keep their engines from freezing. Their lodgings were four miles away, in the rough-edged, gold mining town of Fairbanks. In the evening, they met in restaurants, bars, and rented apartments and talked about their work among themselves and with friends. The radio and news-papers covered the deliberations across the territory in detail, and at the midpoint of the convention, delegates carried a rough draft of the Alaska constitution back to their constituents to gather their ideas and reactions. Debate was sometimes tough and heated, but deal-making and partisan politics rarely, if ever, intruded on the convention—the work was too serious, the purpose too clear, and the consensus too strong.[1] In just three months, they wrote the best state constitution ever written.

Not many years had passed since Alaskans had sought simply to become a state, giving little thought to the conditions of admission to the union. By the time of the convention, however, the thinking of statehood leaders had evolved greatly. In 1952, when Senator Taft helped us kill the woefully inadequate 23-million acre statehood bill, few Alaskans had believed it possible that we could receive a 100-million acre land grant, even if we waited. Now, in 1956, it was a different story. Our pro-statehood group led the Republican Party; a strongly pro-statehood legislature had thrown the territory's full sup-port behind gaining statehood and had called this constitutional convention; and, although legislation remained stalled in Congress, the bills that were being considered all contained some form of a huge land grant. We knew we would get 100 million acres or more.

No one talked at that time about a resource commons or an Owner State, but those were the ideas we were working on just the same. Although united with the other states in the federal govern-ment, Alaskans would collectively own a large part of our great, resource-rich subcontinent. This would be our commons, cared for and utilized—not exploited or wasted—for the benefit of all Alaskans.

The convention forced Alaskans to think in new ways about these resources we would own. We had focused on the freedom and opportunity of owning our own resources; now we must grapple with the responsibilities that common ownership would entail. We would need a new kind of government that could unleash the potential of our land and resources but remain responsive and responsible to the people, shielding our assets from the Outside financial interests who had exploited and subjugated us as a territory. We would need a state government that harnessed the efficiency and innovative genius of the free market to generate the revenues and royalties to build the roads, the schools, and the public buildings that individuals by themselves cannot create. With the prospect of a large statehood land grant, the stakes were much higher than mere statehood.

It was Thomas Stewart's job to organize the convention. The son of a world-renowned geologist and mining engineer, Stewart lived in Juneau next door to Congressional Delegate Bob Bartlett and down the street from Governor Ernest Gruening. A Yale Law graduate, he was an Assistant Attorney General in 1954 when he ran successfully for the Alaska Territorial House as a Democrat to represent the Southeast Alaska judicial district. Alaska's Republican Party was still embroiled in the takeover by our pro-statehood group, and the previous 1953 territorial legislative session, controlled by our party, had performed poorly. Voters overwhelmingly elected Democratic majorities in both houses of the legislature. At a meeting that fall at the home of Democratic National Committeeman Alex Miller, the new legislative leadership came to an agreement about their priorities and assigned tasks to carry them out. Stewart was given the job of writing a call for a Constitutional Convention.[2]

A statehood bill then pending in Congress called for Alaska to be admitted to the union and stipulated that a convention quickly follow. That approach would allow little time to study other constitutions or consider how Alaska's should be drafted. That statehood bill also called for the election of convention delegates from the same districts used by the Territorial House, but those district lines weren't working well. They grouped the cities together with towns and villages, making it unlikely the smaller communities could ever elect one of their own. Besides, after decades of poor federal government of the territory, Alaskans preferred to call our own convention rather than have it mandated by Congress.

Hawaii had drafted their constitution in 1950 as a way of advancing their cause for statehood. Although Hawaii still was not a state, most Alaska statehood advocates thought we should do likewise and draft our own constitution immediately, both as a way to draw attention to our movement and to demonstrate Alaska's political maturity.

Tom Stewart set out across the country at his own expense to find models for Alaska's experiment. Besides Hawaii, the State of New Jersey had recently written a constitution. He met with their delegates as well as with professors at various universities who were constitutional experts. Drawing on the recommendations he gathered, the bill that came out of Stewart's committee called for a convention with 55 delegates—the same number as attended the federal constitutional convention. Unlike the territorial legislature, the delegate election would be non-partisan and would use localized election districts, permitting every community with at least 1,000 residents to have its own representative. Those proved to be wise decisions. The convention's broad citizen representation produced reasoned discussions by men and women with deep Alaskan experience. Just as important, these delegates had the support of their neighbors, so the document they wrote would be widely accepted. Finally, the legislature took the advice Stewart had heard from his New Jersey contacts to hold the convention away from the political hubbub and taint of the capital, and instead set up shop at the state university. New Jersey had used Rutgers University, and Alaska used the University of Alaska campus in College, outside Fairbanks.

The Statehood Committee, an independent body funded by the legislature, would prepare for the convention. Before agreeing to the budget for the work, however, Ken Johnson, chairman of the Appropriations Committee of the Territorial House, obtained an agreement from Statehood Committee Chair Bob Atwood to hire Stewart as its executive director. Atwood also hired the Public Administration Service for some intensive pre-convention research. The PAS, a nonprofit research organization based in Chicago, enlisted national constitutional scholars and experts on subjects to be covered in the constitution. Over the summer of 1955, their team of ten toured the territory, meeting the people and studying their problems. By fall, they had written a series of papers on the issues and problems that would be faced by the convention. They bound their reports in three thick volumes along with model language for some articles, with a copy given to each delegate. The work still stands today as a broad and insightful study of the problems facing Alaska as a new state.[3]

A Florida State University professor, Ernest Bartley, wrote the PAS report on Natural Resources. Correctly predicting Alaska's land grant would be 103 million acres, Bartley pointed out that this unprecedented, Califor-nia-sized land transfer presented challenges for Alaska's constitution. It represented, in effect, the transfer of an empire. "No other state has ever received, dollar wise or acre wise, so great a patrimony," wrote Bartley.[4]

*Ours would be a new kind of state that could stand as a model for resource regions around the world.*

Bartley pointed out that this massive treasure could easily be stolen from an Alaska that wasn't prepared to handle it. He traced the history of land fraud and theft from land grants made to other states. His recent Ph.D. dissertation had covered the subject, and he had seen places in the 48 states that had been literally destroyed by resource exploitation.[5] In Alaska, Bartley wrote, the loss wouldn't necessarily be the result of political corruption, as "the level of political morality has been high in Alaska," but instead would happen by exploitation in the pattern already set by Alaska's colonial past. For example, Bartley noted, the Kennecott copper operation removed $200 million worth of a high-graded ore, with lesser ores disregarded. When management shut down Kennecott during a labor dispute in 1938, the railroad that had been installed for $20 million was ripped up for scrap. A ghost town was all that was left behind.[6]

## A CHARTER FOR PUBLICLY OWNED RESOURCES

Congressional Delegate Bartlett picked up the same themes when he gave the keynote speech at the opening of the convention on November 8, 1955. Bartley, who drafted the speech, said later that Bartlett recognized that Alaska would be a new kind of state, and he wanted the convention to prepare for an unprecedented future. "There was never any doubt what he was going to emphasize,"

Bartley says. "Alaska just wouldn't make it under the traditional approach. There was just no way it could make it financially. It had to go another way."[7] We needed to address resources in the constitution. Other states had private lands and ownership and grandfathered rights.

There had been little public discussion about natural resources in the weeks leading up to the convention, but in his keynote speech Bartlett focused on the resources article (Article VIII) as the most important in the new constitution. He said this was the convention's best chance to create a lasting monument within the constitution.[8]

This in itself wasn't news: a major theme in the statehood fight had been the need to free our resources from federal management, bringing home their control so we could develop Alaska for the benefit of Alaskans. Bartlett, however, also showed delegates the pitfalls of taking over this vast land area. The following words are some of the most perceptive and significant in Alaska history:

> This moment will be a critical one in Alaska's future history. Development must not be confused with exploitation . . . *Two very real dangers are present. The first, and most obvious, danger is that of exploitation under the thin guise of development.* The taking of Alaska's mineral resources without leaving some reasonable return for the support of Alaska governmental services and the use of all the people of Alaska will mean a betrayal in the administration of the people's wealth. *The second danger is that outside interests, determined to stifle any development in Alaska which might compete with their activities elsewhere, will attempt to acquire great areas of Alaska in order not to develop them* until such time as, in their omnipotence and the pursuance of their own interests, they see fit. If large areas of Alaska's patrimony are turned over to such corporations, the people of Alaska may be even more the losers than if the lands had been exploited.[9]

Bartlett went on to show how other states had squandered smaller land grants through fraud, waste, and corruption. Their constitutions failed to take account of the opportunities and risks of resource ownership and included only "pious generalities" about the need to develop resources for the benefit of all the people, not concrete policies and lines of responsibility.

These were sobering warnings. As daunting as the cost of failure, the convention's Resources Committee must write upon blank paper. They had no model to copy. No other state constitution dealt with resource issues in any significant way; only Hawaii's constitution even had a resources article, and it was brief. Most state constitutions were written before the conservation movement; back when public land was open for use or exploitation by the first comer. They gave no guidance for how a state should allocate the wealth of public land, much less how to develop it for the good of all the people, as we must do in Alaska in order to survive.[10]

The PAS paper on natural resources proposed language for the resources article, but the committee, chaired by Ketchikan fisherman W. O. Smith, rejected it.[11] Smith turned to Vincent Ostrom, a consultant from Stanford University hired by Stewart. Ostrom gave a presentation to the committee at the Fairbanks home of another committee member, Ada Wien, wife of aviation pioneer Noel Wien, leading them through a study of resource law and practices used in the American West and northern countries. A discussion followed about what had worked and what had failed in previous frontiers. At the end of the evening, Smith asked Ostrom to write a draft of the article. Ostrom refused to work on it alone, because he didn't know enough about Alaska; so Smith appointed a subcommittee of three to help him, Burke Riley, former Secretary of Alaska (Lieutenant Governor); John Boswell, a Fairbanks mine superintendent; and B. D. Stewart, Thomas Stewart's geologist father.[12]

Work began the next morning, December 6, 1955, in a small classroom at the School of Mines. The subcommittee started from scratch. Members and non-members who attended joined in a free discussion of their ideas of what the constitution should say about resources. As agreement came together on certain words and principles, Ostrom, standing at the blackboard at the front of the room, copied them down, slowly piecing together a preamble and a series of paragraphs that would become constitutional sections. When the words on the board were typed onto paper later that day, the first version of the resources article came into being. Work went on for weeks and the article saw many changes before the convention adjourned on February 6, 1956, but that initial blackboard draft contained the essential philosophy of the final version of the article, and some of the most important phrases.[13]

The resources article the convention crafted was not perfect. Commentators have criticized some of the language as being vague and contradictory; extensive litigation and years of political infighting over some provisions bear out some of that criticism. The article was the work of a committee, and it contained differing ideas and ways of solving the problems of how to use the state's resources. For example, the constitution recognized that the state would at times have to choose who would get to use scarce resources, but it also prohibited giving anyone special privileges or exclusive rights to what is commonly owned. The courts were left to define how that was supposed to work. To cover themselves with their constituents, miners on the Resources Committee inserted a provision to allow prospectors to patent mining claims in the same way they could under the federal Mining Law of 1872. But when Congress passed the Alaska Statehood Act in 1958, it kept underground resources public, calling for a leasing system similar to the Mineral Leasing Act of 1920, and that section of the state constitution did not take effect. In that instance, the Alaska Statehood Act overrode the Alaska state constitution and preserved the commons.[14]

In total, however, Alaska's constitution, and especially the resources section, amounted to an achievement of historic import. Here, for the first time in America, was a state charter establishing ownership of vast resources to be used for all the people, and setting up principles to protect that wealth for their use and benefit. In other words, it set up the Owner State. Section Two of the resources article, which found its way into the constitution with little change from the first draft on the blackboard, said it simply:

> The legislature shall provide for the utilization, development and conservation of all natural resources belonging to the State, including land and waters, for the maximum benefit of its people.

Other sections elaborated on this basic idea. Renewable resources were to be managed for a sustained yield: no longer would salmon runs be endangered by corporate interests taking too many fish in the short term. Public notice was required for all disposals of state land: no insider land deals would occur behind closed doors, away from the public eye. Oil and gas reserves would be leased to generate revenue for the state, not sold or given away. Waterways would always be public and open to use by anyone. And everyone would have an equal opportunity to use Alaska's natural resources. The constitution recognized that some special land should be set aside for parks and game preserves and for historic, cultural, recreational, and scientific value. But the very first section of the resources article showed the delegates' understanding of the primary purpose for Alaska's land grant:

> It is the policy of the State to encourage the settlement of its land and the development of its resources by making them available for maximum use consistent with the public interest.

The constitution established unique rules and philosophical principles for managing Alaska's natural resources, but success in running this great enterprise would depend as much on who was in charge and that person's authority to act as on the words alone. In fact, one of the most contentious debates of the convention surrounded the question of who would have authority over fish and game, resources highly prized by Alaskans. Under the territorial system, two boards responsible to the legislature had authority over fish and game, and these boards appointed the heads of the departments that carried out fish and wildlife management. Fishermen and sportsmen liked the arrangement, because they believed it removed resource decisions from political infighting. At the same time, the system gave these user groups great influence in resource decisions, influence they wished to maintain. Sportsmen supporting a continuation of this system brought to bear the greatest letter and telegram campaign of the convention. As a result, the Resources Committee inserted a provision in the constitution establishing the commission concept for fish and game, giving little authority to the governor over these resources.[15]

But the convention as a whole turned down the plan. It removed the commissions from the final document, leaving it up to a future legislature and governor to decide if there should be a commission for fish and game and how it should be set up.[16] The reasoning was fundamental and philosophical, reflecting the constitution's most important guiding principle: that the power of the governor should not be diluted. The delegates believed the governor should have the authority to run the state and be entirely accountable to the voters for all the actions of the executive branch. Although this idea of a strong, accountable governor did not arise strictly because of concern over resources, it proved to be among the most important aspects of the new kind of government we were creating.

Delegates arrived at the convention wanting a strong executive. Study of other state constitutions added to this preference, but the basic reasons came from experience: Alaskans had lived through lackluster administrations by territorial governors without the authority to carry out their will. Since the governor had been a presidential appointee, territorial legislatures, elected by Alaskans, gradually diluted his power and gave more authority to officials chosen by them or elected directly by the people. At the time of the convention, Alaska elected its attorney general, treasurer, highway engineer, and commissioner of labor, and had boards and commissions over such diverse areas of authority as the Pioneer Homes for the aged, the Alaska Housing Authority, and the State Police. None of these officials had much power, and with authority so diffuse, no one was clearly accountable for the running of the territory. Heintzleman and Gruening, past territorial governors, both called for a strong state governor in the constitution.[17]

With power would come accountability. Under the new constitution, Alaska's government would have no elected attorney general or department heads. The only elected official other than the governor would be the secretary of state (later renamed the lieutenant governor), and candidates for that office would run as a team with the governor in the general election. The governor alone would form administration policy, he or she would appoint and remove those who would carry out that policy, and then the governor would answer directly to the voters for the success or failure of that policy. The strong executive of the Alaska Constitution is the keystone to our unique state government. A committee cannot accomplish effective management of the commons. One person must have the authority to make decisions quickly and aggressively, just as a private landowner would do.

## THE FOREMAN OF THE RANCH

Alaska's governor can be compared to a foreman of a ranch. He doesn't own the ranch, but he has authority and responsibility, explicitly given to him in the constitution, to get the greatest long-term benefit from the land for the ultimate owners—in our case, the people of Alaska. A real ranch foreman says, "We'll plow that forty acres and plant wheat; we're not going to cut those trees because that's where we're going to build the house or preserve some habitat; that other area is not going to be plowed up because it's pasture for the cattle; and that other quarter section will be set aside for summer fallowing." The foreman doesn't exploit the land, and on a working ranch he doesn't lock it up to avoid competing with another ranch down the road.

Alaska's foreman of the ranch must be committed to the people and the land and believe in using natural resources for the betterment of the total. The Owner State needs a leader with the freedom and the authority to act, not only regulating, but also moving forward as the agent for the owners, instigating development or acting to preserve, depending on the situation. Managing for the benefit of the people, this executive, if he's astute, will keep his employers, the voters, informed at every step. When the state needs a decision, the governor has the authority to make it and carry it out. If the governor is corrupt, incompetent, or lacks the resolve to move forward, the state, like a ranch with a poor foreman, will fall on hard times. But the term of the governor is only four years, and then the owners, the voters, can choose a new foreman. In the meantime, the governor has the freedom to succeed or fail.

One of the governor's obligations is to make big decisions about public resources. Controversy inevitably follows. Weak leaders respond by shying away from decisions, by letting issues fester and progress stop, or by appointing committees and task forces as shields against political heat. Others try to compromise with every interest group. This sometimes quiets public debate and can remove the issue from public view, but it can violate the interests of the real stakeholders—the public owners. The best answer isn't necessarily found at some average point between interest groups. In a meeting between extreme environmentalists and determined developers, no one at the table may represent the public interest. If such a group of stakeholders agrees to trade one area to be locked up for another to be destroyed, they might satisfy themselves, but they may not serve the higher goal of balanced, sustainable development on all the land. If what is needed is bold and creative work, a leader with the authority to act has the best chance to succeed.

*Teddy Roosevelt recognized that free enterprise allowed to run totally free will exhaust common resources and eventually destroy itself.*

President Theodore Roosevelt was such a leader. He was a strong foreman of the ranch for America's resources, and the first president to recognize his responsibility to manage and protect our national commons. Roosevelt had the advantage of being an experienced rancher, but also he had something else. He was a populist who wasn't tied to either political party. He enjoyed strong support from the public and used it to gain control of the commons for conservation and to be utilized for the good of the total. His expansion of the National Forests saved the surface resource wealth of forest and range from a fire sale mentality. Today, it's easy to forget the destructiveness of the 19th century's unrestrained private use of those commons. Serious observers feared for the total desecration of the western forests and depletion of the nation's oil supplies through waste. Without Roosevelt's forceful interest in the natural world, and the great power placed in him by his popularity, the conservation of the west might not have occurred. Roosevelt recognized that free enterprise allowed to run totally free will exhaust common resources and eventually destroy itself.

Yet at the same time as the executive of the Owner State must conserve commonly owned resources, he or she must also make sure the economy prospers. Alaska's Constitution explicitly provides that the conservation of resources is for their more beneficial use by the people, not as an end in itself. In today's complex world of entrenched special interests and multinational corporations, it often takes greater executive resolve to make something good happen than to stop something bad. The foreman of the ranch must be an innovator, using his authority to bring natural resource products to market so the owners can benefit. The development of the Prudhoe Bay oil field may be the best Alaska example; we'll cover it in detail in the next chapter. The point to make here is that the State of Alaska had to push through the project for the benefit of its citizens. Without pressure from the governor, the oil companies that owned the leases might never have found that oil. What's more, after finding it they might have left it in the ground and gone to other world oil opportunities without building the trans-Alaska pipeline.

Alaskans won prosperity through the governmental structure they set up. They obtained title to lands likely to produce a whopping oil find, pursued the discovery, cleared the hurdles for a pipeline to take the oil to market, maximized the state's financial return, and distributed the benefits to the citizens through needed services, low taxes, and capital projects. If, instead, those oil resources had been private, the pipeline could have been postponed to the detriment of the Alaska people and the nation—just as Bartlett predicted at the Alaska Constitutional Convention. Indeed, when there is no local Owner State governmental structure, the most likely outcome is inaction. On federal lands both to the east and west of Prudhoe Bay, vast potential oil and gas resources have remained locked up for over thirty years since the state's great oil discovery, despite highly promising prospects.

*Public ownership, private development, people's government.*

The role of industry is pivotal in this arrangement. Ours is not a socialist system in Alaska. Free enterprise is harnessed in the service of the public. Government, necessary as it is to manage and conserve the resource commons, is expensive and inefficient in a democracy. It cannot itself develop natural resources competitively. In today's swirling world economy, a remote resource region such as Alaska can compete best with the help of the razor-sharp efficiency and explosive productivity of capital-rich industrial corporations. Family fishermen and loggers also make a living on our commons, but the bulk of the revenues needed to run a state come from large natural resource enterprises, which require major investment and innovation.

The state enters into a business arrangement with these companies. Rather than a partnership, call it a contract. Neither side owns the other, nor owes it more than each brings to the deal. The citizens benefit twice from the arrangement: they receive the benefits of government services paid for by resource development, and they can be employed in the industrial activity of the corporations that do the work.

The governor's job is to forge these contracts with industry. An obvious potential weakness of this system is that by giving so much power to one person, the Constitution creates the risk of private interests corrupting him. The vote of the public resource owners is the check. Their vigilance depends on their understanding of what is at stake. An effective news media, always part of a functioning democratic system, needs to follow these negotiations closely and let the public know what the state is earning from its assets. A strong campaign finance law also helps keep the leader as free as possible to act in the owners' interests. It is easy for candidates to get trapped by the need for money and find themselves asking for contributions from companies with financial interests in state resources.[18]

Historically, the people of Alaska have stayed close to what their government was doing, but television and the concentration of the population in cities has undermined that connection. Sometimes rural areas of the state that most need the benefits of the Owner State get pushed aside. It is up to our governor to use his power and responsibility to bring about solutions that help everyone.

The Owner State isn't just a government; it is an economic system for a resource province. It is a system in which the public collectively owns the economic mainspring, the natural resources, but in which those resources are developed by the private sector, harnessing the efficiencies of the market system both to extract the region's wealth and to employ its people. To make this system work takes a certain kind of state—one that has proved exceedingly rare around the world.

At the constitutional convention in 1956, these thoughts were not as clear as they are today, but once the Alaska Constitution was ratified in the 1958 Statehood Act, the final march toward statehood gained momentum, and all the promise of a resource-rich Owner State was in place. Soon, I would be shouldering the responsibilities of foreman of the ranch myself.

As a candidate for governor of Alaska in 1966, I simply promised, "There is a better way." My friend Governor Bill Egan, the incumbent, understood and believed in the same kind of Alaska I did. He fathered the state as President of the Constitutional Convention. As our first elected governor, he oversaw the creation of Alaska's basic political and legal structure. Born and raised in Valdez, where he built a grocery business, Egan possessed a practical mind and a legendary ability to remember the names and faces of Alaskans throughout the state. But in 1966, Egan, it seemed to me, was moving too cautiously. With a deep distrust of giant corporations, especially in the oil industry, he was reluctant to act on the opportunities to discover oil on public lands, and he was not addressing Native claims or federal interference in our shipping in the form of the Jones Act. To move beyond our historic dependence on Outside interests, Alaska needed to move forward boldly, decisively, and on many fronts at once. The election was close, tipping my way with a little more than 1,000 votes between us.

## THE CRISIS OFFSHORE

In the mid–1960s, large Russian, Japanese, and Korean fishing vessels were legally fishing offshore Alaska waters, but often making illegal incursions closer to shore. The primary culprits were Russians who entered within the federal 12-mile limit and sometimes even Alaska's 3-mile limit. Their fleets contained huge, ocean-going ships that were technologically far beyond the vessels Alaska fishermen could afford to own and operate. Besides taking our fish, these trawlers destroyed American fishermen's crab pots with their nets.

Since Japanese vessels began fishing in salmon-rich Bristol Bay in 1937, Alaska's long-range strategy was to get the U.S. to expand territorial waters and control ocean fisheries farther out to sea. At one point, we examined the idea of extending U.S. waters all the way to the International Date Line. But the issue of the day was how to deal with foreign fishing vessels that encroached upon the offshore waters we already controlled. Governor Egan had confronted the problem by seizing a Russian ship. I soon faced the same problem.

Just as the legislature was starting its session in Juneau in 1967, a Japanese catcher vessel steamed up the Gastineau Channel in full sight of the Capitol Building and tied up at the dock. The frustrated Alaska legislature had passed a law prohibiting foreign fishing vessels from using our ports to buy fuel or supplies. This intrusion was a brazen demonstration of how little they respected our control of Alaska waters. Alaska State Trooper Dick Burton[19] searched the ship, along with an attorney and one of my aides, while I phoned the State Department and other federal authorities from the Governor's Mansion. The U.S. Coast Guard wouldn't let Burton on board, citing a health concern to quarantine the vessel. He challenged the Coast Guard admiral, on my authority, and said that, if necessary, he'd break the quarantine and ride the ship back to Japan. He was then allowed on board, but the Coast Guard wouldn't let him search the fish hold, which was padlocked. Again on my authority, Dick sent a trooper for a shotgun to blast off the padlock. The Coast Guard again relented, and the search proved successful. They discovered Alaska halibut that had been illegally caught. With this evidence, we forced the Coast Guard to seize the vessel, but the toughest part of the conflict was not confronting the thieves but the U.S. officials. The entire incident proved that the federal administration was more interested in keeping smooth relations with the Japanese government than in protecting Alaska's fisheries.[20]

The next incident came several months later, when the Coast Guard caught a Russian trawler, the STRM 8–1413, fishing a mile off an island near the Alaska Peninsula. Since the vessel was within three miles of Alaska, we had the authority to prosecute the offense, but the State Department persuaded us to waive prosecution and let them handle it, promising they would bring a harsh penalty. I was shocked when the Russians were let off with a $5,000 fine. For a fleet gathering hundreds of tons of shrimp, a fine that small was a minor cost of doing business—especially since the seized ship was allowed to go home with its ill-gotten cargo still in its hold. I denounced the fine as a slap on the wrist, and the national media picked up my comments. Soon letters flooded my office from all over the country applauding our stand. We decided to prosecute the next ship ourselves.

We only had to wait two weeks. The paltry fine obviously had not scared anyone away. Unfortunately, this next Russian ship did not violate the state's three-mile limit and was caught in U.S. waters. The feds hit them with a fine of $10,000, but it still was not enough. The only way to get their attention was to confiscate a ship, or at least levy a fine large enough that it would not be worthwhile for them to return to our waters.

We took control of the situation when yet another foreign vessel, shortly thereafter, came within the three-mile limit. The Alaska troopers seized the ship and brought it to shore. It was time for us to defend our shores rather than wait for the federal government. When the news media reported that a Coast Guard ship was en route to take over the situation, I grabbed the phone on my desk that connected directly to the White House. The direct line represented Alaska's importance as a front line in the Cold War. When President Johnson came on the line, I said, "Mr. President, I just heard that you're sending a cutter out to Kodiak to solve this problem. This is my part of the world, and I want to solve it."

He agreed and canceled the Coast Guard vessel. Later the State Department called asking for a meeting in Washington, D.C., to resolve the situation. Thank you, I told them, we would resolve it in Alaska. In the meetings with the Russians, we levied a fine of $30,000 and signed an agreement that there would be no more incursions.

We also received new respect from Washington. Not long after the incident, Ermalee and I received a dinner invitation to the White House. When we arrived, President Johnson said he wanted to meet the guy who had dared to talk to him that way. Although he had campaigned for Egan in the gubernatorial election, Johnson and I became friends from then on, and Ermalee and I were guests at his ranch in Texas. The President and Lady Bird could not have been more gracious.

## ADDING VALUE TO THE COMMONS

Making things from our resources—or at least taking the first steps toward manufacturing—increases the value of our natural endowment. The work creates jobs and economic activity to enrich the citizens who ultimately own the resources. This simple concept of value-added processing has long been accepted as an article of faith in Alaska, but in most cases our politicians haven't had the know-how or the guts to make it happen. Sometimes, all it takes is an agreement that if someone wants your resources they must process them in state. Other times, more subtle efforts are needed, as the governor becomes a negotiator and dealmaker.

In the mid-1950s, the federal government struck 50-year contracts to sell timber from Alaska's Tongass National Forest to Japan. The Tongass, at 17 million acres, is America's largest national forest, and it had never seen significant harvest of its extraordinary wealth of large Sitka spruce and western hemlock. In the contracts, the Alaska Pulp Company of Japan received a guaranteed timber supply at low prices, and in return built a plant in Sitka, Alaska, for primary processing of the logs. The plant ground the low-grade hemlock into pulp for paper and other products, while cutting higher-grade wood into cants—squared off logs that load efficiently onto ships bound for overseas lumber mills. The arrangement provided raw materials for rebuilding war-damaged Japan, and it employed thousands of Alaskans in steady, well-paying jobs. Tadao Sasayama, a Japanese businessman, organized a consortium of companies to raise the capital to build the Sitka plant. The investment was Japan's first outside its borders after World War II.

A crisis developed, however, in January 1968, when we learned of a U.S. Treasury Department plan to export as many round, unprocessed logs from the Tongass as possible. With Japan's economy booming, its need for timber had risen dramatically. Most of the wood came from Washington and Oregon, where there was no restriction on exporting unprocessed timber. As Japan's needs rose, its purchases drove up prices and created shortages for domestic sawmills in the Pacific Northwest. The Treasury Department's solution was to cap the round log export from Washington and

Oregon and instead allow the Japanese to buy unprocessed logs from Alaska.[21] Treasury's plan would help plants in Washington and Oregon and allow the U.S. to import less finished lumber from Canada, improving the balance of trade. But it would also drive our Alaska primary processing plants out of business, because they wouldn't be able to compete for price with raw log exports. The details of the new plan were to be negotiated at a timber conference in late February.[22]

A fourteen-member task force from my administration and the logging industry went to work on the issue, headed by Frank Murkowski, commissioner of our Department of Economic Development. They traveled to Washington, D.C., to testify to Congress on our concerns. (But we knew we would have to watch after our own interests rather than rely on the federal government.)

Meanwhile, Tadao Sasayama, president of the Alaska Pulp Company, came to see me in Juneau, and we worked out a plan. He returned to his country and contacted the Japanese trading companies that controlled timber imports. The Japanese economic system's cooperative nature worked to our advantage. Their companies didn't want to cut each other's throats by increasing their round log imports from Alaska and driving out of business the mill they had built together. In early February, I flew to Tokyo and signed a document with the four large timber trading companies, which said they could import as much wood as they wanted from Alaska—but only as primary processed cants. They would not import our unprocessed round logs.

President Johnson's Secretary of Agriculture, Orville Freeman, looking for ways to solve Washington and Oregon's problems, followed us to Japan. He and his team were not successful in undoing our deal. They found the Japanese uninterested in importing round logs from Alaska. Freeman's spokesman told a Seattle reporter: "Alaska pulled the rug out from under us."

The most economically valuable of Alaska's resources was neither fish nor timber, but oil. We needed to add value to that product, too. Alaska was collecting cash for our royalty oil—the one-eighth share of the oil coming from state leases in Cook Inlet. We never saw the oil; the producers took it and refined it on the West Coast. There were three problems with this arrangement: first, there was no way of knowing if we were getting the true value for our crude oil because there was no market for it in Alaska; second, Alaskans had to buy gasoline from Outside when we owned our own oil field; and, third, exporting our crude oil without refining meant fewer jobs for Alaskans, just as with round log exports.

Robert O. Anderson, president of Atlantic Richfield, turned down my request for a new in-state refinery. Chevron owned a small refinery on the Kenai Peninsula, but it did not produce gasoline. Chevron President Otto Miller also refused to expand his refinery or build a new one. "Governor, we have a good refinery down here in California," he said. "There just isn't any reason to have a refinery in Kenai." It became obvious that the majors had no incentive to build a new refinery. The Alaska market for fuel was small, and as long as there was no crude oil market in Alaska they maintained the upper hand in setting the price they paid for the state's royalty oil.

But we owned the oil. It was up to me to do something. First of all, I decided to stop selling our 15,000 barrels a day of royalty oil to the majors. We were receiving $2.84 per barrel. I called Miller, "You keep the money. I'm taking my oil." We then put our royalty oil up for sale to anyone who would build a refinery in Alaska. The majors held firm and boycotted our offer. Miller even ridiculed the idea, saying it was uneconomical and that the state might get only $1 a barrel for our oil, or even nothing at all. We pushed ahead, and in April 1968, struck a deal with a group of Midland, Texas, investors, led by Frank Cahoon, and Leon Jaworski, who later became the Watergate prosecutor. They offered more for our oil than we had been getting, and they agreed to build an $18 million plant to be called Big Bear Refinery. Soon those first investors sold out to Tesoro, which built the first of several plants that have produced oil, gas, urea, and other products and contributed to the employment and local tax base in Nikiski to this day. The refinery created hundreds of well-paid, permanent jobs; it also created healthy competition. Not long after the Tesoro refinery came on line, Chevron built its own new facility next door, despite Otto Miller's earlier ridicule. We had successfully used our state royalty oil to create an in-state refining industry.[23]

## DON'T LET THEM STEAL THE COUNTRY

As governor of our young Owner State, I did my best to build an organization of public servants who thought as owners. Every level of the administration needed to understand our Alaskan enterprise and work toward its long-term success.

It was also my responsibility to appoint judges and a U.S. Senator. The challenge was to find individuals who understood we were the stewards of Alaska's wealth and who could be counted on to fulfill that trust. Making selections that way, my choices sometimes surprised people, as in 1968, when a 38-year-old Anchorage attorney named George Boney got the nod to serve on the Alaska Supreme Court. Boney was a spirited person with strong principles who was young enough to last on the court years well beyond my time in office. He was not a close friend, but he fit the bill.[24] When he heard the news, he was as surprised as anyone, and he asked me what I wanted him to do. "Don't let them steal the country," was all I said. He understood immediately. I wasn't referring to any one group, individual, or company. Alaska simply needed to stay free.

One of the fundamental problems facing the Owner State is creating a bureaucracy that knows how to say yes. It's always been easier to change the philosophy of the top level of government than to change the lower levels, where career civil servants do most of the work. The public considers "bureaucrat" a negative term, but the quality of any government largely depends on the competence and integrity of the civil servants who oversee day-to-day business. Some of these people face the tremendous pressures of making important, technical decisions knowing they will anger powerful people. Rarely do they have the staff and funds they need. And the input they receive from the outside world is almost all negative: make a mistake, and the world will know it, but do something right, and you alone will remember. Politicians seek credit for successes, but blame flows downhill. A bureaucrat learns to keep his head down. An Owner State, however, will have little success if its public servants choose to avoid making decisions in order to escape controversy.

Public managers must protect their people and resist threats to their staff and to their funding. Many conservatives think cutting the budget is good no matter what, failing to understand that as in any business, you can't make money developing resources without talented people to do the work. The state's resource departments tend to be the first cut when the legislature or the governor gets the itch to reduce spending. Yet without staff to prepare lease sales, map and inventory mineral deposits, issue environmental permits, and calculate royalties and taxes, development slows or stops, and the abuse of the commons becomes more likely. By demanding smaller and smaller government, budget-cutting politicians tempt private interests to exploit the people's assets.

I once asked how many people ARCO, our largest oil company in Alaska in the 1990s, would have on its payroll if it managed Alaska's 103 million acres of land, 30,000 miles of coastline, and $24 billion in Permanent Fund investments. ARCO had 21,000 people on their worldwide payroll at that time. We had 16,000 in state government to manage the commons and perform a myriad of regulatory duties, as well as deliver all the unrelated services of government, from law enforcement to running the state mental hospital.

It is difficult to estimate the exact number of state employees working on natural resources and other Owner State responsibilities, but it is less than ten per cent of the total. Our government grew after oil began flowing, and I don't fault those who insist on a balanced budget. But I never sided with those who blame government for all of society's ills and demand cuts in its resource management staff regardless of the effect on our commons wealth. In an Owner State, some unique government functions are necessary to maximize value.

Businesses grow only when their owners spend money and take risks. The Owner State is in the business of selling natural resources, and it can only deliver maximum value for its citizens when it learns to act aggressively and positively. Teaching a whole bureaucracy to act like entrepreneurs is not easy, but that's what is needed.

My goal was to bring people into policy positions who would transform their departments into creative branches of our Owner State, from our ferry system to our department of natural resources. The most important was in the area of oil and gas. My predecessor, Governor Egan, took a cautious and deliberate approach. The major oil companies eyeing Alaska saw it as a prospect for a large find, but

Egan didn't trust them, and political pressures within the state were intense. Alaska Native leaders urged the Governor to go slow until their claims to title of their ancestral land could be resolved. Some of that land had high potential for oil and mineral recovery. And local oil speculators also wanted the state out of the picture. They were hoping to grab a piece of the action, by obtaining oil leases and then making a killing by selling them to the majors. Egan hesitated. No one on his staff was able to show him the full potential of the situation—which was simply that Alaska could free itself from colonialism and become financially independent through the wealth of our oil.[25]

Taking office in 1966, it was evident to me that Alaska was in the oil business, but the people handling those assets had backgrounds in government, not oil. Key issues were left unresolved because of a lack of expertise, such as placing the correct value on our royalty oil from Cook Inlet and encouraging value-added processing, as mentioned earlier. After several months, it became obvious that we needed someone with oil industry expertise. Tom Kelly was an executive with Halbouty Oil in Alaska. A hard-driving young man with an oil patch drawl and a petroleum geology degree from Texas A & M University, he would fit in with any group of wildcatters. I invited Kelly to join the administration, and once on board he began tackling these problems. Kelly knew the oil business, but that didn't mean he trusted the major oil companies. On the contrary, he knew how they could take advantage of the state if we let them. Now that he was working for the public owners of the oil, we had his knowledge on our side of the table as we entered the era of big oil.

But the most important appointment of my public life was when Senator Bob Bartlett died just after President Richard Nixon nominated me as his Secretary of the Interior in 1968. The U.S. government still controlled 90 per cent of Alaska, and in the next decade the fate of those lands would be decided. At that point, Alaska had selected 38 million acres of its entitlement land. In 1971, the 12 per cent of Native lands were granted, and not until 1992 were all the 103 million acres of state lands selected. No other Alaska issue came close to the importance to our relationship with the federal government.

Senator Gruening once told me, "Alaska can't afford a statesman in Congress, not for fifty years." We were too small and too weak. We had to use the system to fight for our rights. Gruening spoke from experience. A true statesman, both by education and temperament, he was one of only two Senators to vote against the 1964 Gulf of Tonkin Resolution that brought the United States fully into the Viet Nam War. Partly as a result, he was defeated in his bid for reelection to the Senate in the Democratic primary in 1968. In replacing Bartlett, we needed a person who knew how to fight for Alaska and who could survive, lasting long enough to gain power through the seniority system.

On December 11, President-elect Nixon on live national television from a stage at Washington's Shoreham Hotel introduced his new Cabinet, which would include me at Interior. The broadcast had just ended when reporter Don Larrabee rushed to me with the news that Bartlett had died three hours earlier in a Cleveland hospital. When Nixon heard the news, he said, "Wally, what are you going to do?"

I mentioned three names: Ted Stevens, Carl Brady, and Elmer Rasmuson. Almost instantly, Stevens' name locked into my mind as the right choice. The President knew Stevens, who had served as Solicitor for the Interior Department when Nixon was vice-president. He said, "Wally, do you have the courage to appoint Ted?" Stevens did not have a winning record in elective politics. He had lost to Gruening in a bid for the Senate in 1962, and he had lost again in the 1968 primary to Rasmuson three months earlier.[26] Brady was my closest friend and supporter, a pioneer aviator, a state senator, and a man of principle. Rasmuson, one of Alaska's leading bankers, had been one of the "Young Turks" when we took over the Republican Party twenty years earlier. Like Brady and Stevens, he was both intelligent and capable.

Stevens, the state House Majority Leader, was not a close friend; in fact he had backed my opponent, Mike Stepovich, in the 1966 Republican gubernatorial primary. Years later, when researchers looked for a picture of the two of us together from our years serving the state in Juneau, they couldn't find one. Although he supported many of my initiatives as governor, we kept our distance. But I respected Ted. He was a capable legislator and a survivor, and we needed a survivor in Washington. I didn't speak my mind to Nixon at that moment, saying only, "I want to do what is right."

Stevens clearly was the most qualified man for the job. He knew Washington from his years at Interior, he had legislative experience from Juneau, he was a lawyer with a brilliant mind, and, most important to me, he was young, a fighter, and someone who would last. In the Senate club, seniority is the key to power. Alaska needed a Senator who could win re-election term after term, fighting his way up the ladder until he had the power to force our case with the federal government. Stevens could give us the continuity we needed. For this reason, above all others, I appointed Stevens.[27]

My relationship with Senator Ted Stevens has had its ups and downs over the years. Despite our conflicts over some of Alaska's greatest federal issues, I never questioned my decision. Stevens was— and is—a survivor. As we will see, he led Alaska's Congressional delegation through the fights to settle the Alaska Native land claims, authorize the trans-Alaska pipeline, and extend control of fisheries to 200 miles offshore. I disagreed with his approach that resulted in mammoth set-asides of federal land in single-use conservation units before we could even assess their potential. Today, Ted is one of the nation's most powerful legislators, still fighting in Washington to protect and improve our unique Owner State enterprise.

# 6

# Opening the
# Arctic Frontier

O n May 2, 1967, a DC–3 with a half dozen of us on board flew
through the mountains of the Brooks Range directly over
Anaktuvuk Pass. As I looked over the long, gradual ramp of the
North Slope, where the continental divide slowly merges with the
Arctic Ocean, a vision hit me, or call it an intuition. I saw an ocean
of oil. "There's 40 billion barrels of oil down there," I said.

After four years of searching and some dozen expensive dry
holes,[1] no oil had yet been discovered on the Slope. Atlantic
Richfield was the lone, remaining company still trying, and I'd argued
and cajoled to get them to drill one final well,
which we'd just visited. The other major player,
British Petroleum, had given up and mostly
withdrawn from Alaska. Other companies that
had won North Slope oil leases were also quit-
ting—allowing the leases to go back to the state
by not paying small annual fees. When the vision hit me of 40 billion barrels of oil in this remote, desolate region, most knowledgeable
people in the oil industry worried about my sanity.

*There's 40 billion
barrels of oil
down there.*

Two newspaper reporters were on that flight, and they picked up
on my prediction. Soon oil executives began calling—they wanted to
know if we somehow knew something they didn't. "Do you know
how much oil that is?" one asked, with a hint of ridicule. "More than
has ever been discovered anywhere in North America, by a long
shot,"[2] was my reply.

I was working on faith, as I had so many times before. We owned
whatever lay under the tundra, water, and ice of that part of the

Arctic plain. As governor, it was obvious to me that finding our wealth and getting it to market would be the key to our freedom from Outside control. As far as the oil industry was concerned, Prudhoe Bay State Number One was the best and perhaps last shot.

Petroleum geologists had long eyed the North Slope with interest, but the state had not always pursued that interest to the advantage of Alaskans. When we became a state, the Arctic's potential oil lands were in the public domain and belonged to the federal government. They were unreserved and open to selection by the state as part of our 103 million-acre entitlement. Governor Bill Egan had molded our political system as our first governor, but he wasn't sure he wanted to own the North Slope. He resisted selecting the lands at Prudhoe Bay as part of the statehood dowry after state geologist Tom Marshall had identified them as a region with high oil potential. Instead, Egan urged the federal government to lease the North Slope to the private sector for oil exploration.[3]

*Finding our wealth and getting it to market would be the key to our freedom from Outside control.*

Egan's reluctance reflected, in part, the pressure exerted by local Alaskan speculators who hoped to benefit from oil development—a goal that could hurt the state as a whole. The federal Mineral Leasing Act of 1920 had set up a system of non-competitive leasing for areas where oil had not yet been found. Anyone could obtain a lease by filing and paying a small fee. An oil company that wanted to drill on that particular piece of public land would have to buy that lease from the lucky person who had filed for it. If the company discovered oil, it would pay a royalty to the federal government. Egan reasoned that, under the Statehood Act, Alaska would receive 90 per cent of that federal royalty anyway; assuring the state treasury a large part of the revenue we would get from owning the land. Of course, Alaska's independent oilmen and speculators liked this system. When oil was found on the Kenai Peninsula's Swanson River in 1957, it minted several instant millionaires.

The major oil companies preferred the state's competitive leasing program, in which they bid for the right to look for oil where they thought it most likely to be found. That system cut out the middle-men, and the bonuses paid for leases went straight to the state.

In the spring of 1961, several major companies asked Egan to select the North Slope and offer it for competitive leasing, but he shied away from the decision. Some non-competitive leasing did take place on the North Slope, using a lottery system that allowed some Alaska speculators to take a chance on making a quick killing. The majors drilled on those leases near the north side of the Brooks Range, but they didn't find anything. Geologists wanted their com-panies to explore nearer the Arctic Ocean.[4] Egan urged Secretary of the Interior Stewart Udall to lease that area.[5] In hindsight, that would have been an enormous mistake. If the federal government had owned Prudhoe when oil was discovered, the state government would have lost control of the resource commons that has funded modern Alaska, created the state's Permanent Fund, and freed us to set our own course.[6]

Fortunately for Alaska, the Interior Department stalled. To offer a lease sale along the coast of the Arctic Ocean, its surveyors would have to find the exact outline of the shore, where federal land divided from tide lands owned by the state—statehood had given us ownership of everything offshore, extending out three miles. One look at that shore would convince anyone that surveying it would be nearly impossible: Along the Arctic Ocean the land sinks so gradu-ally into the sea that the two seem at times to mix together like two shades of the same color. Any leasing would be many years away if an accurate survey had to come first. Convinced of the problem, Egan in 1964 finally selected as part of Alaska's statehood entitlement 1.3 million acres along the Arctic Ocean, where America's largest oil field would later be found.[7] Some of that oil land went on the auc-tion block in December 1964 and July 1965, and the leases, won mostly by the major oil companies, brought the state more than $10 million in cash bids—a lot of money at the time.[8]

Exploration on the North Slope was nearing a standstill when my first term as governor began in 1966. Only Atlantic Richfield was active, drilling one well the company called Susie, after which it planned only one more. And Susie, on federal land 60 miles south of

Prudhoe Bay, would soon be abandoned, dry. That well cost Atlantic Richfield $4.5 million.[9] In fact, flying in the rig had cost more than the rig itself. A faction within the company was ready to give up and not drill again. Adding to their frustration, the best prospect for oil stood near 38,000 acres of state tidelands, just offshore, that had not been put up for lease. If Atlantic Richfield found oil at Prudhoe Bay, it would not control the nearby acreage and could lose much of the value of its investment.

Egan had planned to put those tidelands up for lease, but backed off when the Arctic Slope Native Association sued the state on October 4, 1966, claiming title to the North Slope by aboriginal right. Egan stood on somewhat shaky ground with some Native leaders because they were dissatisfied with his position on their land claims. With the general election a month away, he decided not to antagonize them by going forward with the lease sale.[10] I disagreed. As a speaker at the first convention of the Alaska Federation of Natives that October, I asked, "Doesn't it make more sense to go ahead with oil drilling, and settle the question of who the money belongs to later?"[11]

A few days after my inauguration, state minerals manager Pedro Denton came to my home in Anchorage to explain the leasing situation and Atlantic Richfield's reluctance to drill. After listening to him for less than an hour, it was clear to me that we should proceed with the sale as soon as possible. Otherwise, oil exploration on the North Slope could stop. (Atlantic Richfield executive Mo Benson confirmed in 1991 that it indeed would have.)[12] At the same time, I extracted a promise from Atlantic Richfield's District Manager, Harry Jamison, that if we leased the tidelands they would drill a well.

When we announced the sale, late that December, some Native leaders protested.[13] We soon got together and reached an understanding. First, I pledged my support for a Native claims settlement, viewing their claims to their land as a moral issue. I agreed they should sue the federal government to push their claims and directed Attorney General Edgar Paul Boyko to file the papers in court. On their side, the Arctic Slope Natives agreed to let the lease sale go ahead without protest and without having the proceeds deposited in escrow. After all, we agreed, the money would do more good circulating in the economy than sitting in a bank.[14] A week later, less than eight weeks after I took office, the tracts went up for bid, bringing in $1.5 million.[15] More important, exploration on the North Slope was still alive.[16]

Soon after, Atlantic Richfield hesitated. They weren't sure they wanted to spend the money necessary to drill at Prudhoe Bay. I called Jamison and said, "Damn it, Harry, you'd better drill up there. If you don't, I will."

Jamison said, "You mean the State will?"

"Damn right we will," I said.

Of course, the best approach was for the industry to drill the wells. They had the money, the experts, and the know-how. But we needed to press every advantage to get them to act. That was our oil up there. My hunch was that there was plenty of it, and I wanted it found.

The decision at Atlantic Richfield, however, remained in doubt. It was left in the hands of their CEO, Robert O. Anderson. He said yes, he later admitted, without much confidence, but mainly because the Susie rig was only 60 miles away and the well was already planned.[17] A few weeks after the lease sale, a telegram arrived from Jamison saying Prudhoe Bay State Number One would go ahead.[18]

John C. "Tennessee" Miller and a crew of catskinners moved the rig on sleds pulled by tractors through vicious weather to the new drill site. It was a truly heroic effort. Drilling began at Prudhoe Bay on April 22, and my first visit to the site was on that DC–3 flight on May 2. We carried a party of 16 on the chartered plane, piloted by Neil Bergt,[19] including Jamison and other executives from Atlantic Richfield and Humble Oil (Exxon), two reporters, Commissioner of Natural Resources Phil Holdsworth, and Roscoe Bell, director of our Division of Lands. Skies were sunny as we crested the Brooks Range, and Bergt circled the abandoned Susie well site.[20]

Spring breakup had come early that year, and we stepped off the plane at Prudhoe into ankle-deep water on the rough landing strip. Mud was everywhere. To protect the tundra, which is a shallow insulating layer of vegetation over permafrost (permanently frozen ground), drilling is only permitted in winter. We rode to the rig on a gray truck, most of us sitting on the floor of the freight area, and I told the story of Uncle Emil's oil well back in Kansas, where roughnecks used to dip their pants in water to freeze them to stop the wind from penetrating. The drill site was a sea of mud, but there was a tremendous sense of optimism among the crew and all of us.

As we looked at the rig together I said "Harry, drill, drill!" Despite the need to stop for spring breakup, I was confident that bit would soon reach oil.

"Governor, what makes you so positive there is oil down there?" he asked.

I said, "Harry, if it's not there, I'll think it there. Drill! I want that well in by Christmas."[21]

Returning to the plane, we all rode together on a flatbed truck, like a hay-less hayride. Holdsworth, sitting at the back, bounced a good two feet in the air on the bumps, and it took the strong hands of those around him to keep him aboard. After taking off, Bergt circled over the Arctic Ocean in the DC–3 and then headed south in the bright afternoon light. I looked out the window and felt I could see right into the ground, two miles below the surface. That's when I said: "There's 40 billion barrels of oil down there."

We now know there is even more than 40 billion barrels of oil on the North Slope. Without a barrel of oil shipped from either ANWR to the east or NPR-A to the west,[22] more than 13 billion barrels have been exported to the South 48 from state lands on the Slope, with an estimated value of $270 billion.[23]

## DISCOVERY

Alaska changed forever with a great, rushing roar on December 27, 1967, when natural gas shot out of Prudhoe Bay State Number One with the sound of racing jet engines. Tests of the flaring gas and its sheer force told the men on the rig they had found something big, but the drill got stuck in the hole during the tests and it took time before they could drill deeper to find oil. On March 12, 1968, the rig penetrated the Prudhoe Bay field's oil layer, bringing up crude at a rate of 1,152 barrels a day. ARCO rushed to bring in another rig and drill a confirmation well before breakup. They set up at the Sagavanirktok River, seven miles away—an extraordinary distance from the initial discovery—demonstrating their geologists' expectations of the size of the Prudhoe formation. The second well, called Sag River Number

One, hit oil by early June, producing a flow of 3,367 barrels a day. By late July, when the discovery was made public, the field had been confirmed as one of the world's largest.

As national, even worldwide, attention turned to Alaska, the importance of the many decisions that led to this great discovery were evident: we had applied for statehood with a unique constitution, we had won a large land grant with statehood, we had selected potential oil lands, we had leased those lands competitively, we had pushed for speedy exploration, and we had discovered a resource that would help us pay our own way.

Now an oil rush was on for the remaining federal land on the North Slope. Interior Secretary Stewart Udall had frozen Alaska's federal lands pending resolution of Native land claims, but the land office still accepted applications for federal non-competitive oil leases that could be granted after the freeze. These applications now shot up in value. My belief was that it made no sense for a few individuals to get rich off these resources at the public's expense just because they knew the system and filed paperwork at the land office. The Owner State should acquire as much oil land as possible.

With President Nixon wanting me in his Cabinet, I told Natural Resources Commissioner Tom Kelly in December 1968 to select six million acres of federal oil land for state ownership, including two million acres on the North Slope. The selections would eventually force Interior to reject some 1,200 non-competitive lease applications covering half a million acres, including applications submitted by 150 Fairbanks residents who were doubtless hoping to become oil millionaires. This would cause an uproar, but it was the right thing to do. These were public resources, not private property. The displeasure of the disappointed applicants was intense, and some have not forgiven me to this day.[24] The decision essentially brought an end to the old way of doing things: From here on out, the state would acquire and use its resources to get the most from those assets, like any responsible owner should.

When Kelly oversaw Alaska's greatest lease sale on September 10, 1969, the people of the state and the world appreciated for the first time the value of Prudhoe Bay. Recognizing that the previous sales had brought in pennies on the dollar compared to the true value of the oil under the North Slope (not counting royalties and taxes that would amount to many billions), Kelly sought to make up for the previous bargain basement prices paid by the oil industry. The 400,000 acres of state land that he leased brought in bids of $900,000,000 ($4.2 billion in 2001 dollars), a figure beyond comprehension in Alaska at that time. All our previous lease sales combined had brought in less than $100 million.[25] The checks Alaska flew to San Francisco for bank deposit that night amounted to more than our entire annual budget for the previous six years.

The $900 million lease sale represented only a starting point. Once we got the oil to market, Alaska would receive an eighth share in royalties and immense tax revenues. But getting the oil to market would not be easy.

## THE ROAD TO A NEW ERA

My belief in the need for access to the Arctic's resources began well before the Prudhoe Bay discovery. In any pioneering country, access comes first, then development. Judge James Wickersham, the jurist who first brought law to Alaska's interior in the early 1900s during the Gold Rush, was Alaska's first politician to understand the Owner State. He saw the necessity of opening the country as a prerequisite to building an economy. Elected territorial Congressional delegate in 1908, he denounced the Outside trusts that were exploiting Alaska's resources.[26] Among his amazing accomplishments, Wickersham gave a speech that lasted for five and a half hours, to the U.S. House of Representatives on the potential of Alaska and the need for a railroad. Ultimately, he convinced Congress and President Woodrow Wilson to authorize that railroad.[27] Private industry had tried and failed several times to build a railroad across Alaska. Thanks to Wickersham's eloquence and persistence, Congress approved "not to exceed 1,000 miles" of rail line for Alaska in 1914, with the primary purpose to open up the country. The federally built and owned railroad from Seward through Anchorage and on to Fairbanks, about 500 miles, was completed in 1923.[28]

The influence of the railroad on the development of Alaska would be hard to exaggerate. It built the city of Anchorage from scratch and fed the growth of Fairbanks as well as the places in between, including Palmer, Wasilla, Talkeetna, Nenana, and Denali National Park. The railroad aided the supply of Alaska coal to the military in World War II and the Cold War, and the transportation of Alaska coal continues to this day. Building a rail line across this remote territory took eight years. As an investment in Alaska, it yielded extraordinary dividends, yet as a private business venture, it never would have survived. The railroad's revenues covered its operating costs, but the line did not recover its capital costs in bottom line terms. The lesson to learn is that the bottom line is the wrong measure to use in judging a project that opens up a frontier. Instead, these projects should be judged by the cities they build, the resources they access, the contributions they make to national security, and the civilization they create. By those measures, the Alaska Railroad was a roaring success from the very outset. We can only imagine what greater successes would have come if the entire 1,000 miles authorized by Congress had been built. It could have reached all the way to the Arctic. What additions to Alaskans' quality of life would exist today and what improvements to environmentally sound transportation north?

*The bottom line is the wrong measure to use in judging a project that opens up a frontier.*

Once in the governor's chair in 1966, I was determined to extend Wickersham's work and appointed a NORTH Commission—the letters stood for Northern Operations of Rail Transportation and Highways. The legislature shared the dream and appropriated $750,000 for the commission's work.[29] Members included Sargent Shriver, first head of the Peace Corps, aviation hero Charles Lindbergh, and Bill Lear, inventor of the Lear Jet.[30] William Randolph Hearst attended the first meeting, which was held in Fairbanks.[31]

The NORTH Commission was staffed by an Athabaskan in his early twenties, the late Morris Thompson, who became the youngest-ever Director of the Bureau of Indian Affairs and later a Native statesman and CEO of Doyon, Ltd. The commission's mandate was broad: Access. We sought a way to bring transportation to the North for the development of natural resources and a cash economy for Alaska's rural residents. When we discovered oil at Prudhoe, however, we focused more closely on extending the railroad there.[32] The line could carry oil equipment north, and, as a byproduct, open up the corridor for future development so people could see the country.

Then, as now, some people brushed off or ridiculed the idea of a railroad to the Arctic Ocean. In one conversation, Robert O. Anderson, founder and chairman of Atlantic Richfield, questioned the need for a rail line, suggesting that the oil would run out in 20 years. My belief was that Prudhoe Bay was only the start. New fields to the east and west would follow. Thirty years after the Prudhoe discovery, the oil industry still invests billions at the North Slope in new equipment and drilling techniques and has only been allowed to lease a few small plots to the west in the National Petroleum Reserve, and none at all to the east in the "oil reserve" set aside in the Arctic National Wildlife Refuge. Yet the rail line would have been a bargain. We could have paid for it with the money we would have saved on the construction of the $10 billion trans-Alaska pipeline.

Others questioned the technical feasibility of building a rail line north and west. They probably hadn't studied the history, as I had, of the 6,000-mile trans-Siberian railroad, built in more difficult country seventy years earlier. Environmentalists attacked the idea as a threat to the Arctic. Several years later, David Brower, the head of the Sierra Club, apologized for his opposition when we appeared together on a panel on national television. He admitted that a rail line would have been far better for the environment than the road that now extends to Prudhoe Bay. With rails, the spread of people in the wilderness is contained to the towns where they get on and off the train. I've fought against the clutter that often follows highways throughout my public service career, and therefore his admission pleased me greatly that building rails instead of roads is an excellent alternative, especially in Alaska.

Finally, we had to contend with those who claimed that we wanted to build with an old technology, something out of the nineteenth century. That criticism came from simple ignorance. Rail carries more freight, cheaper, safer, and with less pollution and less fuel per pound than any other on-land technology we have today.

The NORTH Commission, and its dream of a rail line to the North Slope, lost its momentum when Nixon took me to Washington.

A decade later, the bold project became much more difficult when Congress passed Alaska lands legislation that deliberately blocked key transportation corridors to the Arctic by drawing the boundaries of national conservation units to include every eligible mountain pass suitable for a railroad. As a result, a great opportunity was lost, or postponed, until a future generation takes a fresh look at the true potential of our north country.

Before I left the governor's office, however, I did start work on the first surface transportation route to the North Slope. The construction of a pipeline to transport Prudhoe Bay oil to market was still in doubt, and Alaska needed to make a bold stroke to demonstrate that Prudhoe Bay was not too far away to be useful. My fellow Alaskans and I were inspired by the example of the world's pioneers. The true pioneer, in any field, changes the thinking of those who follow by setting down the first path across uncharted territory. Before that first route exists, most people see an impassable barrier in each blank place on the map. The great explorers of history did more than blaze the first trails; they opened the eyes of those who would follow. In this way, Lewis and Clark gave us the American West, transforming it forever from the realm of the unknown to the field of opportunity.

I dreamed of doing something similar for Alaska in October 1968, when I met with Alaska Senate President John Butrovich and Representative Bob Ziegler in Room 40 of the Travelers Inn in Fairbanks. "I need a half a million dollars to get to Prudhoe Bay," I explained. "We don't have any way to get there." I wanted to start a Cat train north across the tundra from Fairbanks to Prudhoe Bay. With tractors pulling sleds behind them, we could blaze an ice road to Prudhoe that the oil industry could use to haul the equipment needed to begin developing the field. More important, it would prove that the Arctic was accessible. The road would make the pipeline easier to build and easier to believe in. Butrovich, my long time friend and Republican ally, said, "Governor, we'll get you the money." Ziegler, a Democrat, looked me in the eyes and said, "Yes, sir, I'll be there." We all understood the magnitude of Alaska's opportunity at the North Slope and our responsibility to bring it to fruition. They agreed that, working together, we would make it work. The next month, we polled the legislature, and the road north was launched.[33]

The convoy started at Livengood, just north of Fairbanks. It was early winter and the ground was frozen and snow covered. We planned to build an ice road that would melt without a trace when spring arrived. We fired up the Cats. I drove the lead for the first few miles, dragging a sled behind me that contained the living quarters for the crew. Jim Dalton was the man in charge. My orders were straightforward: "Jim, don't shut this thing off until you get to Prudhoe Bay."

He said, "I won't, Governor. I'll do the best I can."

Before the project had made much progress, however, I had left the state, having accepted President Nixon's appointment to the Cabinet. Dalton's crew made it to Stevens Village on the Yukon River. The state then put the next segment, to the North Slope, out to bid, but then decided it would be cheaper and faster to finish the job with state workers.[34] Unfortunately, supervision of the project did not keep pace with the difficulty of the assignment. I lost control of the job, but I did not lose the responsibility for it. My successor Governor Keith Miller completed the road and then christened it the Hickel Highway.[35] It quickly became the most controversial decision of my career, gaining intense national attention and condemnation. Much of the work was done improperly. Instead of building a pad of ice that would disappear with the melt, heavy equipment scraped away the top layer of tundra. On a return visit to Alaska, I was sick at heart to see a scar running across the land. The arrival of spring breakup had created a ditch in the permafrost. Meanwhile, environmentalists opposed to the pipeline project used the ice road project as a symbol that the state and people of Alaska could not be trusted.[36] The job should have been done better, but I do not shirk the responsibility. The decision in 1968 to create access was the right one. We needed to put a line on the map of Alaska leading to the North Slope, and we did. We opened the door to a new era for Alaska.

## THE ALASKA PIPELINE—UNDER ONE FLAG

After 25 years of operation, the trans-Alaska oil pipeline has delivered more than 13 billion barrels of crude oil from the Arctic.[37] It has worked so well it has disappeared from the consciousness of most Americans, like the underground water pipes that make their faucets work. But building the pipeline was an extraordinary, pioneering achievement. The difficulties of engineering and construction, along with a final cost of almost $10 billion ($29 billion in 2001 dollars), earned the pipeline the title of the largest privately financed project in world history.[38] Yet, for all the difficulties of construction, the challenges of imagination and politics may have been even greater. The greatest barriers lay not in the environment, but in human minds and institutions. Some people didn't want the line built at all, some wanted other land issues resolved first, and some wanted the project but didn't believe we could do it right.

As Secretary of the Interior, I had a unique opportunity to work on these issues as an Alaskan. But now my assignment was much bigger. I had become the American public's trustee for its 600 million acres of commonly owned land, as well as its air, water, energy, and wildlife.[39] My role at Interior had many similarities to the Owner State role of Alaska's governor, but the commons was much, much larger.

Complex issues surrounded and entangled the pipeline project. We needed to motivate the oil producers to make the massive investment needed to build the line quickly, and we needed to keep enough of a leash on them to make sure they did the job right, with proper respect for the environment. On top of these concerns, the ownership of the land upon which the pipeline would be built was in dispute. Alaska Natives believed, with good cause, that they had claim to millions of acres of Alaska.[40] Finally, we had to grapple with national environmental organizations that had taken a radical posture, choosing to fight against all development projects. They would erect every barrier at their disposal to block the construction of the line.

My predecessor at Interior, Stewart Udall, had stopped virtually all federal land transfers in Alaska in late 1966, and in late 1968 issued an executive order that made his freeze into law. Alaska Natives had filed claims to land covering most of the state, and Udall's freeze attempted to stop the clock until the land claims were resolved. Yet, during his eight years at Interior, Udall had made few real efforts to offer the Natives a just settlement. My approach was very different. I supported a fair and generous resolution of the Natives' claims and a prompt solution so we could bring an end to the freeze, which was stifling our chance to build an economy to set us free.

Even with a resolution to the Native claims conflict, the pipeline would need special permits to cross hundreds of miles of federal land. The law allowed for pipeline rights-of-way 54-feet wide. Installing this huge pipeline would take a corridor at least 100 feet wide, and a permanent haul road would have to be built parallel to the line. At the same time, the National Environmental Policy Act (NEPA) was under consideration by Congress and passed in 1969, requiring Environmental Impact Statements for all major projects affecting federal lands—and allowing almost anyone to sue if they felt the impact statements were defective.

As we began planning the pipeline, the oil industry seemed blissfully unaware of the problems we were facing. In February 1969, a loose consortium of seven companies announced they would build the pipeline, expecting to have oil flowing in three years. At that time, British Petroleum's upper management didn't even know about the land freeze or the Native claims issue, according to Hugh Gallagher, who became their lobbyist.[41] On June 9, 1969, my department received the oil companies' application for a right-of-way to build the pipeline, which they turned in at the Anchorage office of the Bureau of Land Management along with a demand that the permit be issued by July 1.[42] The application took no account of the complexities of building a pipeline in the Arctic. There were huge gaps in the needed geological and soils information and nothing on design specifications or construction practices. Provisions for leak detection and shut-off valves were inadequate. Apparently, they assumed the application would be approved automatically.[43]

I put together a task force to work on the problem, led by Under Secretary Russell Train. This group came up with 79 technical questions, but the industry's answers were vague. They essentially asked us to trust them and let them figure it out as they went along.[44]

When five of the top pipeline engineers came to see me, they assured me that they could handle the job. After all, they had built pipelines throughout the world.

"How would you build it in the Arctic?" I asked. They hesitated and then said, "We'll bury it."

I knew at that moment that they didn't understand the Arctic. "Then bury it above ground," I replied.

It was obvious to most of us involved in building and engineering in Alaska that the pipeline would be much more difficult to build and maintain than they expected. Prudhoe Bay crude comes out of the ground at 150 degrees Fahrenheit and has to stay hot to flow through an Arctic pipeline. In much of Alaska, the ground is solid only because it is frozen. This material, called permafrost, turns to mud when it gets warm. A study from Interior's lab in Menlo Park, California, confirmed this, saying, in part, "over distances of several miles on almost imperceptible slopes, in a few years the pipe could be lying at the bottom of a slumping trench tens of feet deep on the uphill end, while at the downhill end, millions of cubic feet of mud (and probably the pipe as well) would be extruded over the surface."[45]

*Bury it above ground.*

It appeared we would have to do much of the planning work ourselves. We set up a technical team at the California lab to study the pipeline and the Arctic conditions it would encounter, led by Bill Pecora, the director of the United States Geological Survey.

Creation of the technical group represented basic stewardship of the commons, and it came to play a crucial role. At the lab, Pecora brought together the best scientists in each relevant field to study aspects of the pipeline's construction and the environmental concerns surrounding it—many of which, we knew, were legitimate. Over the years that followed, long after my departure from Washington, the group continued to work through each technical issue to either solve the problem or determine it was invalid. Slowly, a complete application would come into focus, along with a detailed environmental review. They did a wonderful job. The proof is in the project: the pipeline has been a world model environmentally, without serious detriment to Alaska's land, water, or wildlife.[46]

By late September of 1969, it looked like we were ready to lift the land freeze and move forward with the project. We had developed a set of construction stipulations, the strictest government controls ever put on a private construction project. The oil companies had obtained the right-of-way waivers they needed from Native villages along the proposed route. I went to the Congressional oversight committees and asked for an agreement to lift the land freeze over the pipeline corridor. A misunderstanding shot me down. Members of the Senate Interior and Insular Affairs Committee had been to Alaska and seen construction on the state project extending a road from Livengood, north of Fairbanks, to the Yukon River, where a large bridge would be built for the pipeline. The committee members didn't remember agreeing to lift the freeze for this project, and so thought I had violated our agreement. In fact, the work was on state land, and the committee had approved the transfer.

In early 1970, several environmental groups and some of the same Native villages that had waived their claims only a few months before sued in federal court. The Natives felt the oil industry wasn't living up to its bargain. The environmentalists said the pipeline still was not planned in adequate detail.[47] They were right about that, and I had no intention of issuing a construction permit until the Arctic engineering issues were resolved.

Meanwhile, a letter and telegram campaign from Alaska, augmented by newspaper editorials, demanded to know why Wally Hickel's Interior Department was holding up construction of the pipeline. Many had expected construction to start and had made investments based on a hoped-for boom. Badly overextended, they now saw Alaska's economy slipping into a slump. The villains closest at hand appeared to be the government bureaucrats and me. They were unaware of the struggle we were having with the oil industry and the new requirements of NEPA. The pipeline could not go ahead until we had technical specifications that would effectively construct the line over permafrost and earthquake hazard areas. Meanwhile, the oil industry still had not come to grips with the challenging Arctic, an environment in which they had never built a hot oil pipeline.[48]

How could I motivate them? Their loose consortium of seven companies couldn't even come to decisions among themselves. ARCO wanted the pipeline built quickly and was ready to move fast. The North Slope discovery had invigorated the company, which needed new oil reserves, and its CEO, Robert O. Anderson, was a visionary and a public-spirited leader who wanted to build the pipeline responsibly, and for the right reasons. In 1969, not waiting for either government or his partners, Anderson instigated the purchase of 800 miles of 48-inch pipe, at a cost of $100 million. It sat in storage on the North Slope, and in Fairbanks and Valdez, for six years waiting for the go-ahead. The first segment was put in place in 1975.

But one of the members of the consortium was holding back. Exxon, then called Humble Oil, lacked ARCO's belief in Alaska. My guess was that they preferred to slow down the pipeline, drawing on their oil reserves elsewhere in the world rather than committing to the huge investment of money and effort to bring North Slope crude to market. Besides, Exxon, unlike ARCO, needed oil on the East Coast, not the West Coast; so Alaska oil was not as valuable to them. The company pursued a bold project to carry the oil through the Northwest Passage around the north side of Canada in an ice-breaking tanker called the Manhattan, but it proved unfeasible. As the delays on the pipeline mounted, the Interior Department got the blame. Exxon didn't seem to care.

*"Mike, come back here and sit down."*

In July 1970, two and a half years after the Prudhoe Bay discovery, with progress on the pipeline stalled, I called in the heads of the major oil companies to try to get something started. We still had not received a single sheet of design specifications from them telling us how they would build the pipeline.[49] Robert O. Anderson, Mike Wright, President of Humble Oil (Exxon), and Sir Eric Drake, chairman of British Petroleum, came to my office. It soon became evident that the problem was Wright of Exxon. Wright said, "We're just not ready for it," admitting they would just as soon leave the oil where it was for five years or more.

That bald-faced admission confirmed my suspicions. Wright got up and started to walk out of the room. As he got to the door, I yelled at his receding back, "Mike, come back here and sit down. If you go through that door, I'm going public with what you said." The country would then have learned that Exxon was ready to blockade this vast bonanza of domestic oil production because of their own corporate interests abroad, demonstrating that their loyalty was to no flag but their own. That made it all important for me, as trustee of America's resources, to force our case.

Wright returned to his chair, and we began talking about how to improve the oil companies' ineffective and haphazard pursuit of pipeline approval.

"There is no way I can deal with all of you at one time," I explained. "I want a man I can deal with in that chair in 30 days."[50] Thirty days later, to the day, Ed Patton from Exxon walked into my office. He was an outstanding choice, proving to be the strong and efficient manager needed for the project. He organized the formation of a new company, Alyeska Pipeline Service Company, owned jointly by the seven North Slope oil producers, with the authority to obtain the permits and build the line. Patton had signature authority in the tens of millions of dollars.

This veteran of many large construction projects gave the oil industry the unified voice they needed to break through the political logjam in Congress. In September, he spoke to the Anchorage Chamber of Commerce, telling the assembled business people directly that until Congress settled Native land claims, there was no way the pipeline would be authorized to proceed. When urban business people heard Patton's comments, many who had opposed transferring any land to the Native Alaskans changed their minds and backed a settlement. Land claims and the pipeline now were linked. But even with oil industry support, it would still take another year for Congress to approve a Native land settlement, and two years after that before Congress approved the pipeline.

It would be a long fight. But at least we now had the oil industry and Alaskans working together for the public interest.

## A BOLD ROAD NOT TAKEN: STATE PIPELINE OWNERSHIP

In 1971, Bill Egan, back in the Governor's Mansion, advanced a truly innovative idea. He recommended to the legislature that the State of Alaska should own the trans-Alaska pipeline and charge the oil industry to transport oil through it.

Although Egan and I came from different political parties and had faced off in a tough election campaign, we grew to be friends and to share a similar philosophy regarding Alaska's commons. We both had come through the statehood fight and had absorbed the ideas of that time. The idea of owning the pipeline came out of those same underlying principles.

Egan foresaw in 1971 that the pipeline would be the hammer with which the oil industry could control the value of Alaska's oil. State government would recover Alaska's portion of the North Slope's oil riches through oil taxes and by a one-eighth royalty share of the oil as it came out of the ground. To know how much revenue the state would receive, we had to know how much the oil was worth. The critical number was the value of the oil when it came out of the ground, before it started its journey down the pipeline from the North Slope. That "wellhead price" would determine Alaska's fiscal health for decades. The world oil market would set the price once the oil arrived at a refinery, but, to figure the wellhead price, the cost of moving the oil from the Slope to the refinery had to be deducted. The greater the cost of moving the oil, the less it would be worth at the wellhead, and the less the industry would pay the state in taxes and royalties and the federal government in royalty share.

If the oil companies owned the pipeline, they would be expected to set the price of using the pipeline, called the tariff, as high as possible. The more they charge for the tariff, the lower the wellhead price, and the less they would pay in taxes. In addition, the higher tariff would mean that they could purchase our royalty oil more cheaply. The pipeline tariff would be regulated, but Egan knew that regulation of such a complex operation is difficult, and the industry could easily exaggerate expenses. Moreover, the companies would have little incentive to hold down their costs for building and operating the pipeline.

Egan sought to solve all these problems by thinking like an owner. Instead of letting the industry control Alaska's economic lifeline, the state would borrow the money to build the pipeline—getting tax-free rates on money that the oil industry couldn't access—and then hire Alyeska, the oil consortium, to build the line and maintain it. We would own it, and they would run it.

"The primary obligation of the companies involved is to the stockholders and boardrooms in New York, Los Angeles and Houston," Egan wrote at the time. "Alaskans must be vigilant and forceful in the protection of their own interests."[51]

Egan broke the news to the heads of the major oil companies in a meeting in October 1971, and then made the idea a centerpiece of his program in the next legislative session. The oil companies opposed the plan for the same reason that it made sense for Alaska: It would take away their power to control the price of our oil. They lobbied the legislature hard while Egan received little support from Alaskans, even from his own party. Big ideas often scare politicians and special interests, and their lobbyists can prey on those fears by raising potential problems and concerns—the sorts of details you would work through to resolution if you had the go-ahead.

*Governor Egan's idea was bold but not enough people understood it.*

Financing stood as the largest issue. Alaska probably did not have enough credit through its tax base for general obligation bonds to cover the cost of building the line. Wall Street could lend the money needed against the project's revenues, but bankers wanted a guarantee that the revenues would materialize, such as long-term contracts with the oil companies to carry their oil. The companies refused to make any commitments. Obviously, if we went ahead and built the line, they would have to use it, but they didn't want to help Egan with his radical idea. It was most definitely not in their financial interest.

Meanwhile, the pipeline ownership idea won few advocates in the legislature. It was a costly lesson. Once the pipeline was built, the oil companies did exactly as Egan had feared. The massive construction job proved to be a notoriously free-spending operation, escalating by a factor of ten the original cost, from $900 million to a final cost of nearly $10 billion.

The oil companies' incentive to spend freely showed up vividly at the very outset, with their labor agreements. Jesse Carr, head of Alaska's Teamsters Local 959, dropped by my office in Anchorage before going to a meeting to negotiate the pipeline's project labor agreement with the oil companies. His strategy, Carr confided, was to ask for the moon, throwing in every conceivable expensive provision as a starting point in negotiations. After the meeting, he returned to my office, and he was almost in a daze, his face white. "I got every damn thing I asked for," he said, "and now I have to live with it." From the oil companies' perspective, why not agree to everything? They not only got peace with labor, they could charge the costs—whatever they were—against the tariff with a guaranteed return. Only the State of Alaska and the consumers of the oil in the South 48 were the poorer.

Beyond pipeline construction costs, the oil companies systematically shortchanged the state, and many years of litigation over the pipeline tariff ensued. Bill Egan had seen this coming years earlier, but unfortunately not enough people understood or helped him fight the battle to win legislative support. Egan's idea sounded socialistic. In truth, it was a bold and wise move for an Owner State, but on a scale that most Alaskans could not yet grasp.

# 7

# Caring for
# the Commons

O n January 27, 1969, for the first time, America passionately
embraced the environment. On that fateful day, the oil-rich
formation beneath Union Oil's Platform A in the Santa Barbara
Channel started to leak, and a slick on the ocean surface began
spreading up the California coast. The news swept across the headlines of every newspaper in America. Cormorants coated with crude
oil choked and died on TV. The American people, already alarmed
by smog-filled skies, the degradation of their neighborhoods, and
polluted lakes and streams, were furious. Their simmering concerns
boiled over in outrage, and I had to do something.

Just four days earlier, the Senate had confirmed my nomination
as the 38th U.S. Secretary of the Interior, responsible for the nation's
waters, wildlife, public lands, and parks. President-elect Nixon had
enthusiastically announced my appointment in mid-December.
"Wally Hickel can see beyond the horizon," he said in his glowing
introduction on national TV.

Democrats in the Senate, however, did not share his enthusiasm.
They decided to use my confirmation hearings to try to embarrass the
new President and his Administration. For two weeks, Senate
Interior Committee Chairman Henry "Scoop" Jackson and his colleagues challenged and questioned me, raising a seemingly endless
array of fictitious charges and unfounded claims. Columnist Drew
Pearson portrayed me as an oilman from Alaska interested only in
development. As the debate raged on Capitol Hill, newspaper editors
elevated environmental issues from the back pages to the front, from

the scientific journals to network news, and political cartoonists depicted Wally Hickel as the enemy of all creatures great and small.

At a lunch at the White House, retiring president Lyndon Johnson had warned me in advance, "What's about to happen to you should happen to no one." Finally, old friends from Alaska and from both sides of the political aisle, including President Johnson, stepped into my corner. The momentum shifted, and Senator Jackson told the media, "All the charges against Wally Hickel just blew up." The committee voted yes, and the full Senate confirmed my nomination by a vote of 73 to 14.

## A PRESIDENTIAL SUMMONS

Making the decision to leave Alaska for Washington, D.C., had been difficult, but inevitable. John Mitchell, the attorney general designee, had called and offered me the job, but I had turned it down. So when the President-elect called, nearly a month after Election Day, it was a complete shock. Nixon didn't ask, he simply said he was going to name me. I hung up, and I wept. What about Alaska? With the North Slope oil discovery, my vision of the Arctic was unfolding before our eyes. This was where I best knew how to help. We were on the threshold of building the northern civilization we had envisioned.

Bob Atwood and other Alaska leaders saw the rumored appointment as an opportunity for the state, and they let me know their views. To realize our dreams, several big issues had to be resolved. We had to convince the oil industry to invest billions of dollars to produce oil from the high Arctic, a bold, never-before-attempted enterprise. They would have to invent a new technology of Arctic drilling and engineering, and obtain hundreds of permits and eventually an Act of Congress to build a pipeline from the North Slope south to the ice-free port of Valdez. And we had to assist Alaska's Native peoples to resolve their legitimate claims for a fair share of their ancestral Alaska home.

To get these jobs done, we needed people in Washington, D.C., who knew Alaska. If federal decisionmakers do not understand something, it is much safer and easier to study, delay, and deny than to approve. In Alaska's case, the Washington, D.C., establishment had rarely been motivated by malice towards us, but their ignorance about Alaska was monumental. There were plenty of interests lining up to oppose the development of Alaska oil—both by competing oil firms and by militant conservationists. The largest petroleum reservoir ever discovered in North America was at risk of being shut in by Washington, D.C., never to be opened. It had happened before. As noted earlier, all coal lands in Alaska were withdrawn from entry in 1906 by federal executive order.

The decisionmaking process was shifting from the governor's office in Juneau to the chambers of the U.S. Secretary of the Interior in Washington, D.C. To have an Alaskan in that chair who knew the Arctic could help the President and, through him, the nation, to appreciate and understand our complexities and our potential. It was also an opportunity to help the American people begin to understand what the commons was all about. I accepted the Presidential summons.

## CARING PASSIONATELY ABOUT
## NATURE . . . AND PEOPLE

Still exhausted from the Senate confirmation hearings, Ermalee and I were recuperating at the Camp David Presidential retreat when my executive assistant, Carl McMurray, called to report that the Santa Barbara blowout was rapidly escalating into a major spill. I checked in with the President's staff and sensed immediately that his political people did not want to step into a fight with the oil industry. Chief of Staff Bob Haldeman, told me, "You handle it, Wally."

Most Americans knew little about me other than the unflattering portrait painted by my adversaries during the confirmation fight. They had no idea that having served as governor of Alaska had uniquely prepared me for this job and this moment. Haldeman's orders were music to my ears. I told Carl McMurray, "Get me an airplane."

Carl and I flew directly from Washington, D.C., in an executive Jet Star, arriving in Santa Barbara at nine in the evening. A large, milling crowd carrying posters met us at the airport. Their faces were angry and frustrated as we drove slowly past them and on to the downtown Coast Guard station. The briefing took three hours, and the photos and firsthand accounts disturbed me. Afterward, as we drove to the Biltmore Hotel, I contemplated a shutdown of all oil drilling in the channel. We arrived at one in the morning. Fred Hartley, Union Oil's CEO, was waiting in the lobby, and we were soon in a shouting match that migrated to the beautifully manicured grounds of the famous old hotel.

"Fred, if this is as bad as it looks, I'm going to shut you down," I said.

"You don't have the authority," he growled.

"Well, by God, I just gave myself that authority," I growled back.

The next morning, I climbed into a small Coast Guard aircraft with Ed Weinberg, the holdover Interior Department solicitor. We flew low over the oily waters. As we droned our way up the coast, the slick could be seen extending for miles. It was obvious that a shift in wind would drive thousands of barrels of thick crude oil onto the beautiful beaches. I had to think fast. The implications of this disaster were far-reaching and historic, and the public and the press would demand to know what we were going to do as soon as we landed.

I weighed our options. On the one hand, it was obvious from the faces of the crowd the night before that the local residents were close to violence. They had never liked having those rigs in their lovely channel, and they would leap at the chance to get rid of them. On the other hand, the industry had worked for years to get offshore oil development going. They would use every political, legal, and public relations weapon at their disposal to fight any reversal of policy. I discussed the alternatives with Weinberg. As the department's lead attorney, he told me that we had no legal recourse to stop the drilling, even temporarily.

But my gut told me differently. Something had to be done. The concerns of the people of Santa Barbara deserved to be heard. Their water, their beaches, their waterfowl, their marine life, all needed protection. And yet, there was a fine line to walk, that invisible line that those who serve the public must walk. The people of that part of California needed energy to maintain their quality of life, their businesses, their schools, everything. As we approached the airport, my decision came clear. Our emerging offshore oil industry would not survive this calamity—or to put it more positively, this national awakening—unless we forced them to be more careful. We had to discover how to prevent disasters such as this one. We would shut down all drilling rigs in the channel while we evaluated the situation thoroughly and found a safer way to operate.

A battery of microphones awaited us as we stepped off the plane. I told the nation that the spill was even worse than anticipated. We would seek voluntary suspension of drilling operations immediately. I went to my hotel room and got on the phone. By noon, all six companies with oil rigs in the channel had pledged to cooperate. I flew back to Washington arriving late at night, D.C. time; confident I had made the right decision.

But the next morning, there was bad news waiting at my office. Within hours of my announcement, many of the oil rigs in the channel had resumed operations, and others were getting under way. The Interior Department's chief engineer on the scene, without checking with my office, had made the decision to allow the rigs to start pumping again.

I was furious. I needed more complete technical information and better legal advice. I called in Dr. William Pecora, director of the United States Geological Survey. Bill and his staff studied the records of the rigs operating off Santa Barbara and determined that they were in compliance with existing regulations. The problem they discovered was that the regulations were totally inadequate. U.S. offshore rigs were operating with rules and regulations written years before for onshore drilling. No wonder we were having a crisis caused by a leaking underwater oil structure.

As the rigs began pumping again, the citizens of Santa Barbara became more and more militant. They assumed that I had sold out to the oil companies.

Sitting alone in my large office on the top floor of the Interior Department, I boiled with frustration. The words kept going over and over in my mind, "There has got to be a way." I punched a button and got Deputy Attorney General Richard Kleindienst on the line. Explaining the situation and its urgency, I said, "Dick, find me a way!" At his instructions, a team of Justice Department attorneys worked through the night, researching the leases and the law. About ten the following evening, Kleindienst called: "The opinion is ready," he said. "I think you'll like it."

Kleindienst and his team had discovered a protection clause in the lease giving me the authority to close down the rigs. Ironically, we couldn't stop them for polluting the water, but we could shut them off for "wasting a resource." I knew I had to send a strong signal to the nation. The next morning, I issued an executive order stopping all offshore drilling and production, this time throughout the U.S. That same day we put together a team to write new regulations for offshore drilling and production.

Only when the new rules and guidelines were in place did we give the industry approval to begin operating again. With only one exception,[1] there has not been a significant production-related oil spill offshore in the thirty years since. And when the oil companies sued, we took the heat. Our response to the Santa Barbara blowout illustrated an important truth. Those in charge of America's environment and our publicly owned natural resources must care for the total environment— people, people's needs, and nature. Ecology teaches us that the many parts of an ecosystem depend on each other, and our global environment works the same way. That means that we must meet the needs of human beings as well as the needs of nature. Although this fundamental reality seems perfectly obvious as I write it on this page, few public officials stand up for it.

*People, people's needs, and nature.*

We must care passionately about nature, the intricate web of life and the great beauty that is ours to protect. But a true commitment to the environment also requires an equally passionate concern for the basic needs of the human race, from jobs to energy to vital goods and services. Rather than advocate for only one animal or plant species, one place of great beauty or one industry, we must seek solutions that help them all.

In Santa Barbara, we took a stand to protect nature while finding a way to continue to meet the energy needs of the people of California and the nation.

## THE REASONING ANIMAL

The issues we faced in Santa Barbara were much bigger and the stakes much higher than I had experienced in Alaska, but they were not new. We had wrestled with many controversies over the protection of commonly owned lands and wildlife. Native and non-Native Alaskans depend on the environment for their basic needs. For many, fish and game feed their families as well as keep them in touch with their spiritual roots. If you want to understand how deeply this is felt by the Alaska people, attend a hearing on subsistence hunting and fishing in a rural community, or drop in on a strategy session of the Outdoor Council in Fairbanks, the political organization for Alaska's urban hunters.

*Regardless of the beauty of the scenery, if an individual is cold, hungry, or unemployed, he is in an ugly environment.*

When serving as governor, I urged my cabinet to address the emerging issues of the environment and to do it boldly. We helped set aside the McNeil River Brown Bear Refuge in 1967, a sanctuary where bears from a radius of hundreds of miles gather to feed on salmon. Some of these brown bears or grizzlies weigh 1500 pounds and stand seven feet tall. I signed the bill that created Chugach State Park, a priority of the newly formed Sierra Club chapter in Anchorage. This magnificent half-million-acre park embraces the mountain ranges and ice fields to the east of Anchorage. We eliminated the bounty on wolverines and hair seals, and we took the unprecedented step of arresting and punishing the oil tanker *Rebecca*, not the captain or the crew but the ship itself, for polluting Alaska waters.

God made the human the only reasoning animal. We are the only creatures who can bring balance to the environment. The grizzly bear doesn't care what happens to the raven. The elephant doesn't take care of the lion. It is up to us. I once commented, "You cannot let nature run wild." That statement was ridiculed, but it is a truth that the stewards of wildlife must address and the public must understand. Mother Nature has no compassion when a predator species becomes overpopulated and wipes out its prey. She is oblivious when a species faces extinction. When such situations emerge, only humans can intervene, and they must.

Fortunately, the bald eagle, the peregrine falcon, and the trumpeter swan, three of Alaska's greatest treasures, have recovered from the brink of extinction and have been removed from the endangered species list. Fervent private activism and enlightened government policy brought about this reversal. The tiniest and plainest species, all vital parts in our ecological system, must be identified and cared for, and we must work to save the populations of our large mammals.

One of our most successful efforts in Alaska has been the restoration of the musk ox, one of the most ancient species and beautiful animals of the North. The musk ox has a gorgeous, thick coat that produces soft wool called *qiviut*, the warmest and most expensive in the world. The animals look ferocious, with powerful heads and necks and great horns that appear armor-plated. To protect their young and fend off bears and wolves, they form a circle, heads and horns out, literally building a battlement with their bodies. This defensive tactic helped them survive from the Ice Age to modern times, but utterly failed in a world of gunpowder and bullets. The whalers of the nineteenth century massacred Alaska's musk oxen for their hides, a rare commodity on worldwide markets. Unlike the plains buffalo, they were not just reduced; they were exterminated. In 1865, two years before Alaska was purchased by the U.S. from Russia, the entire Alaska musk ox population had vanished.

In some cases, the human race finds a way to fix its mistakes, and this was one of them. In 1930, biologists transplanted musk oxen from abundant herds in East Greenland to remote regions in Sweden, Norway, Iceland, and Alaska. More than thirty years later, the herd of 33 released on Nunivak Island off the west coast of Alaska had grown to a population of 700. As governor, I was surprised when game guides started to lobby the legislature to permit professional hunting of musk ox on Nunivak. Clients from outside the state were offering as much as $5,000 for hunting tags. I was appalled. Can you imagine urban "hunters," armed with high-powered rifles, walking up to these beautiful creatures, all huddled together, and blowing their brains out? Some sport!

Nevertheless, the Musk Oxen Hunting Bill passed the legislature in 1967. I promptly vetoed it. My long time friend Senator Vance Phillips came to me greatly upset. An ardent sportsman and a spokesman for the guiding industry, Phillips said that my veto would eventually destroy the natural vegetation of Nunivak Island. There were too many musk oxen on the island, and they were overgrazing the food supply. I called in the biologists in the Department of Fish and Game and asked, "How many is too many?"

"There are 150 more than the vegetation can support," they replied.

Adjutant General C. F. "Nick" Necrason and his Alaska National Guard pilots and crews came to the rescue. Within weeks, we transported 150 of the handsome creatures to the North Slope. By the spring of 2001, Alaska's musk ox population had grown to 3,000 animals, ranging over large areas of remote Alaska, including what is now the Arctic National Wildlife Refuge, restoring their dignified Ice Age presence to the rugged landscape.

## RETURN IT LIKE YOU FOUND IT

The portfolio of the Secretary of the Interior in 1969 and 1970 included a broad mandate, encompassing those areas of national life now regulated by the Environmental Protection Agency, the Department of Energy, and the National Oceanographic and Atmospheric Administration (NOAA). Perhaps it was easier that way, because my job was to bring a balance to caring for the national commons, rather than to advocate only for a single use of the public lands and the public resources.

As a result, the philosophy of our team at Interior mirrored that mandate. As we confronted a myriad of issues, we strived to balance the needs of nature with the needs of people and their communities. Environmentalists and their friends in the media did not know whether to treat us as friend or foe; nor did the leaders of business. My message to the 70,000 employees at Interior was simply, "Do what's right, and you'll have no problem with me."

This charge encouraged individuals to initiate exciting and important efforts from nearly all sections and divisions in the once stodgy and mostly ignored department. Led by Carl "Clean Water" Klein, Assistant Secretary for Water Quality, we developed innovative ways to finance water treatment plants throughout the country and slapped penalties on those who were discharging mercury in the nation's waterways. The Bureau of Outdoor Recreation established open spaces near the large population centers in metropolitan areas, such as the Gateway National Recreation Area just outside New York's city limits. We followed up with a "Parks to the People" program, reflecting the same strategy. We outsmarted alligator poachers in Florida's Everglades by cutting off their New York market thanks to the help of New York Governor Nelson Rockefeller. We spoke out against the proposed Devil's Canyon Dam on the Snake River in Idaho, opposed the Supersonic Transport (SST) aircraft and the Cross-Florida Barge Canal, and issued an executive order that banned billboards from all federal lands across the country, a ban that continues to this day.

*I was not their guy. I was not anyone's guy. The steward of the commons must be free.*

When industrial pollution came to our attention, we urged the polluters to clean up the problem and used a legal hammer when necessary. We threatened to sue the City of Toledo, Ohio, as well as four steel companies and three mining companies, for using the Maumee and Cuyahoga rivers as an untreated sewer system. This was not a marginal case. When the Cuyahoga became so polluted that it caught fire, our arguments in court were unnecessary.

The challenge was to analyze each case on its merits and not be swayed by ideology, media interest, or public pressure. We shut down the Blue Lake timber harvest in New Mexico, not for environmental reasons, but because it desecrated the religious meeting grounds of the Taos Pueblo Indians. We stopped the threat of thermal pollution by the Florida Light and Power Company in Biscayne Bay near Miami, not because we opposed the generation of electricity but because we would not let them raise the water temperature to levels that would upset the ecosystem. Our message to the company stands today, nearly thirty years later, as an axiom for using the commons. "Go ahead and use the public water," I told them. "We won't even charge you for it. But return it like you found it. That's the cost of doing business."

The conservationists cheered when we fought against pollution or when we preserved parklands. They attacked when we advanced the trans-Alaska pipeline and a North American energy grid. My friends and associates in business and industry were equally perplexed. I was not their guy. I was not anyone's guy. The steward of the commons must be free—neither beholden nor owned by anyone or any interest.

## THE OCEAN COMMONS

The free enterprise system is the best of all economic systems, but when it comes to public lands and resources, free enterprise allowed to run totally free will destroy itself. Nowhere is this more obvious than among those who harvest the sea. No one owns the oceans. No one will ever buy a lot in the ocean or homestead the ocean. And when no one owns something, no one cares. Fleets of fishermen sail toward the fishing grounds with the attitude of "every man for himself." The result is a mad scramble for the commonly owned riches of the sea. When challenged, a fisherman replies, "If I don't catch the last fish, someone else will." Someone must make rules and enforce them. If not, the survival of the living resource is at stake, and so is the industry itself.

In the North Pacific, Alaska's king crab was a classic victim of unrestrained and unregulated free enterprise. The largest of all crabs, the king is a remarkable beast that spends its lifetime 300 to 600 feet below the surface. As an adult, it can measure as much as six feet from leg tip to leg tip. Its delicious meat became a sought-after delicacy in the late 1960s, spawning a large crab fishing fleet in the Bering Sea and on Kodiak Island. Entrepreneur Lowell Wakefield invited me to visit the fishery soon after it began. He showed me how the fishermen harvested the crab.

They were clearly overharvesting, and I knew it couldn't last. A decade later, the king crab population experienced a "sudden" collapse. Crab fishermen suggested that a disease might have caused the collapse. Yes, it was a disease, a disease called greed.

The king crab fishery's failure was a replay of the tragic story of the whaling industry. Fortunately, many whale species are now making a comeback. My last official act before leaving the office of Interior Secretary was to place all eight species of great whales on the U.S. Endangered Species List. Five of those species were nearly extinct: the Blue, the Humpback, the Bowhead, the Finback, and the Sperm. The Sei and two "Right whale" species were not threatened but at risk. All had been heavily harvested for decades, some nearly to the point of no return. The magnificent Blue whale was being caught and marketed in the early 1930s at the incredible rate of 30,000 animals a year. The Blue measures three times the size of the largest dinosaur, apatosaurus (formerly known as brontosaurus). Scientists estimate that when I put them on the endangered species list, there were only 100 Blue whales left in all the oceans of the world.

## A THREAT TO THE SPACE PROGRAM

Representatives of the State Department and the Sperm whale oil industry had come to see me as we studied the whale issue. That meeting was a turning point. The experts and the industry were adamantly opposed to my placing the whale on the U.S. Endangered Species List. They explained that as the American fleet harvested a relatively small percentage of the world's whales, unilateral U.S. action would hardly make a dent in the kill count. They talked about the American families who were employed in the industry for generations and the communities that would be hurt. I listened carefully to their concerns, but something in my gut reacted when the State Department spokesman surprised me with a new argument.

"Besides, we have to have whale oil for the space program," he declared.

As a strong proponent for space exploration, it took me aback to learn that NASA was using whale oil, let alone depending on it. "What are you going to use when the whale is extinct?" I demanded.

The official began to stammer. "I suppose we'll have to find a substitute."

"Well, you find that substitute," I nearly shouted, "Because those whales are going on the list."

The United States had to take the lead. Whaling fleets around the world were building and deploying high-tech factory ships that could process an 80-ton whale carcass in 30 minutes. If we didn't act, who would?

On November 25, 1970, I released a statement saying: "It would be a crime beyond belief if, in the same decade that we walked on the moon, we also destroyed the largest animal on earth." I signed the order late in the afternoon following the meeting with President Nixon when he fired me. Whether or not my action was legal may be a question, but as long as I still had a key to my office I was determined to win the battle to save the whale.

One of the toughest obstacles was opposition from one of America's heroes, Charles Lindbergh, a man I greatly respected. A strong advocate for the world's whales, Lindbergh had written to me about his concerns. He feared that if we used the Endangered Species Act, we might anger the Japanese and the Russians, the largest whaling nations, and the move might be counterproductive.

*It would be a crime beyond belief if, in the same decade that we walked on the moon, we also destroyed the largest animal on earth.*

Nonetheless, my executive order was printed in the federal register, and the response from the media and the world community, including from some of the other whaling nations, was remarkably positive. Through this unilateral act, our nation had taken a stand. Lindbergh watched this reaction and later graciously wrote me a letter of thanks. "You touched their conscience," he said.

I first met Lindbergh when he came to Alaska in 1967. Alaska State Senator Lowell Thomas, Jr., who had known Lindbergh since childhood, had asked him to speak to a special joint session of the legislature on conservation issues. When we heard he was coming, Ermalee and I invited him to stay with us in the Governor's mansion. Ermalee remembers that Lindbergh, after dinner, asked graciously if the mansion staff would press his pants for him prior to his speech the following morning. Ermalee immediately said yes, although there was no staff on duty. Instead, Alaska's First Lady pressed General Lindbergh's pants and was proud to do so. That visit was the beginning of our long-term friendship.

A dynamic Canadian, Maurice Strong, visited me in 1970 immediately after he was named Secretary General of the first United
Nations Conference on the Human Environment. Strong had
achieved an impressive record as an entrepreneur and as leader of
Canada's External Aid Office, directing Canadian foreign aid initiatives. In my office, he spoke quietly but with great conviction about
his vision for the role of the U.N. in facing the growing worldwide
environmental crisis, and he described the upcoming conference
slated for Stockholm, Sweden, in June 1972. At his request, I partic-
ipated in an early planning session at the Swedish embassy.

In 1972, although I had returned to private life, Strong asked me
to help him with a problem in Australia. The government in
Canberra was hinting that they might not participate in Stockholm.
Strong asked if I would fly to Australia, meet with their government
leaders, and try to turn them around. I welcomed the assignment.
With the help of the Australian United Nations Association, my
aide Malcolm Roberts and I visited Melbourne, Canberra, and
Sydney in three days, held twenty events, including four speeches
and several media interviews, and met with both the Federal
Minister of the Environment, Peter Howson, and the leader of the
opposition, Gough Whitlam, who later became prime minister. We
completed our mission when the Australians promised to attend and
actively participate.

A few weeks later, Strong invited me to be one of six world
observers at the Stockholm Conference. It was a great honor to be on
a list with anthropologist Margaret Mead, author Rene Dubos,
British philosopher Lady Barbara Ward, and the others. But simply
going to Stockholm to sit in the gallery and watch the proceedings
was not appealing. This first effort by the governments of the world
to address environmental needs had to be successful, and I wanted to
help. How could we assure success, and what could we, as private
citizens, do to help? Art Davidson, the Alaska Regional Director
of the Friends of the Earth, came to see me to brainstorm some ideas.
"I want to take one issue to Stockholm and fight for it," I said. "That's
how to win."

Art suggested that we push the United Nations to support a
worldwide moratorium on commercial whaling. I agreed instantly,

and Art and Malcolm began writing a resolution. The draft they wrote called for a ten-year moratorium and a scientific commission that would conduct a study of the whales of the world, the pollution and harvesting practices that endangered them, and the sustained yield levels required to assure that populations of all species recovered and thrived.

Once the resolution was finalized, we wrote a booklet, smaller than a postcard and just a few pages in length, entitled "The Cry of the Whale." Never underestimate the power of stating things simply—the shorter the better. The booklet included the resolution and a brief history of the world's whale populations. For the cover, Eddie Lum, an Anchorage artist and architect, drew an illustration of a Blue whale. We printed several hundred copies, and Malcolm took them to Stockholm a week ahead of time.

Strong and his staff welcomed him enthusiastically and endorsed our strategy. It appeared that the conference would have a rocky start, teetering on the edge of deadlock. Many national delegations, including the U.S. and the Soviet Union, were fundamentally opposed to U.N. involvement in environmental issues, preferring to negotiate bilaterally. They stonewalled many issues of substance, including the moratorium on whaling, which had been discussed at a planning level. Adding to the tension, more than 1,000 young people from many nations had arrived in Stockholm to keep their somewhat skeptical eye on the conference. They were primed to demonstrate if necessary. They established a tent city south of town on some farmland in Scarpnäck and dubbed it "The Hog Farm." The anti-Viet Nam War advocates among them had begun a full-court press to mobilize the world media covering the event.

With the tacit approval of the Secretary General's staff, Malcolm began organizing a demonstration to dramatize the whale issue. Working with Joan McIntyre, director of Project JONAH, an organization dedicated to saving the whale, and Stewart Brand, editor of *The Whole Earth Catalog*, they decided to hold "Whale Night at the Hog Farm" for the day I was to arrive. And they planned a march the next day. Malcolm obtained several large rolls of black polyethylene and chicken wire and delivered them to the Hog Farm, where Brand had lined up volunteers who had agreed to construct a whale out of an old, red hippie bus. This would be the centerpiece of the demonstration.

On June 8, my son Joe, 18, and I arrived in Stockholm in time to participate in Whale Night. When we drove into Scarpnäck, rock music blared from a large stage while a high wind ripped through the tent city. The media surrounded us. Joan McIntyre invited me to speak to the crowd about our actions on behalf of the whale at the U.S. Department of the Interior. I explained the purpose of the whale resolution we had written for the conference and expressed my high hopes for the U.N.'s role in world environmental issues.

Near the end of my comments, the large crowd parted at its outer edge to let a car through. It was not a limousine, but a small VW Bug that bounced and lurched as it came across the rutted field toward us on the stage. Out jumped Maurice Strong, who had left a formal dinner of world diplomats. He joined us at the podium and gave an impromptu but passionate address. The next day the media reported the story of "the Secretary General, Hickel and the Hippies" meeting to discuss the survival of the world's whales while the diplomats dined.

## A NEW SYMBOL FOR THE UNITED NATIONS

There were only three people ready to march the next morning at 9 o'clock, the agreed-upon time for the demonstrators to rally in the parking lot of the Stockholm Museum of Modern Art—and there was no whale. The situation evolved from the pathetic to the ridiculous when Stewart Brand showed up dressed in a cape and a stovepipe hat with a large feather in it. Russ Train, my former under secretary and an official U.S. conference delegate, had heard about the proposed march and cruised by in a large, black embassy car to check us out. Then the Stockholm police notified us that the whale had been detained trying to negotiate the city streets, but the delay worked to our advantage. As we waited, a crowd began to gather. Eventually, someone shouted, "Whale ho!" as a large black whale on wheels rounded the corner and lumbered into the parking lot. Brand's friends had worked through the night. They had covered the bus with the black polyethylene, transforming it into what seemed to us at the time to be a magnificent leviathan, complete with a tail made from chicken wire. As a finishing touch, its creators used masking tape to add a smile to its face and the words "Maybe Dick" to its starboard side, a wry reference to Herman Melville's classic novel and a youthful wish that U.S. President "Dick" Nixon would become an endangered species himself. A public address system in the cab played recordings of a whale's haunting underwater calls, as if this strange creature was pleading with the world's leaders for its survival. Its eloquent message was interspersed with a popular hit of the day, "He Ain't Heavy, He's My Brother."

I took a position in front of the plastic masterpiece with Brand and Joan McIntyre, and the march began. As we paraded down Stockholm's cobblestone streets heading for the Old Parliament Building, our ragtag crowd of marchers grew in numbers, seeming to materialize out of nowhere. It was a sun-filled Saturday morning, and the Swedes on the sidewalks stopped to watch and stare in mute disbelief. The marchers, however, were not so mute. Within sight of our destination, our sound system blew a fuse. Undaunted, the demonstrators used their own voices in loud, unearthly imitation of the cries of the earth's largest creatures.

Outside the Old Parliament Building, where the conference delegates from around the world were in session, the Stockholm police stood at the ready, wearing helmets, clubs, and plastic visors. They formed a line across the street, locked arm in arm, preventing us from getting within throwing distance of the building or even within earshot of the formal deliberations. These precautions were hardly necessary. As we confronted the police, we were not carrying rocks but orange blossoms. Our bus conveniently "broke down" near the Parliament Building, and hundreds of voices rose in crescendo—an eerie, awful wail. The media swarmed to the site and, by the time we disbanded, we knew our message had been seen and heard. The next day photos of "Maybe Dick" appeared in the local press and on the front page of the *International Herald Tribune*. We had made our case.

The day after the march, I met with Swedish Prime Minister Olaf Palme for an hour-long discussion. I gave him our whale resolution and discussed the need for the conference to take a stand. As Malcolm and I left his office, we heard that the whale debate was coming up on the floor of the Resources Committee. We grabbed a cab to the Old Parliament and sprinted up the stairs to the gallery. Many of our fellow demonstrators were already there. The previous night Malcolm and my son Joe had placed copies of our "Cry of the Whale" booklet in the mailboxes of the delegates. As I looked down at the room full of diplomats below us, that small booklet sat prominently on the desk of nearly every delegate, including my successor, U.S. Interior Secretary Rogers C. B. Morton.

Maurice Strong and his lieutenants were convinced that the U.S. delegation opposed any meaningful action on whales, so during recesses or when delegates left the chamber, I lobbied every member I could corner, including old friends Elvis Stahr, world head of the Audubon Society, and Secretary Morton. Whatever their prior position, that afternoon they saw the power of the whale issue and submitted an amendment to the conference resolution that strengthened it, mirroring the draft in our booklet. Twelve countries rose to speak on its behalf. South Africa and Portugal joined Japan in opposition. The resolution went to a vote and passed 51–3, with 12 abstentions. Those of us in the gallery, and many of the delegates from around the world, broke into spontaneous applause when the vote was tallied.[2] The logjam had broken. The following morning, the same committee, which had been incapable of taking meaningful action, flashed through 26 resolutions in 50 minutes. And that day the front page of the Stockholm newspaper *Dagens Nyheter* reported on the whale demonstration, the debate, and the vote. For a graphic, they reprinted Eddie Lum's drawing of the Blue whale from the cover of our booklet. The caption read "New Symbol for the U.N."

## THE MOST PRECIOUS THINGS ON EARTH

The following morning, as we attended the plenary session of the conference, Secretary Strong saw us in the gallery and sent an aide to escort us down to the main floor, seating us in the front row of the delegate section. A member of the Chinese delegation, the Vice-Minister of Fuels and Resources, Tang Ke, rose to take the podium. His speech captured the views of many of the Third World, and I will never forget his words. He attacked the wealthy nations for trying to persuade the poor people of the world, including his own, to slow their development. "We can't stop eating for fear of choking," he scoffed. Family planning was important to the Chinese people, he continued, but population was not the only problem. "In 1948 we had 500 million Chinese and lived in terrible conditions," he explained. "Now we have 700 million, and conditions have improved for all."

*The color of the environment is not just green. It is real.*

Then he made the most important state-ment of the conference: "Humans are the most precious things on earth." I have often quoted that line, and I deeply believe it. I disagree with those who, con-sciously or unconsciously, forget or dislike people. The world includes the wonder of wilderness and wildlife, the rich variety of nature, the glories of a garden or a meadow, moments of solitude, a stunning sunset, and a breathtaking landscape. All these marvelous aspects of this earth and the life upon it fill us with awe. But above all, the most important wonders of this world are people—the elderly person with her wisdom and patience, the happy family with its gift for unselfish caring, the young couple in love, the newborn child. These are the greatest miracles of creation.

When we set out to care for the environment, we must consider all its dimensions. The color of the environment is not just green. It is real. It is the city streets as well as the parks. It is the junkyard down the block. It includes man-made spaces, and the space within our minds. It includes caring for the hundreds of millions of wonderful human beings in China as well as the magnificent whales in the sea. That is the total environment. Our job is to care for it all.

# 8

# The First
# Peoples' Commons

I didn't invent the idea of the Arctic commons and how best to manage them, nor can any individual claim the credit. The indigenous people of the North created this idea—this way of life—at the same time as Europeans were developing the concepts of feudal rule, individual land ownership, and market competition. The concept was born millennia ago on the tundra, and in the rainforest of the Arctic and sub-Arctic, when the first councils of elders sat down to solve the problems of using and caring for the land they shared. It was the natural way to live and survive on this harsh land.

In the high Arctic, property lines make as much sense as they do in the ocean or in space. Wildlife and fish roam freely and thrive on the openness of the land, rivers, and seas. For the sparse human population subsisting from this land, survival requires cooperation and paying close attention to the wisdom of age-old knowledge. Here, care for the total means taking only as much as is needed (to support the community), and wasting nothing.

Life was hard in the prehistoric Arctic. People died young. No one now chooses to live through long Arctic winters in dugout dwellings lighted only with smoky seal oil lamps. Modern health care, education, and material comforts seem even more essential here than in the temperate regions. On the other hand, even our advanced society has much to learn from the people who survived for millennia on the meager resources of this harsh, unforgiving land.

The traditional Native village still governs itself in ways that work best for the commons—essentially with a grassroots democracy. When decisions must be made that will affect the entire community, the village gathers and the elders discuss the issues, and make decisions by consensus. Elders are not elected, but the village accepts their leadership because they have earned respect through their actions and wisdom. Indeed, being old does not by itself make one an elder. Sometimes when an Alaska Native village grapples with important issues, young people speak the most, and much older members sit back. Some young women have become the strongest leaders among the Alaska Native people. In the village, becoming an elder indicates respect and reliability, not age.

Cynics who do not believe a community can manage the commons for the good of all should visit an Arctic coastal village during the Bowhead whale harvest. The whaling captain leads the village into the hunt, and the village pays him the highest level of respect. Directing his crew in dangerous waters, he must know the resource and how to get to it. He needs authority to manage the hunt safely and successfully. When the whale is landed, his authority stops. Neither the captain nor his crew asserts ownership of the catch. Instead, the entire village hauls the whale onto the beach and butchers the mountain of meat and blubber it yields. Every family receives the food they need, with special gifts going to the elderly or the sick who cannot assist in the work.

The Inupiat were careful to take only what they needed, and the whale population was sustained. Until the arrival of square-rigged whaling ships from New England in the nineteenth century—sailed by the first people of European descent seen by the Inupiat—there were abundant whale populations in the Arctic, despite a thousand years of Eskimo hunts. After I placed the eight larger species on the endangered list, some scientists urged that Eskimo harvesting of the Bowhead, a key to Alaskan culture and diet, be abolished. But the Inupiat whalers of the Arctic assured them that the Bowhead population was recovering well, and there were plenty for their annual hunt. To prove their point, the Inupiat established the Arctic Eskimo Whaling Commission to bring science and traditional knowledge together. It wasn't until 1990 that scientists developed adequate techniques for counting whales. At that point, their data supported the Inupiat view. "Technology has validated what the hunters already knew," biologist Kathy Frost said at the time. "We put information in terms that could be accepted by our (Western) culture that was already known in the hunters' culture."[1]

The Inupiat and other whaling Native Americans adamantly oppose animal-rights activists who want to ban subsistence whaling. To other residents of the industrial world, the need to draw on the Arctic's natural resources for survival may seem incomprehensible. But the city dwellers who would deny the Natives' ability to hunt the whale have no understanding of the Arctic commons or the history of the Northern people. Based solely on their own biases, these Outsiders want to stop the harvest of whales to make themselves feel good, regardless of what it does to an ancient culture that functions well to this day.

## WISDOM OF THE WALRUS HUNTERS

Jacques Cousteau and his film crew invited me to join them on an expedition to make a film about the walrus in the early 1970s. We traveled to Gambell, a tradition-minded village on St. Lawrence Island, far out into the Bering Strait. There we lived together in a one-room cabin while they filmed the walrus and recorded the village culture. During that adventure, I had some lively debates with Cousteau's son, Jean Michel, who objected to the Native way of hunting. He wanted to know, if this was a traditional, subsistence hunt, why the Yup'ik people used guns and not spears. I asked in return why Jean Michel wasn't using a box camera to take photos and octopus ink in his pen. Alaska Natives are residents of the modern world like the rest of us. Their way of life adapts their age-old relationship to the environment to modern realities. Those who assume otherwise misunderstand and write off their subsistence lifestyle as a vestige of the past, instead of what it is: the best way to live on their piece of the globe.

Reversing his logic, Jean Michel argued that the Gambell hunters should use aluminum boats instead of *umiaks*,[2] boats of ageless design made from the skin of the female walrus stretched over a frame of bone or driftwood.[3] After all, he said, he could provide all the aluminum boats they might want, avoiding the need to use female walruses for boat building. Then, one evening, the film crew went out for a shoot. They were due back at midnight, but many hours passed without a sign of them. Finally, at 5 A.M. the *umiaks* pulled up to the beach. They had been caught in moving sea ice. Their boats would have been crushed, but the Yup'ik guides and the camera crew climbed onto an iceberg and pulled them up to wait for open water. No boat better than the light, easily dragged *umiak* has ever been invented for these dangerous situations. The flexibility of the boat allows it to lift itself upward when ice presses in on its sides. Not only are heavier, aluminum boats more difficult to carry, their stiffer hulls collapse under the pressure of the ice. The film crew was duly impressed. The weeklong trip was a learning experience for all of us, and my friendship with the Cousteau family lasted for years afterward.

Urban attitudes toward Alaska Natives—including the idea that we know better how they should live their lives—are motivated by both ignorance and outright prejudice. Getting off the steamer in Juneau in 1940, I was shocked to discover that Natives were not allowed in the Baranof Hotel, the capital city's most prestigious establishment. In Anchorage, there was less overt racism, but even there I was chastised for dancing with a Native woman at a Rainbow Girls dance at the Elks Club. It was outrageous to me that newcomers who had just gotten off the boat treated Natives as outcasts in their own land. Some of these attitudes still linger today, although the vast majority of Alaskans recognize such ignorance and prejudice for what it is.

In my bid for governor in 1966, my platform included the recognition that Alaska Natives had been treated unfairly and deserved a major settlement of their claims to Alaska's lands. Although comprising more than 15 per cent of the population, they did not own their ancestral lands. Alaska's history had left most land in federal hands, without Indian reservations or treaty rights found in many other states. During the statewide campaign that year, I visited as many villages as possible, even tiny ones with few voters, and I learned a great deal. The poverty and hardship as well as the hospitality and warmth convinced me we needed to do something significant to improve living conditions even in the most remote villages. I proposed that we create a Department of Native Affairs to aid village economic development and to provide legal assistance to newly created Native organizations such as the Alaska Federation of Natives (AFN).

Various Native groups fought for their lands in the courts for decades, but in 1966 they were becoming more unified and more sophisticated in their approach. The Alaska Federation of Natives gave Alaska Natives a single voice for the first time. The statewide organization held its founding meeting in Anchorage in October 1966 and invited me to speak. The Native land claims issue, to me, was an issue of human rights.

> Those of us who fought for Statehood had high hopes when . . . our state government began on January 3, 1959. . . . We were now no longer second-class citizens. We had obtained the rights we had so long sought. But I charge that those rights were extended to only five out of six Alaskans, and have been denied to the one out of six that are Native Alaskans . . . . No Alaskan can hold his head high as long as we see other Alaskans deprived of their human dignity and human rights.[4]

The incumbent, Bill Egan, had attacked my idea of a Native affairs agency, saying Natives should join the mainstream. Some Native leaders began to throw their support behind my candidacy, especially those who were unsatisfied with Egan's tentative support for their land claims. Speaking to the AFN, I challenged his record, one of the few times in that election. If elected, I promised that the state would be the Native's strongest ally in fighting for their land.

I won the election by a margin of 1,080 votes. Although Egan received most of the (consistently Democratic) Native votes, it is possible that my campaigning in the Bush and my stand on land claims made a difference to a few.

## SETTLING NATIVE LAND CLAIMS

What would a fair settlement for Alaska's Natives look like? Interior Secretary Stewart Udall submitted a bill to Congress in 1967 that would cede 8 to 10 million acres of Alaska's 365 million acres to the Natives by placing 50,000 acres in trust for each village. A court would add an unspecified amount of cash later. This was not enough. But the AFN's own bill also left the amount of money vague and would allow the courts to determine the amount of land.[5] Written by the attorneys for the Native groups, the bill specified a process that would have taken decades to determine what land was involved, tying up the entire state in uncertainty and litigation. It also included a ten per cent take for the attorneys, potentially making them the nation's biggest individual landowners.[6]

The delay over Native land claims had tied Alaska in knots. Even as he offered an inadequate settlement, Udall maintained an "informal" land freeze on Alaska's federal land. No oil lease sales or land transfers to the state could occur on land claimed by Natives. He had received claims starting in 1961 but had approved none of them. By May 1967, the land freeze had chilled Alaska's economy, with partly overlapping claims filed on more than 380 million acres—more than the entire land mass of the state.[7] The freeze was intended to help the Natives, but as we demonstrated in the January 1967 oil lease sale on the North Slope, it made more sense for everyone involved to continue to explore the land while working to resolve the claims.

On February 26, 1967, I called together a day of meetings with Native leaders at the Alaska Native Health Center in Anchorage to work toward a joint position. We had to work through a lot of mistrust. Property lines are foreign on the Arctic commons, but they were needed if we were to carve out pieces of Alaska that the Natives could own. For their part, the Native leaders wanted enough land both to generate income and to continue their traditional lifestyles. How many acres would they need for their trap lines, or to live off the great caribou herds that roam the Arctic and interior of Alaska? How many acres would they require to support new mines and logging operations that could employ their people?

That October, we found a path to a solution at the second AFN convention. My Attorney General, Edgar Paul Boyko, said, "The state needs land. The Natives need land. The state and the Natives should go into partnership."[8] We agreed to form the Governor's

Special Task Force on Native Claims, a group charged with producing a solution that the Natives, the State, and the Interior Department could all agree on. We invited Native leaders from each Alaska region. Some of the members of that Task Force have since demonstrated great staying power, including Senator Willie Hensley of the NANA Region, Byron Mallott of Sealaska, Aleut leader Flore Lekanof, Harvey Samuelson from Bristol Bay, and the first AFN President Emil Notti.

I wanted the Natives to receive enough land so they could carry on their way of life and advance economically. They also needed to receive subsurface rights so they could share in Alaska's oil and mineral wealth. And they should be paid cash for dropping their claims to the remaining millions of acres in Alaska. We needed to allow for a combination of traditional Native lifestyles and economic opportunities. The Native people themselves would decide the final mix over generations to come.

The Task Force proposal, completed the following January, recommended that 40 million acres be conveyed to the Natives through for-profit corporations representing the regions and villages of Alaska. In addition, Natives could continue to use other federal lands for subsistence hunting and fishing.[9] After many twists and turns, most of these ideas were incorporated in the final settlement passed by Congress three years later, but the Task Force expected the cash the Natives would receive to depend on future resource revenues from oil and gas, with a minimum of $65 million. That wasn't enough. Testifying to a U.S. House subcommittee that summer, I called for at least $500 million for Alaska's Native people.

"The recognized judicial basis for the taking of land," I said, "is its fair market value, and I doubt whether the minimum $500 million settlement satisfies that criteria. As a side note, $1 billion is perhaps inadequate to satisfy this criteria."[10]

In joining President Nixon's Administration at the end of 1968, I carried these ideas with me to Washington, but Washington was far behind our thinking. The key committee chairmen in Congress did not take seriously the magnitude of the Native demands. They were working on bills that planned for much smaller land and money settlements.

In April 1969, I asked for a meeting with President Nixon and other members of his Cabinet to determine the Administration's direction on Alaska Native claims. Commerce Secretary Maurice Stans was there, as well as representatives of the Justice and Treasury Departments. We met in the Oval Office, and the other departments presented their views to the President first, giving him reasons why the United States owed Alaska's Natives neither land nor money. Part of the Native argument rested on the belief that when the Russians sold Alaska to the U.S., Native claims were unresolved and not part of the bargain. Many Native tribes had little or no contact with the Russians. They argued that the Russians had sold land they didn't own. But the attorneys told Nixon there was no legal claim: the Russians conquered Alaska and their possession was confirmed by international recognition at that time. America had bought that ownership fair and square. The other departments explained why there was no economic claim. Clearly, I alone would be arguing the Native point of view.

After hearing out the other side, the President turned to me and said, "Let's hear from Wally."

I said, "Mr. President, I agree with my colleagues, there is no legal claim here, nor is there an economic claim. Mr. President, it's a moral claim."

As quickly as that, Nixon's face lit up. I knew that expression well. This was the positive Nixon who enjoyed doing things that were innovative and right, the side of him which, tragically, was lost later in his Administration. He dismissed the arguments of the other Cabinet officers and said, "I'm going with Wally."

> *"Mr. President, It's a moral claim."*

From that day on, Nixon was the strongest ally of Alaska's Natives in Washington. Historians writing on the Native claims have noted that without Nixon's support a settlement as large as we achieved would never have happened.[11]

It's important that we set the record straight on what motivated Nixon's support, and uncouple the oft-repeated link between the trans-Alaska oil pipeline and the Native claims settlement. My support for a large settlement pre-dated the discovery of oil on the North Slope, and Nixon's decision to back my position came before Ed Patton[12] or

anyone else linked the two issues.[13] Later, the pipeline issue strengthened the Natives' cause, and Congressional politics linked the two
issues, but in 1969, when we established Administration policy on
Native claims, the subject of the pipeline never came up. We simply
wanted to settle the claims because it was the right thing to do.

All it takes to introduce moral considerations into government,
on the commons or on any other issue, is for one man or woman with
conviction to speak from the heart. Words so spoken get heard,
either because those listening believe or because they feel ashamed of
their own motivations. Nixon backed me up when I went to Capitol
Hill to testify on pending land claims legislation. The Senate Interior
Committee asked me to appear on April 29, 1969, three months after
I had taken office. The Congress and Natives waited anxiously to
hear the new Administration's position. The bill under consideration
included a payment of $185 million. I announced that the Adminis-
tration couldn't accept that figure. This gave the impression that we
thought the figure was too high. Then, I hit them with a bombshell,
saying we would not support any bill with a payment of less than
$500 million. That figure became the floor in legislation that fol-
lowed over the next two years, and it moved up from there.

The next year, 1970, the Senate passed a bill sponsored by
Senator Henry "Scoop" Jackson and supported by Senator Ted
Stevens that included cash payments of up to $1 billion but only 10
million acres of land. The Native spokesmen knew that wasn't
enough land for their people to continue their traditional way of life.
Feeling they were being treated unfairly, they adopted more extreme
positions. The issue appeared headed for an impasse.

Back home, it took time for development-minded Alaskans to
support a large land settlement. Governor Miller, reflecting a common
view in the business community, thought the Natives should get no
land exclusively for their use and no sizable money settlement. Bill
Egan believed a settlement of five million acres would be reasonable.
But shortly before the 1970 election, in which Egan defeated Miller
and returned to office as governor, Egan changed his mind.

Governor Egan explained his reasoning later. When the land was
in federal hands, as in territorial days, the resources were abused, or
put off limits. Through the statehood fight, we were promised 103

million acres for the state, and we had brought in the Prudhoe Bay oil discovery on property we selected. If the Natives got another 40 million acres, then the federal government would have that much less land to mismanage or ignore. Native leaders wanted a better life for their people, so they could be counted on to care for their land and to use it productively. This was one reason Egan began to advocate strongly for a generous settlement, including an AFN proposal that was even larger than the final bill.

Other forces also joined with the Natives. By 1971, the pipeline issue had become inextricably linked to their land claims. After the showdown in 1970, when the oil companies committed to build the pipeline and hired Ed Patton to do it, they threw their support behind a settlement satisfactory to the Natives, because that would help clear the legal tangle ensnaring the pipeline corridor. Nixon met with Don Wright, president of the AFN, and after hearing Wright's impassioned plea, Nixon committed to veto any bill that the Natives felt didn't meet their needs. The Administration then introduced a bill calling for 40 million acres and $500 million; with terms close to those my state Task Force had advanced three years earlier.[14]

On December 14, 1971, the Alaska Native Claims Settlement Act passed Congress, ceding 40 million acres of land and $962.5 million to 13 regional Native corporations and many village corporations.[15] This was, by far, the largest settlement ever received by indigenous people anywhere in the world, and set a new standard in human history for the fair and moral treatment of First Peoples.

Before he would sign the bill, President Nixon wanted to know if the settlement was agreeable to the Native community; so the AFN called a special meeting on December 16, 1971. Two days later, the Native representatives present voted 511 to 56 to accept the terms, in which they would receive title to one ninth of Alaska and nearly $1 billion.[16] I was present as President Nixon was connected by telephone to a meeting hall at Alaska Methodist University in Anchorage to receive the news of the Natives' vote. Nixon said, "I want you to be the first to know I have just signed the Alaska Native Claims Settlement Act."

Nixon invited me to attend that meeting. I'd been back to Washington a few times to help with the bill since leaving Interior a year earlier. My most important role, however, had come at the beginning by helping to set the standard for the size of the settlement and by winning the President's support. I was proud to stand with hundreds of Native delegates in the hall listening to Nixon's transmission. A historic photo of the meeting shows all of our faces turned toward the speaker emitting his voice. I recall my surprise when the President thanked me specifically for helping bring about the settlement. But the victory belonged to Alaska's Native people. They had fought for their own land; no one had given them self-determination. They had won it for themselves.

## ONE COUNTRY, ONE PEOPLE

In the thirty years since the passage of ANCSA, this innovative, never-tried-before approach to resolving aboriginal claims has worked extraordinarily well. Most of the Alaska Native regional corporations have succeeded far beyond expectations, and the outlook is strong. Fourteen of the forty-nine top Alaskan-owned and operated businesses are Native business ventures. In 1999, they provided 13,470 jobs and generated $2.2 billion in total gross revenues.[18]

*Our population, including our Native peoples, represents many backgrounds and cultures.*

One of the most interesting aspects of the Settlement Act is a provision that requires that 70 per cent of the revenues earned from harvesting timber and subsurface minerals be divided among the 12 regional corporations.[19] This concept, foreign to traditional capitalism, was born from the Native understanding of the commons and the traditional concept of sharing the bounty of nature. Those regions fortunate enough to have natural resources on their lands are required by Section 7(i) of the Act to share the benefits with the others. Several regional corporations would not exist today if 7(i) hadn't kept them afloat during hard times.[20]

Progress has also been made in addressing social issues. In 1971, when ANSCA became law, 41 per cent of Alaska Natives lived below the U.S. poverty level. By 1990, 23 per cent were so listed by the federal government[21] (still far too many, but a significant im-

provement). The percentage of Alaska Natives over 25 who had finished high school nearly tripled from 1970 to 1990, rising from 21 to
62 per cent, and the infant mortality rate was one-third of what it was
in 1970.[22]

Other problems continue to plague rural Alaska, including alco-
holism, drugs, teen pregnancy, domestic violence, and suicide. Fetal
alcohol syndrome is two-and-a-half times the rate of the overall
North American population. Natives make up 16 per cent of the
Alaska population and yet account for 33 per cent of the prison population. The connection with substance abuse is clear, as 80 per cent
of crimes in rural Alaska are alcohol and drug related.[23] The good
news is that Native Alaskans themselves are addressing these social
issues through innovative nonprofit health and family support organizations. The Federal government has also assisted and lent financial
support. The sobriety movement, founded by Alaska Native elders
over a decade ago, has been remarkably successful in changing
accepted standards of behavior on many levels. Over 100 Native villages have voted themselves dry, prohibiting the sale of alcohol, and
nearly all major Alaska Native conferences and celebrations are
"alcohol free."

Some militant voices among the Native community advocate
Native self-government, or even a separate Native state. But few
Alaskans, Native or non-Native, see separation as the answer. The
South African experience has shown the world that when a society
divides along racial lines, the opportunity to build a healthy and fair
society is lost. Furthermore, our population, including our Native peoples, represents many backgrounds and cultures, not just Native and
white. Like other parts of the United States, Alaska has become the
home for thousands of Asians, Hispanics, African Americans, and a
growing Polynesian community, and many have chosen to intermarry.

My vision for Alaska is "one country, one people." If we work
together and respect each other, our future will always be filled with
promise. Rather than the classic American melting pot, blending
cultures and personalities, the vision shared by most Alaskans is
closer to a pot of chowder or a mixed salad in which each flavor
remains unique and is appreciated for what it brings to the mix.
There is an important difference. The Alaska Native Heritage

Center, which opened in Anchorage in 1999, is an excellent example of retaining one's values while sharing one's wisdom and tradition with others. This beautiful "gathering place" provides an introduction to visitors and Alaskans alike to Alaska's Native cultures as practiced today, and illustrates how appreciation of one's heritage can inspire and strengthen the wider community.

## FREEDOM FOR THE COLONIES

One of the benefits of a long career in the public arena has been the opportunity to see similar events repeat themselves at different times and from different perspectives. I was appointed Interior Secretary in 1969, only ten years after we won statehood for Alaska. With the office came the same powers over other U.S. territories and trusts that Interior Secretaries McKay and Seaton had wielded over Alaska during the statehood fight, when all Alaskans were powerless territorial citizens. Although the remaining U.S. territories were far from the Arctic commons, the experience taught me much about the relationship of colony to landlord nation. It's worth examining how that relationship looks from the landlord's perspective.

As Secretary my duties included wider responsibilities than overseeing the territories, but few issues struck as close to home. I had lived in a colony controlled by a distant democracy in which it could not participate. Understanding that relationship from the receiving end compelled me to get directly involved in helping those other territories where I now had jurisdiction.

It would be an exaggeration to say that these territories suffered the same abuse and neglect as Alaska had before statehood. Puerto Rico, the Virgin Islands, Guam, American Samoa, and Micronesia lacked Alaska's resources, and simply didn't want statehood or independence as badly as we did. What they did want—and what every people wants—was fair treatment and self-determination. They wanted the same legal safeguards for their land and economic activities as other Americans and the same fairness and active concern from their government.

One of my duties on taking office was to appoint new governors of the U.S. Virgin Islands and Guam, just as Secretary McKay had done for Alaska when Eisenhower won the presidency in 1952. Remembering that experience, I traveled to Guam and appointed Carlos Camacho, a dentist, and then announced, "Okay, now you elect your own." Soon after, I appointed the U.S. Virgin Islands Governor, Melvin Evans, M.D., and made the same announcement, "Now you elect your own." They both did for the first time in 1970.

Puerto Rico and American Samoa already had the right to elect their own leaders. These changes demonstrated America's ideals of democracy, brought power home to the people in these remote territories, and cost us nothing. Yet, without having lived under the colonial system, no previous Interior Secretary had been sensitive to this issue and taken these obvious and important steps.

The Trust Territory of Micronesia presented greater problems and demonstrated a worse example of federal abuse. The roughly 100 inhabited islands of the 2,141 Mariana, Marshall, and Eastern and Western Caroline Islands suffered from poverty, neglect, and economic disadvantages imposed by the U.S. government. We had exploited their remoteness and strategic military value as surely as the canned salmon industry had exploited Alaska. Spread over an ocean area comparable in size to the Lower 48 states, the islands were out of sight and out of mind. We had seized the islanders' land for military bases without compensation, and we had conducted nuclear tests on their remote atolls. Marshall Islanders were evicted from Bikini and Enewetak for dozens of blasts, lasting from 1946 to 1958, and have never been able to return to their radioactive land. In perhaps the most extreme example of appropriation of native lands, one island in the forty-island Enewetak Atoll was completely vaporized in a 1952 test, leaving only an underwater crater 1.2 miles wide.[22]

At the time those blasts were taking place, Alaskans were fighting the Eisenhower Administration's plan to make the north half of our territory a permanent military reservation. The parallel is chilling. As discussed earlier, in Chapter 4, we fought Eisenhower's partition plan, knowing that if it were carried out, our state would be stillborn, without the basic resources to live. A colonial power can exploit a colony's land in many ways. National security might seem a more compelling reason than greed but can have the same effect.

For centuries, the islands of Micronesia were pawns on the chess-board of the Pacific, traded from one great power to another. Held by Spain until the late 19th century, they were sold to Germany after the Spanish-American War, when the U.S. took Guam. After World War I, the League of Nations placed the islands under the control of Japan, as a trust, and the Japanese then appropriated them for military purposes. After the U.S. conquered the islands in World War II, the United Nations Security Council placed them under our strategic trusteeship. This Trust Territory was administered by the Interior Department, but Defense and State had a significant interest too—Defense, for the bases on the islands, and State because, under the trust, the U.S. was obliged to report annually to the U.N. on how well we were handling our trustee responsibilities.

We hadn't handled the trust well at all, and most members of the U.N. wanted the islands to gain independence. In March 1969, I received a disturbing report on living conditions. The islanders' political status was even worse than we had suffered as Alaskans. They weren't U.S. citizens and were treated as foreigners for travel to the mainland or for immigration. Although they were forced to pay tariffs on trade with the United States as if they were a foreign nation, investment by any nation other than the United States was forbidden. U.S. governance had been ineffective and lax. Some Japanese-built roads had fallen into disrepair, schools and sanitation were inadequate, and the infant mortality rate was high. Micronesians held few positions of power in their own government—none in the top or second level—and workers were paid less than their white counterparts in identical jobs. Most egregious of all, the islanders had not been paid for the millions of dollars of damages incurred during the war, and the American military had taken their property without compensation and had designs on taking more.[23]

When I arrived on the scene, the departments of Defense and State were calling the shots. These departments had been fighting for five years over the future of the Trust Territory. There was no apparent concern about the abuse we were inflicting on these islanders. The only significant political pressure to improve the situation came from the United Nations. It was clear that our next report to the U.N. was not going to look good.

I sent Edgar Kaiser, a White House fellow and the son of the steel magnate, and Ron Walker, a talented assistant who later became a presidential advance man,[24] to Micronesia. They did a brilliant job sizing up the situation and put together a package of proposed physical improvements and political concessions. Then I decided to inspect the situation and implement the needed changes. President Nixon backed me up, saying, "You've lived in a colony most of your life. Go on out there."

The trip was memorable. With plans for change in hand and the funding and manpower necessary, we offered equal pay for Micronesian and non-native workers, construction of roads, docks, airfields, water and sanitation projects, appointment of more Micronesians to key positions, and, most important, payment for land needed for U.S. defense or other government purposes. We would also ask Congress to remove duties from Micronesian trade and offer free travel and immigration to the U.S. The trip brought these issues to the President's attention, forcing their resolution.

In the capital of Saipan, I swore in Hawaiian Ed Johnston as the Trust's new high commissioner, a ceremony that had always occurred in Washington before—and announced the changes to a large audience there. My message was that Micronesians should decide their own destiny, and the Islanders said they sensed a whole new kind of relationship with Washington. Although I didn't find out until decades later, one woman at the speech was pregnant at the time, and decided to name her son Walter. He even became a builder.

When a reporter asked about statehood, I said, "It's an ultimate dream. It could happen."

The reporter said, "For Micronesians? For their sake?"

"I wouldn't say what they should ask at this point," I said. "It's up to them, just like it was up to us in the territories before we became states."[25]

I went back to Washington with a sense of optimism. From my discussions with the islanders, it seemed clear that if the U.S. offered self-determination on the model of Guam or Puerto Rico, and respected their land ownership and their decisions, they would agree to U.S. sovereignty, allowing our military bases to continue. That would be a far better outcome than continuing the shaky trust that existed, or the slide toward independence that would cost us our bases.

Returning to Washington, my momentum ran into the molasses of government. Negotiations begun between the Micronesians and various Administration officials in October quickly bogged down. The Micronesians resisted allowing the U.S. to have the power of eminent domain over their lands. A culture with so little land was naturally unwilling to give up rights to it, and our past pattern of taking their land without paying couldn't have helped. To try to move the issue forward, I suggested a compromise: if they would agree to permanent association with the U.S., we would obtain land only from willing sellers. After all, that was how we built bases in other countries. The Micronesians liked it.

I pushed my idea with other Cabinet officers whose support was needed. If we met the Micronesians' requests, I assured them, we could obtain the necessary land through lease or purchase. Henry Kissinger and Secretary of State William Rogers rejected the concept.

In one debate, Kissinger said, "There are only 90,000 people out there. Who gives a damn?"[26] Rogers said there was no need to rush anything. He wanted us to negotiate at a leisurely pace. Without decisive action, the Administration's policy became one of staying just ahead of outside forces that might make us move faster. The existing situation suited U.S. interests, so why change?

I imagine that this was exactly the kind of meeting that occurred in Washington when Alaskans were seeking statehood. From the perspective of the colonial overlord, it's easier to continue the relationship as is until forced to change. The wishes of people who are so far away don't seem to matter. It is a formula for abuse.

Kissinger got his way on Micronesia, but the slow, unresponsive approach didn't work out as he had hoped. Micronesia's people became more and more rebellious under the trusteeship, and the opportunity evaporated for the compromise I had suggested. After so many years of being misgoverned by the United States, they would accept nothing less than independence. Only the North Mariana Islands chose to become a part of the U.S. In 1986, they joined the U.S. as a commonwealth, like Puerto Rico, as I had proposed two decades before. The other Trust Territories split off in groups and became various independent nations.

   Decades after I went to Saipan, I received a visit in Anchorage
from Howard Willens and Deanne Siemer, attorneys who worked
with the islanders and later wrote an extensive history of their struggle. In hindsight, they said, I arrived just as the Micronesians were
becoming fed up with their colonial treatment. By making small concessions then, the U.S. could possibly have kept the islands as our
territory.[27] Perhaps it's typical of distant colonial governments that
the Nixon Administration couldn't understand that possibility,
despite my efforts. At many times and places in history, distant colonial powers have been unable to hear their colonies' legitimate
complaints. And many a colony has then been forced to rebel.

# PART FOUR

## The Challenges

# 9

# Setbacks
# to the Dream

Twenty years after winning Statehood, we had much to celebrate. We had a land base of 103 million acres, a world-class oil facility at Prudhoe Bay, settlement of Native land claims, a 200-mile zone for offshore fisheries management, and an oil pipeline generating the revenues needed to upgrade our communities. But we soon plunged into a series of struggles and made some mistakes that threatened the very foundation of our Owner State. In Washington, D.C., a national effort, prompted by the loss of wilderness lands in the South 48, captured the attention of Congress. In the process, the promises made to us in the Statehood Compact were ignored and even violated. At home, government giveaways partially squandered our newfound wealth, and a new generation of politicians played politics when they should have been building a culture. As mistakes can be our greatest teachers, these battles are worth describing.

## FIGHTING OVER THE ALASKA COMMONS

Russian legend has it that when God created the earth, he journeyed around the globe spreading resources. When he reached the Arctic, he slipped on the ice and spilled his bag of treasures. Myth often follows fact. The Russian north, the Canadian archipelago, the North Sea, and much of Alaska contain vast deposits of gold, silver, diamonds, copper, oil, coal, gas, and nearly every strategic mineral.

Some of these reserves are remarkably rich. Untapped ore located in Alaska's Ambler District in the Brooks Range is 15 per cent copper. Arizona miners profitably mine 0.5 per cent copper. To the west of Ambler, the Red Dog Mine is the world's largest known concentration of zinc, with reserves reputed to be 25 per cent zinc. North of Red Dog lie coal deposits estimated to contain the energy equivalent of Saudi Arabia oil. To the east of these coal formations are the proven oil and gas reserves on the North Slope, including Alpine, Kuparuk, West Sak, Milne Point, Prudhoe Bay, Lisburne, Endicott, and the unproven but highly touted Coastal Plain of the Arctic National Wildlife Refuge. Alaska's resource potential, though breathtaking, is dwarfed by the natural wealth of Siberia and the Russian Far East. Much of northern Canada has never been explored and may contain similar riches.

God created these riches, but mankind must find and retrieve them. It's not easy in the Arctic, and the challenges have inspired ingenuity. Geologists, seismic workers, engineers, heavy equipment operators, and people with hundreds of other skills have learned to work in darkness and extreme climates. For most of the year, the surface of the land is hidden beneath ice and snow, and the soil is always locked in permafrost. Prospectors and producers must protect sensitive environments that require innovative and expensive care. In these conditions, only mineral reserves of enormous quantity and value are worth pursuing.

*This Alaska is a great country. If they can just keep from being taken over by the U.S., they got a great future.*
*—Will Rogers*

The most sensible approach to sustainable development in the North, or in any large commons, is to begin with a thorough inventory. Owner States should survey their assets, all of them; the mineral riches mentioned and the beautiful landscapes, the wildlife, the habitat, the fish, the timber, the fresh water, rivers, and lakes. One would suppose, in today's enlightened age, that everyone would agree on the importance of such an inventory. Not so.

Prompted by a handful of conservationists in Alaska, several national organizations set out in the 1960s to reserve as much of the new state as possible in federal conservation units, and they opposed all activities that might disturb Alaska's wild lands and wildlife. They set out to persuade Congress that Alaska's highest and best use was to be set aside and left alone.

These naturalists opposed the exploration and production of Alaska's resources. Indeed, they viewed a comprehensive inventory of the mineral wealth of Alaska as a threat to their mission. If no one knew the extent of Alaska's resources and where they were located, it would be easier to persuade Congress to place a large percentage of Alaska in conservation status.

## PARKS WITHOUT PEOPLE

The naturalists' motivation for what became a national movement grew out of frustration about the changes taking place in the South 48. Some of the most beautiful lands in the western states had been preserved thanks to the bold actions of President Teddy Roosevelt and others. But National Parks were overcrowded, and urban Americans from coast to coast were losing touch with the land. To address this problem, as Secretary of the Interior, I launched the Parks to the People Program, establishing National Recreation Areas bordering large urban areas. These steps were widely applauded, but a new constituency was building of advocates who wanted something entirely different. Their goal was to create great wilderness set-asides that were not for people at all. Wild lands were vanishing in the continental U.S.; so they targeted Alaska.

As the debate began, it appeared that this small interest group wanted only the most beautiful and sensitive areas. As time progressed, it became obvious that they wanted it all. Backed by wealthy, philanthropic families,[1] foot soldiers from the ranks of the environmental community launched an offensive in Congress on three fronts: first, to delay and, if possible, kill the trans-Alaska pipeline; second, to slow down the Alaska Native land claims settlement;[2] and third, to include as much of Alaska as possible in federal conservation units.

When the Native land claims legislation gained momentum, the environmental community changed course somewhat, throwing their weight behind Alaska's Natives on the condition that Congress would consider larger conservation land set-asides. They lobbied Senator Henry Jackson and his staff who were drafting the Alaska Native Claims Settlement Act (ANCSA). As a result, Bill Van Ness, Jackson's chief of staff, asked David Hickok to draft some language about conservation lands to add to ANCSA. Two years earlier, Hickok, one of several authors of a study for the Federal Field Committee for Development Planning in Alaska, had called for setting a high priority on the "development of National Wildlife Ranges and Refuges and National Parks in Alaska."[3] As a result, Hickok wrote what became Section 17(d)(2) of ANCSA, a 136-word sentence buried deep in the 73-page Claims Act. It directed the Secretary of the Interior to withdraw "up to but not to exceed" 80 million acres of Alaska suitable for addition to the federal system of national parks, wildlife refuges, and other conservation regimes.

Eighty million acres is an area too large to visualize. Yellowstone National Park is just 2.2 million acres, and Yosemite is less than one million. This section in ANCSA dealing with "national interest lands" had enormous implications for Alaska's future, but it was only a footnote in newspapers of the day. There had been no public discussion, no hearings, and no debate. Only a handful of Alaskans were even aware that it had been written into law. And yet the so-called (d)(2) provision proved to have an enormous impact on Alaska. Our state, created and managed over time as a seamless commons, first by the Native peoples and then by the federal government, was transformed into a patchwork quilt of land patterns and jurisdictions. The result is a system so complex that even the federal and state managers assigned to administer it do not understand it.

Within three months of the passage of ANCSA, my successor, Secretary Rogers C. B. Morton, unleashed a process that would redraw the map of Alaska. He exempted all federal lands from public land laws, stopping the state from selecting the remaining 77 million acres of the 103 million acres we had won with Statehood. Alaska's new Native regional and village corporations began to organize and begin their own complex land selection process, and a parallel study of national interest (conservation) lands was launched. The ensuing controversy, acrimony, and legal struggles among competing interests kept Alaska on center stage of the national environmental debate for years, divided Alaskans into warring camps, and created a political and economic battle that is still being fought thirty years later.

The race for control of the land was partially a product of fear—a fear born from painful images ingrained in the national consciousness: images of smokestacks in the industrial East billowing soot into pristine skies, overuse of the rich Midwestern farmlands of my youth, the desecration of lands, lakes, and rivers in the Far West, and a vanishing wilderness. The American public, motivated by activists both within and without the national media, feared that this kind of overuse and abuse would engulf Alaska.

The battle for control of the commons in Alaska was also motivated by the hunger of federal bureaucrats as they saw a rare opportunity to expand their empires, in some cases by more than double. The land rush was reminiscent of the 1889 Oklahoma "sooners," but this time it was federal agency personnel, not homesteaders, who raced each other to carve up the state. Instead of horses and prairie schooners, they mainly used helicopters and riverboats. In his bestseller *Coming into the Country*, John McPhee chronicled how state and federal biologists and planners, environmentalists, and celebrity authors like himself camped throughout the wide reaches of Alaska, taking photos, fly-fishing, and drawing lines on the map.[4]

Through the (d)(2) process, the promises of land and royalties won by our young state to make it a viable community, free of Outside dominance, were pushed to the back of the bus. Governor Bill Egan, who in 1970 had been voted back into office, took up the fight for Alaska's rights. Concerned that the value of Alaska's 103-million-acre entitlement would be eroded by ANCSA and (d)(2), he filed for the state's remaining 77 million acres. The Interior Department denied his filing, so the governor sued. The federal and state governments eventually settled out of court, and 41 million additional acres were added to the state's approved land selections which at that point totaled 36 million acres.[5] The final 26 million acres were selected in 1992, although title to most of those lands has not yet been transferred to the state.

## MAPS ON THE LIVING ROOM FLOOR

Under the terms of ANCSA, the Interior Secretary had just nine months to withdraw "up to 80 million acres" for submittal to Congress as possible parks, refuges, and other conservation units. A group of environmentalists in Alaska worked day and night compiling their own wish list. Encouraged by Joe Fitzgerald, Chairman of the Federal Field Committee, they became known as "the Maps on the Floor Society," as roughly drawn maps were spread out in the apartment of Margaret "Mark" Ganapole, wife of a Texaco oilman, and a founder of the Anchorage chapter of the Sierra Club.[6] Ganapole and her friends enlisted National Park Service, and Fish and Wildlife Service employees familiar with the remote areas of the state. Several of them had done preliminary studies of possible additions to the lands held by their agencies.[7] Juneau environmentalists recommended acreage in the National Forests that they felt should be reclassified as wilderness and placed off limits to logging, and Fairbanks groups focused on the Arctic to establish vast areas where there would be no airplanes, no motorized vehicles, no resource development. Hickok recalls that the group had a difficult time coming up with even 60 million acres that could be honestly justified as the "crown jewels of Alaska," and he told that to Congressman Morris Udall, who was leading the effort in Congress. But Udall wanted 80 million, so the team eventually found 83 million acres that they sketched onto their maps as possible National Parks, National Wildlife Refuges, National Forests, and Wild and Scenic Rivers.[8] Of course there was a great deal of guessing and blind estimation.

To deliver their recommendations, Ganapole enlisted Walt Parker, Alaska's commissioner of highways, who was heading to Washington, D.C., for a meeting with Interior Secretary Morton. Soon afterward, the Secretary asked his staff how they were coming on the land selection project, and they threw up their hands. They complained that the timeframe was too short. So Morton handed over the "Maps on the Floor" draft for them to review, and it was essentially that map that Morton submitted to Congress.[9]

The task of evaluating the quality of what were now Morton's recommendations fell on the shoulders of the federal agencies. The Park Service, the Fish and Wildlife Service, and the Forest Service all fielded study teams to tackle the assignment. Environmental insiders on the Secretary's staff, who were pushing for "single use" (preservation) of Alaska's lands, kept the Bureau of Land Management out of the process.[9] BLM personnel were more familiar with these lands than those of any other federal agency, as they were responsible for overseeing the federal commons in Alaska. But the Bureau was not a welcome member of the team. Its mandate was to make decisions based on "multiple-use" of lands and resources, and the environmental community wanted "single use" only.[10]

Meanwhile the Joint Federal-State Land Use Planning Commission, created by ANCSA, was charged with looking at all land use in Alaska, natural resource values, and the needs of both the Native and non-Native peoples. This commission, staffed by professionals from both Alaska and outside the state, studied, mapped, and held public hearings for eight years, seeking to make sound judgments on the vast reaches of Alaska. It was a tough assignment in the midst of the scramble among federal and state agencies, 12 Native regional corporations, and more than 200 Native village corporations.[11] Most of the Land Use commissioners knew Alaska well, and they included miners as well as conservationists. The majority believed in a multiple-use approach, drawn from their Alaska experience. It was common sense that the Alaska commons be managed so that they could be accessed for a variety of uses, from recreation and wildlife habitat to mining and timber, depending on the nature of the lands in question and the best interests of the state and nation.

But Presidential politics trumped the Land Use Commission, and its recommendations were doomed to obscurity. In 1976, Jimmy Carter was elected president, and his Interior Secretary, Cecil Andrus, working with like-minded members in Congress, took over the process. Once again, distant politicians and interest groups dictated Alaska's destiny. Some of the acreage they recommended for preservation had unquestioned environmental merit, and Alaskans and knowledgeable land use experts would have agreed with those selections. But hardly any of these massive withdrawals had been explored for minerals and other valuable resources. In violation of the concept of sustainable development, many of the areas designated for park and wilderness status were already known or suspected to contain enormous mineral and petroleum resources. Their value could be in the tens or even hundreds of billions of dollars.

These decisions were not all made out of ignorance. In August 1977, several of BLM's most experienced Alaska hands, having been shut out of the process for several years, were flown to D.C. and asked by Interior Assistant Secretary Guy Martin to provide maps of the most highly mineralized areas in the state. The team consisted of George Schmidt, Jules Tileston, and Sal DeLeonardis. The implied understanding was that these resources, important to the nation, would not be included in national parks and preserves. But when the Alaska National Interest Lands Conservation Act (ANILCA) was eventually enacted in 1980, Schmidt and his colleagues were aghast to discover that the new conservation units encompassed all of the high-potential mineral lands they had identified. The minerals information had been used for the opposite purpose than intended.[12]

*. . . two kinds of exploiters— those who abuse and those who lock up.*

Andrus, a former governor of Idaho, was bent on "saving" Alaska from the damage he had seen mining companies inflict on his state. He was living in the past. National environmental legislation had ushered in a new era in America. Backed up by state laws and regulations, damage to the environment in Alaska or anywhere else in the U.S. would no longer be tolerated. Mining techniques had already been vastly improved. This struggle with Andrus reminded me of Bob Bartlett's warning to the 1955 Alaska Constitutional Convention when he described two kinds of exploiters, those who abuse and those who lock up.

The irony of this battle was that the primary conservationist goal in Alaska was something to which almost all Alaskans subscribed. We supported protecting the wildlife habitat and the world-class splendor throughout our "Great Land." But we opposed locking up great sections of Alaska that were featureless in landscape, sparse of vegetation and wildlife, and potentially laden with mineral resources. Our concerns were more than economic. What about other values? What about the freedom to explore, to roam, and to seek adventure without living in a permit lifestyle? What about the ability of the individual to live off the land, make a living from its bounty, and improve one's quality of life?

Meanwhile, a D.C.-based lobbying group that called itself the Alaska Coalition was assembling "the largest and most powerful citizen conservation organization in American history."[13] They launched a massive campaign. Their goal was to place as much of

Alaska as possible in restrictive conservation units. Few of these ide-alists truly knew Alaska, had spent a winter, run a business, or served in local or state government here. They had little concept of what it takes to live in an Arctic or sub-Arctic environment and to meet the needs of both the Alaska people and their environment. They organ-ized a group of celebrities—"Americans for Alaska"—and used their fame to raise funds with national newspaper and magazine ads. They assured the American public in their ad copy that once the (d)(2) lands were set aside, "90 per cent of Alaska will be OPEN for oil pro-duction and other resource development."[14] As we shall see, these promises were patently untrue.

Nevertheless, their strategy was effective. Sympathetic to the plea to protect Alaska from those who would "rape, ruin and run," the majority of the American people agreed with the message. The average citizen assumed that "Americans for Alaska" had done their homework and that the legislation was balanced.

Here in Alaska, we were appalled by the rhetoric and the way that otherwise credible people endorsed it. We watched in dismay as exaggerations in Congress and in the national media became out-right distortions. Our values and lifestyle were under attack. Did the Iron Trail, the railroad from the sea to the copper mines in the early 1900s, desecrate Cordova and Kennecott? Did the fish canneries, now abandoned, deface Montague Island? Do subsistence and sport hunting and fishing have to be abandoned to placate urban values elsewhere in the nation? Is a prospector's cabin on the Yukon a pleas-ure to discover or an unsightliness?[15] Must the guilt of what others have done or failed to do elsewhere be inflicted on Alaska? Taking away Alaskans' pioneering life and giving it over to "sportsmen" from Outside or to no human visitation at all—is that the American spirit?

## FENCING OFF ALASKA VALUES

Alaskans spoke up, but the American public did not hear us. Congress heard, but chose not to listen. On January 4, 1977, Representative Morris Udall of Arizona (D), Chairman of the House Interior Committee, introduced House Resolution 39, an Alaska lands bill that would place not the "up to 80 million acres" called for in the (d)(2) provision of ANCSA, but 116 million acres of Alaska in conservation units and stipulated that those units were all to be wilderness, as defined in the Wilderness Act of 1964. Federal wilderness status allows little human activity and precludes resource development of any kind. Motor vehicles are forbidden for virtually all purposes. House Resolution 39 would exclude most Americans from nearly one third of Alaska. Recreation and tourism activities would be possible only for those young and strong enough to explore by foot and affluent enough to dedicate weeks of time to their outings.

In response to this extreme measure, the opinion leaders of Alaska forged a common position, establishing seven consensus points to guide our congressional delegation as they fought to amend or kill Udall's bill. I served on a Blue Ribbon Task Force convened by Lieutenant Governor Terry Miller that drafted these points, but I argued that we would be better off leaving the entire federal land estate in Alaska in "multiple-use" regimes. Federal biologists, geologists, and planners could then inventory Alaska for all of its many resources. I argued that the proposed Conservation System Units (CSUs) were mostly arbitrary, hastily drawn lines on a map that served mainly to lock up the state.

Chairman Udall's bill was a direct attack on the victories we had won with Statehood. Moreover, there was a philosophical issue involved. If you separate humans from the land, you destroy them both. In speeches and articles, I implored our national leaders to have faith in people, especially our Alaskan people.

"Never in our wildest imaginations will we ever know (Alaska's) true value or its true potential by fencing it off with a federal law . . . . We should look at all of Alaska for its potential as a free land, not study its potential as a locked-up land. Alaska has an opportunity to show the whole world how free men can be responsible for the land, care for it, use its riches and be proud of what they have done."[16]

Our cries went unheeded. On May 19, 1978, the United States House of Representatives passed Udall's bill with a resounding 246-vote margin. Alaska's sole Congressman, Don Young, fought valiantly.

Udall proved his strength in the U.S. House, but his efforts did not sway the Senate. Senator Paul Tsongas (D) introduced a companion bill to Udall's H.R. 39, but the junior Senator from Massachusetts admitted that he had never been to Alaska and didn't plan to visit "for at least 10 years."[17] The deadline for congressional action on (d)(2) land selections, December 18, 1978, loomed on the horizon, and Senator Mike Gravel, Alaska's junior senator, threatened a filibuster if any (d)(2) bills came to the Senate floor. Gravel's talents for disrupting the Senate were rightly feared. Senate action on (d)(2) came to an abrupt halt.

Seeing that the delay in Congress might doom any hopes for a bill to protect conservation lands in Alaska, Interior Secretary Andrus convinced President Jimmy Carter to approve large wilderness withdrawals in Alaska. Carter's floundering Administration needed a "win." Using a plan outlined by Andrus, the president designated 56 million acres of Alaska as National Monuments by invoking the 1906 Antiquities Act. He also directed Andrus to name an additional 40 million acres of Alaska as wildlife refuges and instructed Agriculture Secretary Robert Bergland to close mining in 11 million acres of the Tongass and Chugach National Forests. Once again, the majority of Alaska's federal lands were frozen, and only Congress could do something about it.[18]

The following May, the Joint Federal-State Land Use Planning Commission issued its final report, representing nearly a decade of work. Their study represented some of the best and most thorough research ever published on Alaska, its lands, and its potential. They urged that the boundaries of conservation units follow Alaska's natural systems and topography and avoid major natural transportation corridors. It recommended a flexible approach that would allow for development of highly mineralized areas with special care taken to protect the primitive nature of the land. President Carter, Secretary Andrus, and Congress chose not to follow their recommendations.

In Alaska, we felt ourselves slipping back into colonial status. Our frustration was reminiscent of the nearly 100 years of helplessness we had experienced as a territory. But, reminiscent of the statehood battle, we rallied our people. Former Governor Bill Egan and I became fast friends during the ensuing months of struggle. In 1979, to mobilize the intellectual and moral strength of Alaska, we co-founded Commonwealth North, a public policy forum and think tank. It was, and is, a meeting place for Alaskans of all political backgrounds who agree to check their special interests at the door to work for the good of the state. As one of Commonwealth North's first priorities, the Board of Directors studied the (d)(2) issue. We held a series of briefings, including separate meetings with Senators Ted Stevens and Mike Gravel.

Both Stevens and Gravel had worked with Senate Interior Committee Chairman Henry "Scoop" Jackson on Senate Bill 9, a new version of the Alaska lands bill. It created 106 million acres of federal conservation units, 57 million of which were to be designated wilderness, while inserting Alaska-specific "protections" to accommodate subsistence hunting and fishing in conservation units, mineral assessments in those units, and a specific procedure for access, and it protected valid existing rights of miners and other in-holders. Stevens attended every mark-up session and worked hard to amend the bill. But Gravel, who was running for re-election, reversed directions and took a "no bill" approach. He believed, correctly, that President Carter would be defeated in the November election and a new Republican administration would be closer to the philosophy of most Alaskans.

*Our sessions with the two senators were intense and emotional.*

Our Commonwealth North sessions with the two senators were intense and emotional. The meeting with Stevens included many Alaska leaders—Max Hodel, Carl Brady, Sr., Loren Lounsbury, Sue Linford, Bob Hartig, Bill Tobin, and Malcolm Roberts. It was one of the most difficult moments of my life. We met Stevens in the boardroom of the Alaska Mutual Bank in downtown Anchorage.[19] He and his legislative assistant, Steve Silver, came prepared with maps and graphs, showing the shape of a different Alaska, after the new and expanded conservation units were in place. The Alaskan leaders in the room were upset and combative.[20] So was Stevens. He argued that S–9 was the best chance we had to include adequate protections for Alaskans, especially in the face of the much more extreme bill that had already passed the House.

We wanted to know why the hurry, especially with Ronald Reagan favored to be elected president in the fall. We felt we had every right to obtain our full state land entitlement before more than 100 million acres were permanently designated as parks and wilderness and tens of millions more were blocked off through lack of access. We implored him to consider the impending tragedy if Alaska became divided in this way.

Stevens held his ground. After an hour of argument, in frustration, I stood up with tears in my eyes. "In my lifetime," I said, "we may never be able to straighten this out." I walked out of the meeting and out of the building.

In June 1980, the Commonwealth North Board made a unanimous decision that S–9 failed to meet Alaska's bottom line—the seven consensus points. We backed the "no bill" approach.

In 1952, we had proved we could defeat the inadequate statehood bill. We felt it was important to say no again, even if it meant suffering the uncertainty of delay. We mobilized four waves of Alaskans, 73 in all, to fly to D.C. at their own expense, to buttonhole senators, office by office. We held public rallies to explain the weaknesses in the legislation, briefing our citizen lobbyists before they left for the East Coast to try to kill the bill.

*How can any state or nation build a sustainable economy without access?*

A pivotal provision concerned us. Title XI, the access title, would greatly affect Alaska's future. How can anyone enjoy Alaska without access? How can any state or nation build a sustainable economy without access? The bill gave half a dozen federal agencies the power to review and veto any access project that by necessity would touch or cross a conservation unit, such as a rail, highway, or pipeline corridor. Regardless of how important to the people of Alaska, it was doubtful that federal bureaucrats would approve a major transportation or utility project that would enter their jurisdiction. Moreover, if any of the agencies gave the project a "thumbs down," the applicant's route of appeal was to the President of the United States— a daunting proposition. If that appeal were successful, the final step made the entire process a charade: a joint resolution supporting the

President's decision was required by both houses of Congress within 120 days.[21] Alaskans were well aware how difficult it was to pass federal legislation on their behalf, let alone in 120 days.

How much of a state should be dedicated to wilderness and removed from all economic uses? Five per cent? Ten per cent? Fifty per cent? What if half of Texas were off-limits? How could the residents of that state create a viable economy? And what if they had limited access to the remaining lands available for use?

In spite of the efforts of many Alaskans, S–9, with all its flaws, was taken to the Senate floor and passed. After months of work to amend the bill, Senator Stevens ended up voting against it.

With the final days of the Carter Administration winding down, Udall and his allies in the U.S. House watched the Presidential election closely. The American people were increasingly frustrated with President Carter's inability to free U.S. hostages in Iran, interest rates had climbed to nearly twenty per cent, and the beleaguered President was dropping in the polls. When Reagan won the election, Udall knew he had to compromise. He sacrificed his bill, HR 39, in exchange for the Senate bill, fearing that if both bills passed their respective houses and went to a conference Committee, the conferees would deadlock and both bills would die. Through this maneuver and some intense lobbying, the House approved the Senate Bill on November 12.

Shortly thereafter, on December 2, 1980, nearly a month after he had lost his bid for re-election, President Jimmy Carter signed the Alaska National Interest Lands Conservation Act (ANILCA) with great fanfare. The law was the most sweeping preservation act in history. It established 36 federal conservation units throughout the Alaska commons in addition to 22 wild and scenic rivers. It more than doubled the land holdings nationwide of the National Park Service and tripled the lands managed by the U.S. Fish and Wildlife Service. It put to an end for a generation, perhaps more, multiple use of the enormous federal estate in Alaska.

## STEALING THE COUNTRY

President Carter wrote in his memoirs that Secretary Andrus persuaded him that ANILCA was balanced. In his message to the nation, Carter proclaimed that the bill would allow for development of Alaska's vital oil and gas and mineral and timber resources. "One hundred per cent of the offshore areas and 95 per cent of the potentially productive oil and mineral areas will be available for exploration or for drilling," he announced as he signed the bill.[22] These were bogus numbers and empty promises.[23]

ANILCA placed more than 100 million acres in conservation units, governed by Alaska-specific provisions that purport to provide balance, but these exceptions have been mostly ignored. The passage of this legislation set the tone for federal policy toward the entire federal commons in Alaska. For twenty years, there has been little resource development on the 217 million acres of federal properties in Alaska. That's an area larger than two Californias. Neither a single barrel of oil nor a cubic foot of natural gas has been produced from these lands since Carter signed the bill. Only one major hard rock mine, Greens Creek near Juneau, has operated on federal property. Small-scale gold mining on federal property that used to provide livelihoods for hundreds of "mom and pop" operations has been greatly reduced and the timber cut in the Tongass National Forest has diminished steadily because of federal policies in the mid-1990s.[24]

With the passage of ANILCA, history repeated itself. In the 1880s, well-meaning missionaries divided up Alaska into spheres of influence to "save" the Native people from their traditional cultures and religious practices. In the 1980s, an army of federal caretakers, also well meaning, moved into the state. Their mission: to save Alaska from Alaskans. Colonialism had returned.

Senator Stevens, now 77, commands great respect in Washington, D.C., and he may yet fight another round on this issue. Shortly after President George W. Bush was declared the winner of the 2000 campaign, Stevens told an Anchorage audience about his disappointment with the federal government's management of Alaska lands.[25] He specifically mentioned their failure to permit, even encourage, access across conservation units, and their virtual shutdown of resource development on all federal lands in the state. Stevens, along with his Alaskan colleagues Senator Murkowski and Congressman Young, may yet be able to bring reason and balance to how Alaska's lands and resources are cared for and used.

## THOSE WHO DARE TO LOOK AHEAD

A future generation will one day take a fresh look at the federal land laws and regimes that govern much of Alaska's commons. When they do, they will see that the decisions made in 1980 with the writing and passing of ANILCA were motivated by fear, not reason. They will replace the existing jumble of systems, laws, and regulations with something simpler and more suited to the Arctic and sub-Arctic.

Here is a suggestion for those who dare to look that far ahead. Because the federal land systems used in the Lower 48 do not fit the North Country, Congress should create a new land regime that could be called the Alaska Land Management and Conservation Service. The current lines and boundaries on Alaska's federal properties should be erased. In their place, we should create a management system that fits the unique characteristics of Alaska's climate, geography, geology, people, and wildlife. Mineral assessment and wildlife habitat would be given top priority throughout. In those locations where mineral reserves are found in economic quantities, simple access should be permitted, so that needed resources could be extracted.

Most geologists agree that the combined acreage disturbed by this activity would be less than two per cent. The remaining 98 per cent of the 217 million acre federal estate would be managed for other purposes. In other words, the rich natural resources that God placed in Alaska, or spilled, if the Russian fable is correct, would once again be available to meet the needs of people, and a much greater area than exists today would be managed for hunting, fishing, subsistence, and its natural beauty. For this to happen, the Alaska people must maintain their commitment to wise resource development practices and win the trust of the American people, our fellow owners of the federal commons. When that day comes, a true Owner State will exist not only on state lands, but throughout Alaska.

# 10

# The Challenges
# of Wealth

In the 1980s we faced a new challenge as difficult as the fight over our land: how to use our resource wealth wisely. One of our great successes was the creation of the Alaska Permanent Fund, an investment account that transformed one-time oil income into a renewable financial resource. But the Fund's very success brought with it an unexpected downside—an entitlement mentality in our people.

Some of our politicians had never taken the time to understand the history and fundamentals of Alaska's Owner State. They spent our oil revenue bonanza unwisely and failed to invest our new wealth in projects that could improve and diversify our economy. Worse, some came to think of the common wealth from our oil resources as the personal wealth of individual residents. We began to watch the mailbox for a handout rather than watch the horizon for the next opportunity. We risked losing the pioneering spirit, the collective endeavor in managing the commons, and the unity of purpose that had made us successful in the first place.

These problems were not unique to Alaska. They have often emerged when states and nations develop their natural resources successfully. When The Netherlands received a windfall of petrochemical money in the 1960s and 1970s, the government spent the surplus on social programs instead of investing in job-creating capital projects. By the late 1970s, the economic distortions of those government programs pushed unemployment up and industrial output, exports, and corporate profits down. Economists started calling it "the Dutch Disease" and warned other governments against the path of simply paying out resource wealth to the public.[1] Norway's North

Sea oil led to a similar pitfall, as spending drove wages up, the work-week down, and made the currency too strong. That reduced the competitiveness of other domestic industry until oil had to support the entire economy. Venezuela used its oil money to prop up its currency, allowing the middle class to import luxury goods and amass large overseas investments. That policy did little for the nation's economy.[2] Other nations lost immense fortunes to fraud or fiscal mismanagement.[3]

Alaskans began discussing how to handle the expected influx of money not long after we discovered oil at Prudhoe Bay. The allocation of $900 million in receipts from the 1969 oil lease sale added urgency to the discussion of how to be responsible with the money. Even the $900 million alone seemed inexhaustible. By way of contrast, the state budget in 1967, my first year as governor, was only $96 million. We had struggled since statehood, financing government from taxes on our small population and modest oil lease sales. Now we had the opportunity to address many needs that had gone unmet for years. The money built schools, highways and sewers, and funded programs such as generous student loans, payments to the elderly, and reductions in local property taxes. The $900 million was spent in a few years, and soon the state found itself forced to borrow to fund its annual operating budget. Although much of the spending had merit, the public became concerned that the $900 million had been frittered away. Leaders started looking for a way to save something when the oil pipeline was finished and real money started to flow.[4]

Many Alaskans also hoped to use some of the coming revenues to smooth out our boom-and-bust economy. Since the 1898 Klondike Gold Rush, Alaska's fortunes rose and fell drastically according to natural resource discoveries and military expenditures. In 1976, the *Fairbanks Daily News-Miner* editorialized:

> What could be more exciting than the prospect of true economic stability for Alaska? What Alaskan wouldn't like to see the boom and bust cycle that has transformed the state and territory since the turn of the century be transformed into a relatively smooth line on the economic chart.[5]

Two ways of smoothing out the economy were available. One would be to use our new wealth to encourage new development of our resources. The other way was to save money from peak periods and use it to fund government and stimulate the economy when we fell into economic valleys. The savings fund could be a counter-cyclical force.

Done right, a permanent savings fund could work both ways. By setting aside excess revenues during rich years, the fund would help cut off the peaks in the boom-and-bust cycle. By spending earnings during the low years, it could awaken a flagging economy. If that spending in the low years was invested in transportation infrastructure and public utilities, it would strengthen the foundation of our economy and resource development, especially in remote regions, and we would broaden the economy at the same time we smoothed it. In keeping with the pioneering spirit of Alaska, we needed to do more than level an up-and-down line on the economic chart. We also needed to make that line move gradually upward.

In 1976, a group of Alaska legislators including Oral Freeman, Clem Tillion, Clark Gruening, Terry Gardiner, and Hugh Malone[6] proposed that the state create a permanent fund. No one knew what would happen when the wealth of Prudhoe Bay began to flow into the state treasury, but it was a fair guess that there would be enormous pressure from all parts of the state to spend it. Legislative bodies operate by compromise as the representatives of diverse districts and interests come to agreement. In the budget process, compromise often means escalation—adding one more project or program after another to gain the support of a majority of members. The Alaska Constitution's check on this process was the governor, who was given a line-item veto to carve waste out of the budget and bring it back within bounds. Unfortunately, when oil revenue and government spending quadrupled during Governor Jay Hammond's terms in office, no one said no.[7] Ironically, the permanent fund concept was partly to blame. In his autobiography, Hammond says that he allowed the unprecedented spending spree as a way to win approval for his version of the permanent fund.[8]

Hammond had been thinking about this issue for some time. He called his plan Alaska, Inc. His approach, which received little support, was to issue Alaskans shares of stock in a corporation that would receive half of Alaska's oil revenues. The legislature went forward with their own concept, which they passed into law by simple statute. Hammond promptly vetoed the bill, demanding that the fund reside in the constitution so that it could be altered only by a vote of the people.

*"You are establishing a fourth branch of government," said constitutional expert John Bebout about a dedicated permanent fund.*

Some delegates of the 1956 Constitutional Convention counseled against passage of such a constitutional amendment. Meeting at a 20-year reunion in Fairbanks, they recalled that they had written a prohibition against dedicated funds into the constitution and had done it for good reason. In other states, such funds had proved to be a serious mistake, imposing past priorities on future leaders who might be faced with different problems. These mandated funds took on lives of their own and were difficult to amend. Delegate Katherine Nordale asked constitutional consultant John Bebout what he thought of the permanent fund proposal. He replied, "You are establishing a *fourth* branch of government." She was shocked. The more one ponders the comment, the more one realizes that he was voicing a serious problem facing Alaska. She wrote that "great power attaches to the control of so large a sum of money."[9]

Nordale's concern at the time was the management of the Fund, which proved to be a challenge but not a problem. The Fund ranks high in investment performance. But Nordale's warning about the danger of such a large dedicated fund proved insightful. The writers of the Alaska Constitution had faith in the state's future leaders. They gave the governor and legislature great power because they believed elected leaders, given the chance, would try to do what was right in the unique circumstances in which they found themselves. That philosophy of trust is the foundation of democracy. To succeed in our new kind of resource-funded government, our leaders would sometimes have to take dramatic actions. A constitution that took away the ability to act boldly might avoid some mistakes but only at the price of a cumbersome process. That's why Alaska's constitution does not allow for elected cabinet officers, strong boards and commissions, or dedicated funds—all would take away from the power of the governor and legislature.

Nevertheless, the voters overwhelmingly approved the amendment to the constitution that created the Alaska Permanent Fund in 1976. It stipulated that 25 per cent of Alaska's oil royalties and lease payments be deposited into the Fund to buy income-producing investments. The legislature and governor would be free to use the income from the Fund as they saw fit. How the Fund would be managed, what sorts of investments it would make, and how the earnings would be spent were to be left to future legislatures to resolve.

As a result, a fourth of Alaska's oil royalties began to flow directly to the Fund, its principal out of reach of elected leaders. What we didn't realize at the time was that the earnings would also become, for all practical purposes, off limits as well.

## A SERIOUS FLAW

The Permanent Fund has proved to be an excellent idea in that it took money off the table during a rush of oil income and created an investment account which itself has become a commons for the benefit of Alaska. By saving a portion of our petroleum wealth, we were able to transform it into a renewable resource.

But Governor Hammond's goal was not to make additional funds available for needs faced by future legislatures and governors. His motivation was to prevent government from using even the earnings from the fund, especially for major capital projects that would encourage the development of Alaska's natural resources. Once the voters approved the fund, he unveiled a device that would keep that money forever out of government's hands. He called it a "dividend" to be sent to every Alaskan every year. This had been an integral component of his earlier Alaska, Inc., idea. He later wrote, "The dividend concept is based on the Alaska Constitution, which holds Alaska's natural resources are owned, not by the state, but by the Alaskan people themselves. My proposal was to grant each Alaskan, in essence, one 'share' of dividend-paying stock for each year of residency since statehood in 1959, when they had acquired ownership."

At the same time, he hoped the dividend would make the Fund a sacred cow that politicians could never touch. Voters would be seduced by their annual checks from the government and prevent any other use of the Fund's earnings. In essence, the Fund would absorb billions of oil dollars but instead of putting the earnings to public use, Hammond created a dividend-paying machine.

"Wally Hickel likes to refer to Alaska as an 'Owner State,'" wrote Hammond. "I prefer to term Alaskans as an 'Owner People' to reflect our constitutionally mandated public, rather than state, resource ownership."[10]

*Alaska received 103 million acres so that the new state could pay for vital government services.*

Hammond's reading of the constitution and the Statehood Act were dead wrong. Alaskans did not receive 103 million acres from the federal government as individuals; we received the land as a state. The land and its resources were allocated so that the new state could pay for vital government services. The idea of dividing up the spoils and passing them out to individuals would have horrified the original statehood advocates and constitutional delegates, let alone the Members of Congress who wrote and passed the Statehood Act. In Alaska, we needed government to manage the commons for the common good, on behalf of the people. True, the people in a constitutional democracy are the ultimate owners, but their obligations as owners of the commons require them to give, not take. Their responsibility is to care about the needs of the entire community, the economy itself, and those individuals, too young, too ill, or too aged to help themselves. Their ownership did not mean that they could pocket the state's resource earnings.

Delegate Bob Bartlett stated this reality in his famous 1955 speech to the Constitutional Convention.

> "State government in 1955 must provide a wide variety and array of services. Today's citizen expects and demands that government be not only a policeman but a service agency as well. One may disagree with this philosophy but its existence and the extent of its influence is an unarguable fact of modern life. So, *extensive land grants to the State of Alaska will*

*be made in order that this new member of the United States may start off in a sound fiscal position, capable of meeting the requirements of service placed upon it by its citizens."*[11] (Emphasis added).

The 1979 Iranian Revolution shot oil prices up to $30 a barrel, and the unexpected revenue spike kicked off a spending frenzy in Alaska's Capitol. The legislature abolished the personal income tax the next year, and, disregarding Bartlett and the writers of Alaska's Constitution, passed the Permanent Fund Dividend into law.

But it hit a bump. Hammond's concept would reward the most those who had lived in Alaska the longest. This idea stalled in court when Anchorage attorneys Ron and Penny Zobel asked whether longer-term residents should be entitled to be paid more than recent arrivals. While the litigation dragged on, the spending spree in Juneau became wilder. In 1981, $6 billion came into the state treasury from Prudhoe Bay (about $12 billion in 2001 dollars), which amounted to more than $15,000 per resident ($30,000 in today's dollars). Legislators scrambled to grab the most money they could for their districts as the longest session in state history dragged into the summer. In 1982, the legislative leadership simplified the process. Individual legislators received allocations they could spend however they saw fit, and simply typed their projects straight into the capital budget without further review or public hearings.[12]

*The obligation of the people as owners of the commons requires them to give, not take.*

This behavior gave extra support to those who wanted to pass a Permanent Fund Dividend without legal problems—simply a mandated payment each year of half the fund's earnings divided among everyone who had lived in the state for at least a year. Hammond threatened to use his line-item veto on the pet projects of any legislator who prevented this bill from reaching the floor of either house. The arm-twisting worked, and once on the floor, the bill passed unanimously. Checks for $1,000 went in the mail to every Alaskan that summer. Although they wrote the dividend into the statute books—not in the constitution—the result would be as permanent as

any constitutional provision. As Hammond predicted, once the dividend started flowing into people's pocketbooks, it would be secure
for as long as there was money in the fund.

The damage done to Alaska by that decision appeared more
quickly than anyone expected. In 1985, oil prices crashed as suddenly
as they had risen—with a quick and drastic dive. Suddenly, the state's
budget was wildly out of whack. The spending of the oil windfall had
superheated Alaska's economy. State-subsidized loans had driven
construction activity to an unsustainable level, and real estate prices
reached an all-time high. Alaska floated on an expanding economic
bubble, and the force inflating that bubble was state spending,
unplanned and often misguided.

In hindsight, state leaders should have taken steps to avoid
making matters any worse than necessary. Reducing state spending
gently would have softened the intense economic pain that loomed
on the horizon. The Permanent Fund offered a perfect opportunity to
intervene and orchestrate what some were calling a safe landing.
Despite giving away half the earnings in dividends and reinvesting a
large portion of the remainder to offset the impact of inflation on the
fund, an account of excess earnings had amassed more than $1.1 bil-
lion. Even without altering the dividends, the state was free to use
this money to cushion the decline in public spending. By doing so,
the legislature and governor could offset the destructiveness of the
coming economic crash.

But the voters already had been seduced. Because of reappor-
tionment, 58 out of 60 members of the legislature were up for
re-election, as was Governor Bill Sheffield, and they feared doing
anything that could be perceived by the voters as reducing dividends.
The state faced a $1.1 billion shortfall in a budget of $2.4 billion.
Incredibly, with much fanfare and beating of chests, the legislature,
led by Governor Sheffield, took the $1.1 billion in the earnings
reserve balance and deposited it in the corpus, or principal account,
of the fund where it couldn't be touched.[13] Instead of providing a
counter-cyclical cushion for the economy at the very time it was
most needed, the fund had become a vacuum, sucking money out of
Alaska and sending it to Wall Street.

Peter J. Smith, a Canadian political scientist who came to Alaska to counsel the Permanent Fund Trustees in 1988, expressed his confusion at what appeared to be a great failure for our experiment.

> While acting as savings account, the Fund was [also] intended to provide an income stream to be decided by law. It is here that the decisions of the state are debatable, or, better to say, for an outsider inexplicable. In 1986 and early 1987, for example, the State of Alaska found itself in a position where, due to declining oil prices, it was forced to cut millions from its capital and operating budgets. The state was also considering laying off or reducing the salaries of its employees. This, at a time when citizens were sent dividend checks totaling $295 million and the legislature had authorized the transfer of $1.26 billion of the Earnings Reserve Account to Fund principal . . . . Few legislators, it appears, demonstrate a willingness to alter the popular dividend program by transforming the dividends from a means, that is making citizens more aware of the Fund, into an end in itself.[14]

This was the tragedy of the commons in a modern form. In order for each Alaskan to attain a small individual gain, we sacrificed the larger public good. And, like the shepherd on the overgrazed village commons, we suffered more from the economic collapse that followed than we received in the small, incremental gain of slightly larger dividends. Dividend checks essentially privatized the commons of our Permanent Fund investments. Capital sums that could have upgraded our communities and diversified our economy were dispersed as bonuses for each resident. We paid the price by losing our ability to use our resource wealth to meet the needs of people, build infrastructure, and diversify the economy. We failed to benefit from our Owner State because our leaders forgot why we had obtained ownership in the first place.

*The Fund had become a vacuum, sucking money out of Alaska and sending it to Wall Street.*

We reaped the harvest of that shortsightedness soon enough. Alaska's economy crashed into an unprecedented recession. Just as our state government had brought us prosperity by properly managing our commons, now we had a period of economic desperation brought on by misguided state policies.

Uncontrolled spending on state programs and subsidized housing loans had superheated the economy. The state spent $17 billion above a maintenance rate during the boom years, and even while spending those billions through the budget process, it borrowed $5 billion more for subsidized housing loans (combined, more than $30 billion in 2001 dollars). Private mortgage lending disappeared—most bankers, unfortunately, turned to riskier loans—and the construction industry exploded, more than doubling in employment in a few years. The booming job market drove up wages and lured more than 60,000 new people to the state. Economist Scott Goldsmith has shown that the great majority of this growth came directly from state spending, not from the oil industry or any other basic economic activity.[15]

When the state suddenly cut off the spigot because of plunging oil prices, nearly everything stopped. In two years, 19,000 jobs disappeared, seven per cent of the state's employment. The construction industry dropped to below its pre-boom level. The population decreased by at least 26,000.[16] Many of those who left walked away from their homes and mortgages. Foreclosures and personal and business bankruptcies hit record levels. Newly built subdivisions stood empty. Foreclosure sales flooded the market; by mid-1987, the beleaguered lending institutions had foreclosed on seven per cent of Alaska's housing.[17] Of course, the bottom fell out of the real estate market, and with it the equity of Alaska's banks. Before the end of the decade, a majority of our banks and savings and loans had failed—fourteen in all. Those who lived through those dark days will never forget the painful, personal stories of financial ruin. As one writer said late in 1987, "We'll know the recession is over when we can open a newspaper and see no mention of layoffs or banks on the brink of failure; when we go to a store we haven't been to in six months and find it still in business; when we can drive around and see no notices for garage sales that say: 'Everything Must Go— Leaving State.'"[18]

It took more than five years to recover. When we did, economists like Goldsmith were able to look back on what Alaska did as a perfect example of how *not* to manage an economy. Among his findings: of the billions that flowed through the state government during the bubble years, 28 per cent had been spent on services and payments for migrants who had been induced to come north by the excessive spending, a large number of whom left again when the lights went out.[19] They'd all collected their Permanent Fund Dividends while they were here, but not a penny of the Fund's excess earnings had been used to cushion the fall for those left behind.

Far more important than the economic cost of the mistakes of those years, however, was the loss of our pioneering spirit. The Permanent Fund Dividend cost us as much psychologically as it did economically. In earlier years, Alaskans prized their individualism, but they also knew how to pull together. The statehood movement was one of our brightest hours, and the recovery from the 1964 Good Friday earthquake and the 1967 Fairbanks flood weren't far behind. We had been willing to pitch in to help each other, if that meant paying for what we needed together as a state, or if it meant paying for the state's needs out of our pockets or rolling up our sleeves to help our neighbors rebuild. We counted on the better side of human nature, and our faith was rewarded time and time again when we were building our state. The dividend played to the opposite, self-serving side of humanity. The primary rationale was this: only by appealing to the citizens' self-interest could we get them to care. Otherwise, they would sit back and allow their elected leaders to waste their resources and plunder their savings. Our citizens came to care about the dividend, the way a drug addict cares about getting his fix. The public looked at government as the source of an annual handout, not as a way of solving collective problems. A new generation of Alaskans saw little need to strive for new pioneering accomplishments.

*"Everything Must Go—Leaving State."*

The dividend strategy worked politically. In 1999, when the legislature and Governor Tony Knowles finally asked the public for permission to spend a portion of Permanent Fund earnings as part of a long-range fiscal plan, they were turned down in a landslide—83 per cent to 17 per cent. The Permanent Fund, now containing more than $25 billion, yielded more money annually in earnings than the state received in oil revenues. Yet these earnings were used for only one purpose: paying dividends to individuals.

## TWO DIVIDENDS—PERSONAL, AND COMMUNITY, TOO.

Other Owner States would do well to establish permanent funds—however, they should factor into the enabling legislation a "community dividend" before implementing a personal dividend. I recommended a community dividend in Alaska in the late 1990s, and some interest is finally being shown by our legislature. The goal of a community dividend is to dedicate a portion of the wealth of the commons to the common good for which it was intended. This dividend would be paid directly from the fund each year to local governments and villages to allow them to meet their shared needs, in schools, health or sanitation facilities, docks, roads, or airports, or anything else they need to help the community as a whole.

It's staggering to consider what we could accomplish by pooling the amount of money currently distributed in personal dividends. In 2000, the high water mark to date, the state paid more than $1 billion in PFDs. That was $1,964 for each Alaskan. Put it together, on the other hand, and a community of 565 people would have $1 million to work with—enough to make a significant improvement to their quality of life. In my town of Anchorage, community dividends would total $400 million—enough to renovate all of our old schools and build needed new schools—in a single year.

It is difficult to win support for community dividends after a personal dividend program is in place. Many Alaskans now feel so entitled to their individual dividends that they resist any change to that system as vehemently as if their basic rights were under attack. However, both dividend programs can work side by side in Alaska. We can do this by capping the personal dividend at current levels and paying the added earnings each year in community dividends. At the end of a short period of time—seven years by one estimate—the two dividends will be equal and will increase side by side, and both individuals and communities will benefit directly from our resource commons.

## LOSING OUR WAY

In 1978, Jay Hammond sought a second term as governor, and I was determined to replace him. Rarely have Alaskan voters faced a clearer philosophical choice between two candidates or a time when those differences mattered more to our future. Alaska was riding a rising wave of wealth thanks to our success at Prudhoe Bay. The next governor would be responsible for how a flood of state revenue was used or mismanaged.

I believed in developing Alaska's commons and using the resulting wealth to build a great Alaskan civilization. Hammond wanted to slow our growth and had strong support from those who were nervous about our economic successes, including the national environmental community. The battle over the use of Alaska's federal lands was reaching a climax, and our governor would be a major player in the shape of Alaska in the future.

Alaskans also were excited about building a natural gas pipeline to carry the North Slope's abundant gas to market. Construction of the oil line had just been completed, and here was a big project that could pull us together again and harvest the Owner State's resources. I supported an Alaskan route for the gas line. It would provide a flow of gas for in-state use and a new industry at the downstream end of the pipeline, producing petrochemicals and other products that would add value to our resources and employ Alaskans. Hammond, however, favored routing the pipeline through Canada. A Canada line would reduce the value of the gas for Alaska. Less of the pipeline would be built within our state, generating less revenue for Alaska, the owner of the gas, and any chance to process the gas in state would be lost. This issue, along with the land and permanent fund issues, lured me back into the race for governor.

Hammond ran a strong, well-financed reelection bid. Although few Alaska businessmen would contribute to his campaign, those backing construction of a gas pipeline on a Canadian route supported him. In 1977, President Jimmy Carter had used a new federal law to

select the Alaska Highway route across Canada. Most Alaskans preferred the all-Alaskan route from Prudhoe Bay, but Hammond
dubbed the Canadian project "the only game in town" and gave it his
full support.

Hammond instinctively didn't like resource development projects, but as an able politician he appeared to support them to win
votes in development-minded Alaska. In his autobiography, he writes
about how he publicly backed a petrochemical plant in Valdez while
hoping it would never be built. The Alpetco plant, a joint venture of
Dow Chemical and Shell Oil, would use Alaska royalty oil to produce value-added products. Hammond says he knew it would not
work as planned, and when the Alpetco project he had endorsed ran
into expected trouble and asked for a discount on the royalty oil,
Hammond refused, and got what he wanted—the project collapsed.[20]
Was the Canadian gas line also intended to fail? The concept proved
impossible to finance, and by pursuing that illusion we lost critical
years when high oil prices gave an Alaska gas line an excellent
chance of obtaining financing.

When the votes were counted after the August 1978 primary
election, the newspapers declared me the winner, with a lead of 900
votes. But as the days passed, ballots kept coming in for Hammond.
When I returned from a post-election vacation, I had lost by 98 votes.

Our suspicions intensified as the election slipped away. A recount
left the results unchanged. Edgar Paul Boyko, my former attorney
general, represented me in court, assisted by volunteers investigating
suspicious ballots. Under pressure, Hammond's Attorney General
Avrum Gross ordered an audit of the Division of Elections, and on
September 25 found 247 ballots in a locker in their Anchorage office,
votes from one of our strong areas, the Matanuska Valley.[21] Then, a
box of uncounted votes turned up in the trunk of a car belonging to
the son of the Director of the Division of Elections. It had been
parked in front of his house in Anchorage.

These were the most notorious irregularities, but there were
many more. Our investigation found more than 4,000 problem ballots, more than enough to question the election results. Absentee
ballots flowed in long after the election, undated, without postmarks,
and impossible to trace. We got affidavits from postal workers in rural

communities, Hammond's strongholds, saying many non-absentee ballots were mailed after Election Day, in violation of Alaska law. In 68 precincts, more ballots were counted than voters signed the rolls, and 480 ballots were missing in other precincts where more voters signed than voted. In the villages of Kotlik and Kwethluk, an assistant attorney general had to dig through the garbage for ballots so they could be recounted, but couldn't find them all.[22] If someone had stuffed the ballot box, there was no way of catching them—the entire election was a mess.

Superior Court Judge Ralph Moody reached the same conclusion and threw out the election. But the Alaska Supreme Court, two of whose members had held fund raisers for Hammond in their homes but didn't recuse themselves, reviewed the same material and, while agreeing that the election process was flawed and the outcome unknowable, said we hadn't proved that the errors benefited Hammond. The Supreme Court refused to call for another election. Judge Moody remarked to the press, "They made the final decision, not the right decision."

A few weeks after the fiasco of the primary election became evident, I ran as a write-in candidate in the general election. Although I handily beat the Democratic nominee, Chancy Croft, Hammond still won re-election.

Alaskans still admire Jay Hammond, as do I. He did what he thought was best. But in the decade that followed we reaped a harvest of economic disaster sowed during his years in office, and Alaska faced some of its bleakest days. We not only lost our prosperity, we lost our way.

## SAYING "YES" TO THE FUTURE

As mentioned in the previous chapter, former governor Bill Egan and I created an organization in 1979 called Commonwealth North to think about and teach the history and implications of the Owner State. The name captured our aim: to bring the goals of the statehood movement to the next generation. A great Alaskan consensus created the Statehood Act and the Alaska Constitution: a consensus that our resources were meant to be used to build the state, not exploited, divided up, or locked away. In the late 1970s and 1980s, we had lost that consensus. Commonwealth North's mission was to help us recapture that spirit.

It gave Alaskans a forum to discuss their thoughts and hopes. It pushed for responsible development, and it blew the whistle on the federal government's violations of our Statehood Compact. In a book we titled *Going Up In Flames,* a team of 19 prominent Alaskans documented the violations of the Statehood Act by post-statehood federal laws, regulations, and land use decisions.

By 1992, the most promising Owner State project of that era—the natural gas pipeline—had failed to come together as Wall Street and gas buyers balked at the project's costs. Governor Hammond turned to Governor Egan and me to form the Governor's Economic Committee on North Slope Natural Gas. We studied the barriers to building an all-Alaskan gas line in 1982 and produced a report the next year suggesting that Alaska aim for Asian markets, which we had pioneered with liquefied natural gas (LNG) in 1969. We presented our report to incoming Governor Bill Sheffield and to President Reagan's new National Security Council advisor, Bill Clark. Reagan brought up the issue with Prime Minister Yosuhiro Nakasone, and they formed a U.S.-Japan energy working group, which we hosted in Alaska for its first meeting. By the end of 1983, Egan and I formed a company called Yukon Pacific along with ARCO's Robert O. Anderson and two other investors.

The Alaska gas line's largest hurdles weren't technical. It would be considerably simpler to build a cold gas line through the Arctic than the hot-oil pipeline built in the 1970s. Instead, our challenges came from the regulatory system, from domestic and international politics, and from the major oil companies that controlled the gas. Obtaining the permits to build the line would cost many millions. We also faced the barrier of a federal export ban.

In 1988, President Ronald Reagan signed a "finding" allowing export, clearing our largest legal barrier. In the end, Yukon Pacific won the right to build the pipeline, and still has those permits and approvals, a feat that could not be duplicated today for under $100 million. We had created tremendous value in that company, selling a controlling share to CSX in 1989 to raise more capital.

The pipeline still has not been built, despite our efforts and an attractive market in Asia, because the oil companies in control of North Slope gas have preferred to pursue other overseas interests. At this writing, there is a renewed interest in a cross-Canada project. In the late 1980s and 1990s, as Asia's market growth outstripped our 1982 optimistic estimates, the oil companies looked elsewhere. Exxon had reserves in Indonesia, ARCO was also there and in the South China Sea, and British Petroleum was in Australia and Qatar. By re-injecting Alaska's gas into the ground they kept it from competing with those other holdings. Alaska didn't force the issue. For whatever reason, our governors were unable to force the oil companies to release our gas for sale. When I returned to the Office in 1990, I was constrained from taking an aggressive role on the gas line by my past involvement on the project.[23]

Alaska is a stable, industry-friendly democracy with a huge supply of gas, but multinationals often prefer to deal with strong individuals, even if their system is corrupt or a dictatorship. I have argued this issue with the heads of the oil companies with interests in Alaska. This is a shortsighted policy even in terms of their own self-interests. In Indonesia, the Suharto family became fabulously rich from the country's resources. But citizens will only stand for corruption for so long, and Suharto was deposed by a public revolt, and his handpicked successor was turned out of office at the next election. When uprisings occur, oil companies often are seen as the allies of the old regime, and their assets may be confiscated or their taxes increased, costing them millions. In Alaska, producers are assured of political stability over the long term. A pipeline built across Alaska would yield benefits for decades to come, with complete certainty it would be secure. As Owner State ideas begin to catch on around the world and more local democracies come to control their own resources, this kind of arrangement will spread. Those oil companies that take notice and develop a preference for dealing with responsible, democratic regimes will profit in the long run.

We worked hard through Commonwealth North and Yukon Pacific to remind Alaskans of our Owner State obligations and to restart the exploration and development of Alaska. But in the mid–1980s the state sank into the economic depths of a many-year recession, exacerbated by the continued worship of the Permanent Fund and the personal dividends. Our collective spirit nearly flickered out, and little resource development took place. The legislature and governor focused almost entirely on how to divide up and distribute the money that was still coming in from our earlier pioneering at Prudhoe Bay.

*We have been so busy counting our money, we have lost our guts.*

These issues occupied my mind in January 1986, as I worked on the gas pipeline and wrestled with the problems facing the state. We were in the midst of a wrenching economic recession. Many had given up hope. In a speech given in Sitka that year, I spoke from the heart when I tried to rally Alaska to our former purpose in a speech that said:

- We used to say "North to the Future" in this state . . . and believed every word of it. We were always trying to prove our potential. We thought big ideas, and we were willing to put in the grunt work to make these ideas happen. I sense a different mood now [1986]. Since Prudhoe Bay, which was the most exciting opportunity this state ever had to say "yes" to the future, we have turned into a state of moneychangers.

- We used to say, "Let's go." Now we say, "Give me." We used to say, "North to the Future." Now we ask, "Do we have a future?"

- We've been so busy counting our money, we've lost our guts.

- In the 45 years I've been Alaska, I've learned one basic lesson. It's a lesson they don't teach in school. It's a lesson of the street. A survival lesson. There is no wealth without production. You cannot save yourself rich. You can only produce yourself rich . . . .

- For nearly twenty-five years now, virtually all of Alaska's economy has come from one oilfield. How many other economies, cities, states, or countries can you name that are based on one project?

- Money is not secure wealth. It is merely a medium of exchange to acquire assets that produce. Alaska's citizens have become like the children of *Dynasty* on television, shoring up an inheritance instead of creating a new future for themselves.

- We have a Permanent Fund all right, but not a permanent economy. While the Permanent Fund is a good idea, just having a savings account is not enough.

- We own our land. Let's behave like we own it. For the past few years, Alaska has been described as the "last great battleground between developers and the conservationists." Baloney. This is an artificial battleground. We have the technology to reap the riches of the land without raping it.

- Alaskans must rediscover the spirit that existed before Prudhoe Bay, when we thought we were rich beyond our wildest dreams . . . and that richness was of the spirit.[24]

# 11

# Reclaiming
# the Dream

The arms of the coastal mountains east of Anchorage encircle Prince William Sound, the greatest marine recreation area in the world. Its islands and passages enfold seemingly endless miles of naturally protected, uninhabited shores and deep clear waters. Bears, backed by thick, green forests, feed on the beaches during summer months. Pods of Orca whales live in these waters year round, and Humpbacks visit from Hawaii every summer. Bald eagles and a wonderful variety of other wildlife share the bold and rugged environment.

In northern Prince William Sound, on Good Friday, March 24, 1989, the tanker *Exxon Valdez* on its journey south from Valdez ran into a charted rock, opening a large gash in its side. Eleven million gallons of North Slope crude oil poured into the pristine waters, ultimately oiling more than 1,000 miles of shoreline, killing a quarter million sea birds and more than 2,500 sea otters—the most wildlife ever destroyed by an oil spill.[1]

Over the week following, Exxon, Alyeska Pipeline Service Company, and the state and the federal governments were all in disarray. As we watched the aftermath of the disaster, I talked to Governor Steve Cowper. Someone had to force the company to accept responsibility for the disaster and move quickly to retrieve as much of the oil as possible before the damage got worse. Alyeska's response barge sat covered with snow while the slick spread. In the face of indecision, disagreement, and confusion, fishermen and residents, acting on their own, were doing some of the most effective work. Someone had to take charge.

Through Senator Stevens, I pushed to get President George Bush to "federalize" the spill—to take it over, clean it up, and send Exxon the bill. About two weeks after the accident, Governor Cowper also asked Bush to take over the cleanup.[2] Bush hesitated. Exasperated by the confusion, although a private citizen, I offered to take command myself, thinking of the 1969 Santa Barbara spill. Instead, state and federal bureaucrats fought among themselves over who had authority, and no one forced Exxon to tackle the cleanup while there was still time to make a difference. Finally, the President sent the Coast Guard's top admirals to Valdez to manage the response personally. With this decision made, Exxon, to their credit, threw themselves into the cleanup task, eventually spending more than $2 billion to carry out what was asked of them. Unfortunately, they weren't prepared, and by the time the work began, most of the damage had been done.

Leaders of an Owner State must understand that any company like Exxon has an intense focus on its own profits, especially when that company is among the world's largest. The company's investments did much to build Alaska, but its corporate establishment made little effort to build rapport with the Alaska people. They kept a low profile, operating with single-minded discipline to the rule of the bottom line.

The crew of the *Exxon Valdez* was a case in point. On the night of the spill, they were stressed and exhausted from working around the clock. A captain with a known alcohol problem had not received the counseling and oversight from his employer he required. That night he left a third mate on the bridge who lacked qualifications for the Sound's waters. The third mate, in turn, commanded a shaky helmsman. The huge, technologically advanced tanker foundered because these individuals made a series of mistakes. The crew simply drove it onto a charted rock, a navigational error that a weekend recreationist would not make. Something was terribly wrong on that ship, and not on that ship alone. The disaster was a symptom of a mentality that had invaded our economic system. Focused on the bottom line, Exxon ignored its obligations to its employees, to society, and to the unique and precious environment of Prince William Sound.

It would be too easy, however, to blame Exxon alone for the oil spill. The tanker may have belonged to Exxon, but the waters of Prince William Sound did not. Government agencies, federal and state, controlled those waters and failed in their obligations of ownership. Coast Guard personnel, who historically have done a wonderful job in Alaska, did not require the obvious precaution of having tugboat escorts for the tankers leaving Valdez. They failed to monitor the ships as they sailed through the Sound and made little effort to stop alcohol abuse by the crews. We had long known that tankers with double hulls would prevent spills, but the federal government backed off from making that a requirement because of the high cost to industry. The State of Alaska attempted to regulate tanker traffic and to offer large incentives for double hulls when the pipeline was completed, but it lost that right in federal court. And yet, where it did have power, the state did a poor job, allowing the companies involved to relax their readiness. Spill response equipment was not available when it was desperately needed.

Local activists in Valdez were demanding better tanker safety right up to the eve of the disaster—demands that, if complied with, would have prevented the spill. Why didn't the state government listen to those concerns and force industry to act? The answer goes back to our foundation as a state and our development since. After a river of oil started flowing through the pipeline, and each Alaskan was content in his enjoyment of a much-improved economy, we basically ignored our responsibilities of ownership.

## LEADING A REVOLUTION

Alaska's Owner State faced considerable peril in 1990. The federal government had violated our Statehood Compact, as we have seen in earlier chapters, while Alaska's people and their leaders seemed too busy with their own lives to care. The worst environmental disaster in our history shook our confidence and our credibility. We could sense that our pioneering spirit was fading. By raising and debating these issues at Commonwealth North and other forums, I had hoped to inspire new leaders to pick up on the ideas and run for office. We needed to find new and future statesmen who would bring wise management to Alaska.

Unfortunately, as the gubernatorial race moved towards the primaries of the summer of 1990, it was obvious that the frontrunners of the two major parties did not understand the special responsibilities that come with leading Alaska. We were in a time of crisis, and the available leadership was not up to the assignment. The Democratic nominee, Tony Knowles, was an astute politician but lacked guiding beliefs of his own. The Republican nominee, former State Senator Arliss Sturgulewski, a well-liked civic leader who stood for good government, had no real agenda to address Alaska's serious economic problems. Both were said to be environmentalists but, to my dismay, they were competing with each other to win the support of the oil industry. The message seemed to be that whatever was best for the oil companies was best for the state, a dangerous view for the person charged with handling the state's total assets.

As I fought the impulse to run for governor throughout the spring and summer of 1990, something inside me knew I had to do something. James Rockwell, a young Anchorage businessman, kept trying to convince me to run, but the filing date had long past. Just prior to the primary election, John Lindauer, the nominee of the small Alaskan Independence Party, contacted James and offered to drop out if I would take his place on the ballot in the November general election. State law permitted this process if the head of the party in question approved of the replacement.

Neither Lindauer, nor his party chief, Joe Vogler, asked me to support the platform of the Alaskan Independence Party. They would have been wasting their time, as the planks included secession from the United States. As for James, he simply wanted my name on the ballot because he didn't like what was happening to Alaska. Meanwhile, the Republicans already had their elected nominee.

Seven weeks before the general election, Senator Jack Coghill called me at midnight to tell me that the next day was the deadline to accept Lindauer's offer of a place on the ballot. Coghill was the Republican nominee for lieutenant governor and, therefore, Sturgulewski's running mate. He was also the patriarch of the Interior town of Nenana and known as Alaska's "Mr. Republican" throughout Alaska. But he offered to join me as my running mate if I would run against Sturgulewski as an independent. He had spent the previous evening talking to Sturgulewski and had found her vague and non-committal on many of Alaska's most important issues.

As I wrestled with the decision the next morning, word got out I might jump in the race. Around noon, my secretary told me that John Sununu, President George Bush's Chief of Staff, was on the phone. I wouldn't take his call. Half an hour later, John Snow called. He was CEO of the conglomerate CSX, majority owner of Yukon Pacific, the firm we had founded to advance the Alaska gas pipeline project. Snow said words to the effect, "What in the hell are you doing? The White House Chief of Staff called to say he's going to squash this pipeline because you won't take his phone calls."

That made me mad. Damn mad. After years of fighting for Alaska statehood and struggling to free ourselves from Outside interests, East Coast politicians were still attempting to blackmail us by shutting off our ability to decide what was best for our state. When Sununu called a third time, at about 2:30 P.M., I took the call in a side office. Only Ermalee was with me. Sununu, famous for his temper, told me with high emotion and heated language what he would do if I ran, repeating the threat that he would stop the gas pipeline. He was loud; so loud Ermalee could hear his voice from where she was sitting. Finally I blew up, "John, when I'm elected, you'll see what tough is all about." I slammed the phone down with a bang. Ermalee walked over and said, "Wally, you have to go." That turned the corner. All my life I had been fighting for Alaska against Outside interests and the federal government. Sununu wasn't just threatening me. He was threatening the common interests of Alaska's people.

I walked into my main office in something of a daze. Many of my family and friends were waiting. To no one in particular, I said, "I have never heard Alaska threatened by Outsiders like I just heard. I'm running for governor."

The race was on, literally. We jumped into a car and headed for the Division of Elections at 4:30 P.M., half an hour before the deadline. The Hickel-Coghill team got our papers in with only minutes to spare. Less than an hour later, I announced my decision to a hastily called press conference in the Endeavor Room at the Hotel Captain Cook. The Alaska news media were stunned. "Let's put the spirit back in Alaska," I proclaimed. "This will be a 48-day campaign to bring Alaska's destiny home."[3]

The state's political establishment went crazy. "You got two old dogs who want to bay at the moon one last time," said Republican state Senator Tim Kelly. Jim Crawford, a former Republican Party Chairman, said the party had "exploded." The current party chairman, Grant Doyle of Fairbanks, quit to join my campaign. Senator Ted Stevens, who said he was "too pissed off" to call me, sent my long-time friend Carl Brady to ask if I had lost my mind, and confronted my aide, Mead Treadwell, in a U.S. Senate hallway a day later to say I'd just handed the election to the Democrats. But while party officials, consultants, and editorial writers were busy worrying about how Jack and I got into the race, a spontaneous revolution took place all around us.

## STAYING FREE

In Alaska in 1990, the oil industry had strong influence in both major political parties. Oil companies and executives were by far the largest contributors to political campaigns. Those donations paid for themselves many times over, most notably when the industry persuaded the legislature to restructure oil taxes in 1981 from separate accounting to a unitary tax. In 1990, the new governor would be responsible for many oil industry issues, including oil spill litigation and billions of dollars of back taxes owed to the state.

For these reasons, my campaign did not accept contributions from oil company executives. About ten days before the election, when I had passed both Knowles and Sturgulewski in the polls, several representatives of oil and oil support industries came to my office and offered financial support. Skip Bilhartz, the president of ARCO Alaska, was one of them. It was a crazy, hectic point in the campaign, and he was excited. I said, "Skip, I'll be fair to you, no problem, but I don't want anything." I didn't put the oil companies down, I just said no. ARCO and BP threw their support to Sturgulewski.[4] I also turned down other money that came in when the polls said I was a sure winner. We assembled a team to send back a flood of special interest checks. Of course, I welcomed the donations in tens and twenties that came from individuals who just wanted good government. But in the end, I paid for most of the brief campaign myself.

Just six weeks after the experts had discounted my entry into the race, a surge of populism swept me into office by a large margin of victory over Democrat Knowles and Republican Sturgulewski. On November 6, 1990, after 22 years back in the private sector, I was reelected governor of Alaska. At 71, I would be the nation's oldest governor. The first congratulatory call came from former President Nixon. The second was from President Bush, "We [the Republicans] have been watching your campaign since the day you started," he told me. "And we came in third!"

In the twenty years since I was last in office, Alaska had grown much richer materially but poorer in spirit. The years had changed me, too. Two decades out of public office gave me forty days in the wilderness to study and think about the commons. Through Commonwealth North and my own thinking, I had refined the Owner State idea that had been the key to Alaska's success. Now I had the chance to put those ideas into practice.

In Juneau, Judge Ralph Moody administered the oath of office on December 3, 1990, and I used the opportunity to explain my philosophy:

> We will not allow others to violate our Statehood Compact, an agreement that we have with the U.S. Congress and the people of Alaska. We expect, and we'll demand they keep their part of the bargain. And those who play fair are going to be welcome, as they've always been welcome. In fact, I invite them now to come on up and help us create this new day and this new civilization that's going to be in the North Country. Together, we'll show the world how an Owner State can be developed and the environment protected. Not just protected, but in many cases enhanced. But I think we're going to insist—I think the people of Alaska want that— that they play by our rules, with our understanding of this great country. Because this is a unique state of ours, every

citizen is an owner. Each of us, from my friends from Ketchikan to Kotzebue to my grandchildren in Anchorage— each of us shares the responsibility and deserves the reward of being a part owner of this great country.[5]

With this surprising and spontaneous campaign behind me, I relished the fact that as governor I was a truly free man. No political establishment had a claim. Most of those who had worked on the campaign, including Alaska Independence Party Chairman Joe Vogler and his rank and file, simply wanted good government and were content to let me get the job done. I owed nothing to any industry or resource developer. I was beholden to no environmental organization. I could care for Alaska's commons, both its beauty and its resources, and represent all Alaskans with a free heart.

## "GIVE ME SIXTY DAYS!"

Once in office, my first task was to sort out the maze of problems we inherited from the *Exxon Valdez* disaster. In the previous 18 months, the oil spill had turned into a lawyer spill. The state was spending $1 million a month on attorney fees,[6] and by the two-year anniversary of the spill, government costs in suing Exxon were expected to exceed $100 million.[7] I wanted that money spent where it belonged, enhancing Prince William Sound. The attorneys were unlikely to bring the legal warfare to closure as they were earning huge fees on a case that could go on for years. The Justice Department in D.C. had tried to settle their criminal case against Exxon in August 1990 without telling Governor Cowper. That deal would have undercut the state's position in court and, fortunately, it leaked to the public and fell apart.[8] Now the bureaucrats and lawyers within the state and federal governments were so distrustful of each other that they were not even sharing scientific information—in some areas, both governments were studying the same things, and wasting millions of dollars in the process.[9] The people's elected leader needed to take charge for the good of the total.

It didn't take us long. We set the ground rules. We needed a universal settlement. We had to settle the *federal* charges as well as the *state's* civil suit: there was no way to separate the damage to a state-owned salmon from the harm done to a federally managed sea lion. On January 8, less than five weeks after being sworn in, I met in Juneau with Interior Department officials and asked them to take my ideas for a settlement back to Washington, D.C.[10] Later, I called Dick Thornburgh, the U.S. Attorney General, and said I wanted absolute authority for 60 days to find agreement among the state, the federal government, and Exxon. "Dick, just give me 60 days to put this together," I pleaded.

Thornburgh said, "I'll give you 60 days." He thought it would take six months or six years—it was easy to give me 60 days.

In my experience as Interior Secretary, I had dealt with Exxon many times. I understood their professionalism, their power, and that they knew what they wanted. I had received word—just call it talk around the office—that Exxon was thinking that $460 million would be a reasonable dollar amount to settle the suits. That's a lot of money, but I felt we should ask for more. Alaska had other issues with Exxon. I wanted them to relinquish state oil and gas leases they controlled but had not developed at Point Thomson on the North Slope. Exxon had outstayed its time on those leases without producing the state-owned resources. As an owner, it was time to get tough.

I already had a friendly acquaintance with Larry Rawl, Exxon's CEO. This would be our first contact since my election as governor, and I wanted to set the tone. It had to be clear that I was representing the owner of the oil and of Prince William Sound, and he was representing the company that had spilled our oil on our beaches. The meeting had to be orchestrated in a way that would establish where Alaska and Exxon stood in this relationship. Unlike some other governors, I did not fly to Houston to meet Exxon in their offices. We set up the meeting for 9 A.M. in my office in Juneau on Tuesday, January 15. Normally, the company's executives would fly in for a meeting and out the same day. By my calling the meeting for 9 o'clock in the morning, they would have to come in from Texas the night before. Then, accidentally, my staff put the meeting on my calendar for 9:30. Without my knowing it, Rawl and Exxon President Lee Raymond, the top two men in one of the world's most powerful companies, sat in my lobby waiting for half an hour.

When they finally came into my office, I got to the point. Rawl and Raymond sat right across from me, and my Chief of Staff Max Hodel sat to my left and attorney general Charlie Cole to my right. Everything was intended to show, gently but clearly, who owned Alaska.

"Larry," I said, "I want Point Thomson back." I said it just as clean, simple, and direct as if I had told one of my sons, "Eat your oatmeal." I watched his eyes, because the eyes reflect the mind, just as the face reflects the heart.

Very clearly, without animosity, Rawl said, "Governor, could you give us a little time?"

"Sure, Larry, I'll give you time, but you know the terms of the lease." He knew, and he didn't say, "You're not going to take Point Thomson." It was a cordial exchange, but we had established a clear relationship he understood, and he knew I knew.

Then we got to the *Exxon Valdez*. I was talking and watching. I spoke about the enormous problems we had and yet the great opportunity of what we could do by settling the claims and moving on. "It's going to take a lot of money." I was watching his eyes. I had been planning to go for a billion dollars, but the words that came out of my mouth were, "Larry, it will probably take a billion-two to do this." Throwing in another $200 million gave me a little wiggle room. My comment just blanked him out. You don't have to remember the words; you have to remember what you see in their eyes. I read it as acceptable—you can always tell the difference between acceptance and angry denial. I didn't stop talking—if I did, that might focus the conversation on the $1.2 billion figure—and for a minute or more I kept watching his face and eyes. He seemed intrigued when I said we weren't interested in punishing Exxon. The money was for restoring and enhancing Prince William Sound.

> "A billion dollars is an awful lot of money."

I said, "Larry, we're going to have these meetings, and we're going to solve it in 60 days. So let's have an agreement. You will be at no meeting if I'm not there, and I'll be at no meeting if you aren't there."

Rawl agreed. Then, as he left the room, he turned at the door and said, "A billion dollars is an awful lot of money."[11] I didn't blink. I just smiled and said goodbye. The meeting had lasted only forty-five minutes.

During the following weeks, I met with Rawl several times in Washington, D.C., and, good to our agreement, neither of us met on the issue without the other present. Indeed, when Lee Raymond, Exxon's president, called a week later, I asked Attorney General Charlie Cole to handle the call. I would only deal with the top person, including on the federal side.[12] That was one of the keys to settling the case quickly.

About that time, the U.S. Department of Commerce called Cole and invited us to Washington to meet with the heads of the departments of Commerce, Transportation, Interior, the EPA, and the National Oceanic and Atmospheric Administration, the federal team they had put together. I called Rawl, who was in Chile, and we agreed to meet the next Monday in Washington, D.C. When I arrived in Washington Sunday afternoon, however, we had word that Interior Secretary Manuel Lujan didn't want to meet with Exxon. He didn't feel ready to enter into negotiations. I called Lujan at home Sunday night and laid out my idea for the settlement. On that basis, he agreed to attend, and the meeting convened the next day, January 28, in the office of Secretary of Transportation Samuel Skinner. Secretary Skinner and Charlie Cole were the only attorneys in attendance.[13]

After that meeting, talks started continuously at Cole's level, establishing the details of a joint state-federal offer. A week later, I was back in Washington for another meeting. In a two-hour session with Cabinet members and Rawl, the state and federal governments presented a detailed $1.2 billion settlement offer to Exxon.

There were many more meetings. At one of them with Rawl and the Cabinet officers, Lujan said out loud to the group, "Where did we get this billion dollar figure?" No one said anything, and the conversation went on to other topics. We had an army of scientists studying the oil spill and tallying the animals poisoned or suffocated by the crude oil. But how do you put a dollar value on a dead otter or an eagle? There was no way to measure it. The lawyers preparing the case for trial understood this problem. They were even doing surveys to learn how much each animal was worth to the typical member of the American public. Lujan knew all about that, and I had been briefed on the studies as well. Again he said, "I don't know if the figure is right, too high, or too low, or what? I don't know where we got the figure." I still said nothing. Finally, Lujan turned to me and said, "Governor, where did we get this figure?"

I pointed to my forehead and said, "Out of my head." The number didn't come from studies of the wildlife nor by trying to analyze how much it would take to return each bay in Prince William Sound to the way it had been before the spill. No one knew how to do that, much less how to estimate the cost. I instinctively knew it had to be a billion dollars or more to be acceptable—to the Alaskan people and to the nation.

The negotiations were intense, and they came close to falling apart more than once. My primary concern, other than the amount of money, was how we were going to spend it. At one meeting with the federal Cabinet members, including Attorney General Thornburgh, they discussed using the settlement money:

- to buy out the timber rights in the Sound from Native landowners,
- to pay back the federal and state governments for out-of-pocket costs,
- to fund more cleanup, and
- to continue scientific studies.

I supported those things, but I said, "I want the word *enhancement* in there." They talked about it, but the idea didn't get anywhere, so I said it again. "No, I want the word *enhancement* in there."

They didn't get it. It wasn't enough to take trees off the market. I wanted to obtain the knowledge and develop the facilities to study, protect, and use the Sound in the future and make it better. We needed to invest the money to build a research center to understand the environment and educate the public—to have the environment serve mankind. We needed to know how the Sound works, not just to cry over the spill or dish out punishment.

The bureaucrats were stuck on punishing Exxon and trying to do something for the wildlife. As a dedicated boater on Prince William

Sound for thirty years, nobody loves the otters and whales more than I do. But to save nature is to understand and enhance it. You move forward and do something positive.

*Together, we'll show the world how an Owner State can be developed and the environment protected . . . and not just protected, but enhanced.*

Failing to get the attention of the others, I finally said, "I'll refuse to go along with this thing unless you put the word enhancement in there." They reluctantly put it in. That saved the deal and, over the years, will be the key to balanced, wise management of the Sound.

By the end of February, the settlement had taken shape, but in early March a federal judge enjoined us from signing it until we promised it would not affect the Alaska Natives who were also suing Exxon. I didn't disagree with that. The injunction was lifted on March 12, and the U.S. Treasury Department asked me to fly to Washington immediately. We met at the Treasury Building at 11 P.M. that night. Dick Thornburgh, Larry Rawl, and about thirty others were there. Dick turned to me and asked, "Governor, what day is it?"

I said, "I think it's Tuesday, could be Wednesday." I had flown across the country, and it was 11 o'clock at night, so I wasn't too sure.

"No it's Tuesday," he said. "I asked what day is it?"

"I think it's Tuesday."

He said, "No, Governor, it's the fifty-eighth day. You asked for sixty."

We settled it that night. Everyone signed off. I had never counted the days. I had told him sixty days, and we did it in fifty-eight.

Larry Rawl admitted he didn't think it could be done.

At half past midnight, we held a press conference. I said, "Exxon should be commended, the federal government should be commended, and Charlie Cole should be commended. This is a very good deal for the state of Alaska, the federal government, and the environment of Prince William Sound."[14]

The settlement would bring $1 billion to compensate the governments' costs for the spill and to restore and enhance Prince William Sound. A six-member board of trustees would control the money, with three state members and three federal members. To do anything, all six would have to agree. Although I had the power to approve the settlement on the state's behalf, I asked the legislature to ratify it. We had some false starts there and in court, but on December 9, 1991, the settlement received final approval from a federal judge in Anchorage. It was the largest settlement of its type in American history, and the largest environmental fine ever levied, by many times.[15]

Three years later, in 1994, private plaintiffs suing Exxon— 16,000 of them—won a much larger award: $5 billion for punitive damages. Some people said we should have taken our case to court and tried to get that much for the government. But my goal never was to punish Exxon; it was to restore and enhance Prince William Sound. As this is written, more than a decade after the spill, the private plaintiffs are still in litigation—they haven't seen their first dollar, and a federal appeals court has ruled that the $5 billion judgment was excessive. Meanwhile, we've used our settlement money to protect 650,000 acres of spectacular coastal forest, an area almost as large as Yosemite National Park,[16] including 1,300 miles of shoreline and 280 salmon streams, along with beautiful Kachemak Bay State Park.[17]

We did a lot more with the *Exxon Valdez* settlement, including the creation of the Alaska SeaLife Center, a world-class marine research and education center in Seward, which opened to the public in 1998. My words from the dedication ceremony are on the wall above the throngs of visitors who come to see the live exhibits featuring Alaska's marine mammals, birds, and fish of the North Pacific, and to watch scientists conducting research.

> We must use, understand, enhance and protect
> the commons of the North Pacific
> for the benefit of the total.
> The cost is to care.

This statement explains the purpose of the SeaLife Center. When it is projected to the commons of the world, it is the fundamental challenge mankind faces at the dawn of the 21st century.

## STORING THE FISH IN THE OCEAN

In my more than twenty years out of office, times had changed, but the basic issues remained surprisingly similar. We still were presiding over Alaska's commons on land and sea, and we still faced personal and corporate greed as well as federal policies that were simply misinformed, sometimes written by Outside bureaucrats who thought they knew what was best for us, whether we liked it or not.

Back in 1966, we had fought the federal government to protect our offshore waters, which were then defined as Alaska's three miles of territorial waters within the U.S. 12-mile limit. During the 1970s, Alaskans pushed for an extension of the 12-mile limit to 200 miles. We wanted to regulate and, if necessary, ban the foreign ships that were plundering the fish and crab atop our continental shelf. I added my voice to the debate, and Senator Stevens and Congressman Young dedicated a major part of their careers to this issue. By 1976, the Magnuson Act was in place to allow only American control of the fishing off our shores.[18] It took twenty years, but we met the first of our obligations of ownership by getting control of the commons of our offshore fisheries.

But in 1990, major problems remained.

The fisheries for halibut and black cod (also called sablefish) had deteriorated into a classic tragedy of the commons. Anyone with a boat and a hooked line could commercially fish these valuable bottom fish, and many did. As the years passed, more and more fishermen pushed for a limited catch quota, and the fishing season grew shorter and shorter. By the start of my second term as governor, halibut seasons lasted just 24 hours and came only two times a year. If a storm blew up on the chosen day, the Coast Guard struggled to save the lives of fishermen who risked disaster rather than miss the one-day derby. Some died during these openings. The system also made no sense for the public. The stores carried fresh halibut from Alaska only a few days a year. The rest of the time, we had to settle for frozen fish. Only large processing companies could afford to buy enough fish for a year's sales and keep the catch in cold storage, and that limited the competition. The consumer paid the extra cost of cold storage and the debt incurred by fish buyers, which could exceed the cost of the fish itself. Often, restaurants in Alaska had to import fresh halibut from Canada.

When too many entrants chase common resources, someone has to act or the resource will be depleted or destroyed. Whether the solution comes from government or private corporations, it has to be enforceable. The traditional solution has been a government approval to limit entry in some way or to limit the efficiency of fishing gear. You can sell access by auction, as we usually do with oil; you can distribute it by lottery, as game managers do with special hunting permits; or you can give it to the first to arrive, as we do with hard rock minerals, homesteads and, often, fisheries.

*"Can you put fresh halibut on the table in America year round?"*

When Alaska's salmon fisheries came under pressure in the 1960s, a limited entry system awarded fishing permits only to those who had fished in the past. The voters amended the Alaska Constitution in 1972 to allow this system of limited entry, and the program began in 1973. Holders of the permits won the opportunity to catch fish, but competition among fishermen still determined who got how much. They could sell their permits, but no new permits would be created. Soon the price of those permits rose as high as $100,000 each. Access to the commons was no longer free: you had to buy your way in. But once in, you could take as much as you could catch during open seasons.

*"Yes, if you can take the heat."*

Back in office in 1990, I turned to Clem Tillion to solve the halibut and black cod problems. A crusty, crafty fisherman and the father of the Kachemak Bay community of Halibut Cove, Clem had served in the legislature for seventeen years, retiring as President of the Senate in 1981. I knew he cared deeply about the issue and that he would do what he thought best for the resources and the people. Indeed, the only lure I had to take him away from his comfortable kingdom on Kachemak Bay was the opportunity to solve the problem, a temptation he could not resist.

I asked him, "Can you put fresh halibut on the table in America year round?"

He said, "Yes, if you can take the heat."

I told him, "Clem, you have absolute authority. Take it from there."[19]

Immediately dubbed "Fish Czar," Tillion understood how a foreman of the ranch has to behave—decisively and aggressively. I was not disappointed. By the time of my inaugural celebration in Kodiak, one of many we held around the state, Clem had that fishing town up in arms over his ideas to solve the halibut and black cod crisis.[20]

These fish, mostly caught outside the state's waters, fell under federal control, regulated by the North Pacific Fisheries Management Council. The National Marine Fisheries Service, and ultimately the Secretary of Commerce, carried out the council's advice. Membership of the council primarily represented segments of the fishing industry, but as governor I had some influence over who was appointed. Tillion was my representative, and he may have been the only member without a conflict of interest.

For halibut and black cod, Tillion's solution was a form of limited entry that would privatize the resource, but deliver far greater benefit to the public, the ultimate owners of the commons. Instead of racing for halibut, everyone who had caught some during certain past years would receive an Individual Fishing Quota (or IFQ) in all future years. That quota was each fisherman's portion of the catch, available for harvest at any time of year, whenever weather and markets dictated. If a fisherman landed one per cent of the total halibut catch prior to the new system, he or she would be entitled to the same portion forever on. Or the fisherman could sell that quota on the open market—essentially, selling a slice of the former commons before the fish were ever harvested. Federal observers would regulate adherence to the catch size.

The system would allow fishermen to deliver their catch year round. Instead of storing the fish in freezers, we would store them in the ocean to take as needed, and we would be able to serve fresh fish. Smaller processors would be able to buy the fish—they wouldn't have to buy so much at once—and the cost of borrowing money to buy and freeze the catch would be reduced.

When the council passed the plan, less than a year after Tillion took on the challenge, he said, "We have begun to change the way the United States looks at fisheries. We have operated for centuries under the tragedy of the commons."

A fisherman who was listening shot back, "You've given away my fish."[21]

But of course, it wasn't his fish. It belonged to the public, and the public was not able to use it because of the way we were harvesting it. The old system benefited the most competitive fishermen, those who could win in the 24-hour derbies, but for the true owners of the fish it was a mess. As we have seen since, prices for the consumer have stayed the same under the new system; while the prices fishermen receive have risen substantially, because the middlemen are taking less of the profit.[22]

Some criticized the transferability of the permits, asking why fishermen should be allowed to sell the right to fish. Tillion argued that ownership of the fishery makes fishermen better stewards of the resource. As he says, "The American farmer beats every farmer in the world because he owns his farm. You don't have any conservation ethic if there's no gain to be made by taking care of the resource." This approach, setting a limit determined by biologists and allowing the market to set the value of quotas, is known as "cap and trade." It is supported nationally by groups as diverse as free-market foundations and the Environmental Defense Fund.

Another problem we faced troubled me even more than the need for year round fresh fish. Congress, through the efforts of Senator Stevens and Congressman Young, had begun to rid the 200-mile limit of foreign fishing ships, but most ordinary Alaskans still got little value from the fisheries. Huge factory ships fished for months out of sight of Alaska's shores, rarely touching land. They pulled in pollock and other plentiful bottom fish from the Bering Sea, processing it on board into fish sticks or surimi, a fish paste used to make imitation crab and other products. When they came ashore to refuel and unload frozen cases of finished product, they usually passed by Alaska entirely and landed in Seattle. Alaskans deserved to benefit from the resources taken from our waters, and not only with menial jobs on the processors' floating slime lines. We needed to capture a portion of this commons for Alaska's towns and villages on shore, some of which were struggling in poverty.

I remember standing on a beach years ago on Saint Lawrence Island looking out at the ocean at night with several village leaders. Lights filled the horizon. A city of Russian ships sailed just a few miles offshore, dragging the bottom and scooping up tons of seafood. One of my companions seemed to speak out to the sea when he said, "They fish all the time, and we don't even know what's there."

Tillion worked on this issue, too. I told him about standing on that beach with my friends on St. Lawrence Island, and said: "Get them involved." Our solution came from Alaska-based Bering Sea fishermen themselves. A group came to see me and recommended that we push the federal government to set aside a Community Development Quota, or CDQ. Unlike the IFQs, which would give individual fishermen the right to catch the fish, Community Development Quotas would give towns and villages on the shore the right to 7.5 per cent of the bottom fish the big factory processors hauled from the ocean. They could use these quotas to force onshore processing that would employ their residents—the kind of value-added processing we had created with our Cook Inlet royalty oil—or they could exchange the quota fish for jobs, equity in fishing ventures, and money that would aid their communities. With consummate skills, diplomatic and political, Tillion got this plan through the council, too.

When the CDQ plan was forwarded to Washington, however, it ran into problems. We had no way to know why the plan was running into trouble, but it felt much the same as in territorial days, when the federal management of salmon tracked influences originating from Seattle. The Seattle factory trawlers didn't want to give up 7.5 per cent of the catch, and they used their influence to get the Secretary of Commerce to turn down the plan. Senator Stevens called me and said we had lost the battle. I thought about it overnight, and then called William Reilly, administrator of the Environmental Protection Agency, catching him on his car phone as he left the White House on Friday evening.

After hearing about the situation, he said, "Governor, that's a Commerce decision."

"No, Bill, it's an environmental decision," I argued, explaining how these ships were catching and discarding millions of pounds of edible fish a year. The waste from this bycatch was horrendous. We could be better stewards of the marine ecosystem if Alaska communities had a stake in it.

Over the next weekend, John Sandor, Commissioner of Environmental Conservation, and Carl Rosier, Commissioner of Fish and Game, led a team that produced a series of briefing papers and faxed them to Reilly. Somehow, within a few days, Reilly helped get the decision reversed. We had won. Alaska had Community Development Quotas.

These programs work. Local people, mostly Native Alaskans, won the right to use the commons to improve their lives, and the wealth of the ocean commons comes home. The IFQs provide year round, fresh Alaskan halibut and save lives that otherwise would be lost when storms hit during the one-day fishing seasons. The consumer gets a better product for the same price, and fishermen make more money and work under better conditions. In exchange, we gave up the freedom of allowing anyone with a boat and tackle to become a commercial halibut fisherman. We took the path from pure freedom to freedom tied to collective responsibility, and our commons won. Congress should allow this approach to extend to other fisheries in Alaska and the United States.

## WATCHING WHAT YOU OWN

When I came into office in 1990, Commissioner of Revenue Lee Fisher and Attorney General Charlie Cole brought to my attention a staggering backlog of unpaid tax and royalty bills owed to the state by the oil industry. Our state government had failed in one of its primary obligations, to watch what we own. Some of these back oil taxes had been in dispute for more than a decade. Private attorneys hired by the state made millions working on these extraordinarily technical cases while the oil industry made millions using the unpaid taxes as if they were low-interest loans.

We charged an interest rate of twelve per cent on these contested, unpaid tax bills, without compounding. That meant that if the state won its case in court proving that some of these long overdue taxes were owed, we would recover only about half of what we could have earned by collecting the money earlier. In other words, each year the companies failed to pay, the effective interest rate decreased. In the 1990 legislative session, State House Speaker Sam Cotten tried to add compounding to the back-tax interest rate and to make the rate vary with interest rates nationally. Oil company lobbyists killed his bill in the State Senate. Incredibly, senators justified their action by saying that Cotten's bill would cost the oil industry too much—by charging a *normal, compounded* interest rate.[23]

Soon after taking office, settling these tax cases became one of my top priorities. At the same time as we negotiated the *Exxon Valdez* settlement in Washington, we worked with Cotten, who had been elected to the Senate in November 1990, and pushed a compounded interest rate bill through the legislature that June. It set the interest five points above a benchmark federal rate, and compounded it quarterly. The new rate would take effect October 31. The grace period gave the oil companies time to settle with us before they began paying a market interest rate. If they refused to settle, the state wouldn't suffer too much: we would be getting a good return on our money.[24]

Attorney General Cole and his successor Bruce Botelho focused much of their time on these settlements. Over the four years of my administration, we brought in an average of $3 million a day from this initiative. We negotiated aggressively, getting as much as we could while always working toward a successful end result. With the pressure of the new interest rates, we had the oil companies' attention, and they were interested in a solution. And they weren't as hostile as previous governors had feared. When it was all over, Dick Olver of British Petroleum, BP's Chief Executive in North America, whose company eventually paid the state approximately $2 billion to settle these cases, sent a note thanking me for bringing the issue to closure. In total, we brought nearly $4 billion into the treasury though oil tax settlements. The monies were placed in a Constitutional Budget Reserve Fund that was used to bridge a growing state fiscal gap for years to come without disrupting the state's economy. This money ended up doing what the Permanent Fund had been intended to do—it supported Alaska's vital government services through our rainy days in the late 1990s.

## ONE SIZE DOES NOT FIT ALL

When it comes to caring for the environment, there's an important line to be drawn between setting national environmental standards and ignoring local wisdom and conditions. In Alaska, so different from the states with temperate climates, one size definitely does not fit all.

In many cases, national standards are imperative, as they prevent economic interests from pitting one state against another and bidding down environmental quality to attract industry. A small state could make a reasonable decision to accept a certain amount of pollution in return for economic development, but as that pollution drifts over another state, the cost-benefit calculation breaks down. As Interior Secretary, I championed national environmental policies when state governments did a poor job of conserving their own environment.

President George H. W. Bush was taking that federal approach when he stepped in to stop the loss of valuable wetlands across America. The South 48 had allowed nearly 80 per cent of their wetlands to be filled and paved.[25] As a result, ground water was vanishing and waterfowl habitat suffered. I can remember as a child watching geese land on a small pond that formed in a dip in a field on our tenant farm in Kansas. When we drained that dip, the geese never returned, a loss that I felt deeply. In those days, farmers didn't think twice about reclaiming wetlands like that pond. Families would benefit financially from filling those few acres of wetlands. It seemed to make little difference if those wetlands were preserved, as they represented such a tiny percentage of the habitat available for migrating waterfowl. The end result appeared to be inevitable—a classic example of the tragedy of the commons: no more ducks, geese, or swans.

The federal solution was to mandate a "no net loss" policy. If wetlands were destroyed, they had to be replaced somewhere else. That was a good idea in Kansas and most other states, where a large percentage of the wetlands were already gone. But in Alaska, it's a different story. Nearly the entire state of Alaska is either wetlands or snow, ice, and mountains, and only a small fraction of one per cent of our wetlands has been built on or used in any way. With virtually all of Alaska owned in common through the state, the federal government, and the Native corporations, we would never run short of waterfowl habitat. Here, a no-net-loss policy is costly and unnecessary, another example of the distant, ill-informed power of Washington, D.C., taking away our rights for no good reason.

We fought hard for an exemption to President Bush's policy. Public projects such as schools and airport safety improvements had been cancelled or put on hold. Late in his term, I met with Bush in the Oval Office and persuaded him to grant an exception for Alaska. But Bill Clinton took office soon after, and Bush's order was reversed, forcing Alaska to adhere to "no net loss," when it made no sense at all.

Working with me on all these environmental issues was Commissioner John Sandor, his deputy Mead Treadwell, and a competent staff. I never met a better cabinet officer than Sandor. He had served in federal service all his life and came out of retirement to work on Alaska's needs. Steady and strong, his policies were balanced and his demeanor professional. Where many Alaskans would be so outraged by the abuses we faced that they would become marginalized, Sandor kept a steady hand, and the results of his work were remarkable.

Another example was his dealing with the air pollution requirements of the Clean Air Act of 1990, which created an absurd situation in Alaska. Neither John nor I had argument with the law's standards—setting standards is a legitimate federal activity—although the reasons for having standards didn't apply to Alaska, where our population is so widely dispersed. Unfortunately, the law did not stop at standards, nor did it allow for reasonable decisions at the local level. The law mandated we install expensive air pollution technology on small electric generators and follow complex permitting processes in tiny Native villages located hundreds of miles from any population center—while those same villages still lacked basic sewer systems. Despite serious efforts over the years, many Alaska communities were still using five-gallon buckets for toilets, dumping the contents in lagoons at the outskirts of their towns. As in the Third World, these conditions created disease. Using community agreements, we worked with each village to prioritize environmental problem-solving so funds would go to the most serious problems first. But sometimes we were forced to spend manpower and resources on paperwork on the smokestacks from the town generators instead.

The same Clean Air Act mandated an expensive additive in the gasoline sold in the winter in Anchorage and Fairbanks. Due to the cold weather inversion phenomenon, which holds air pollution near the ground, neither city was able to meet federal carbon monoxide standards several days a year. We received word from the Environmental Protection Agency that if we didn't use methyl tertiary buthyl ether, or MTBE, we would lose our federal highway funding. MTBE increases the oxygen in gasoline so a car's engine burns gas more completely, producing less air pollution. No one knew the health effects of MTBE in a northern environment, or even if it would work to reduce carbon monoxide in cold weather. I wrote to Bill Reilly, the EPA administrator, asking for a waiver. It was denied. We were told to do it just like everywhere in the country, and in November 1992, we did as commanded. Reports immediately began arriving from Fairbanks that people were getting sick from the stuff, with headaches, coughing, a burning sensation in the nose and throat, eye irritation, and even vomiting and dizziness. Led by the state epidemiologist, Dr. John Middaugh, a study by the Alaska Division of Health and Social Services, the Center for Disease Control, and the National Center for Environmental Health confirmed that there was a link between MTBE and the illnesses we were experiencing. The report said 25,000 people might be getting sick in Anchorage from breathing MTBE.[26]

We suspended MTBE in Fairbanks, but the EPA insisted we keep using it in Anchorage, even though we were getting reports of illness there, too. The next summer, an additional study by the CDC and the state found that Alaskans had MTBE in their blood, and those

*The law required us to poison our people to save them.*

with more MTBE had more symptoms of illness. I again wrote to the EPA, saying it would be irresponsible to continue this way. Senator Stevens joined in the fight and was able to win legislation that forced EPA to back off and to study the issue.[27] When a major, interdepartmental study finally was completed in 1997, it confirmed that MTBE might indeed be causing serious illness. Recent studies show that MTBE has polluted lakes and groundwater all over the United States. Twenty per cent of the nation's urban water wells are contaminated.

An exposé by Steve Kroft on 60 *Minutes* in January 2000 warned that MTBE could become the greatest U.S. environmental crisis of the decade.

The point of the story is to illustrate the consequences of imposing the same solution everywhere, regardless of local conditions or preferences. The Arctic is different. We could and did solve the problem better ourselves, by adding ethanol to our gas. I'm proud that in Alaska, where we are used to thinking for ourselves, we blew the whistle on MTBE. The rest of the country, sadly, buckled under the federal mandates and is desperately trying to solve this unnecessary problem.

## TAKING THE FEDS TO COURT

Our battles with the federal government continued—indeed, they were more intense—in my second term. The reach of federal interference in state affairs had grown worse since my gubernatorial tenure twenty years earlier. In the territorial and early statehood years, we fought economic interests—coal, copper, freight, and fish monopolies—that used their influence in Congress to advance their colonial exploitation of Alaska. Now the nature of the problem had changed. In the '90s we faced a government that had decided it needed to protect Alaska from the Alaskan people. The federal bureaucracy ballooned in size as Congress mandated national solutions to local problems. At the same time, Congress forgot the promises made at statehood.

We had become a state with the understanding that Alaska's resources would be used for the good of the people, not set aside or locked up. We were due 90 per cent of the revenues from the use of the resources on and under Alaska's federal lands. Yet ANILCA (see Chapter 9) set aside more than 100 million acres in federal Conservation System Units (the "Map on the Floor"), and the federal government treated most of the rest of its land as de facto parks and wildernesses as well. This meant that virtually no resource development had taken place on 217 million acres of Alaska belonging to the federal government. The statehood agreement looked like an empty promise.

Where was the outrage over this immense deception? Taking away the revenues from resource development on hundreds of millions of acres of resource-rich land was among the largest thefts in world history. It is a funny thing about human nature that if you steal $10 from a man's wallet, you're likely to get in a fight, but if you steal billions from the commons, co-owned by him and his descendants, he may not even notice. The theft of so much of Alaska's future simply was too large and too abstract for most people to understand.

I decided to fight back. We launched a barrage of federal lawsuits against the United States government, demanding Congress abide by its Compact with Alaska. History and the law were on our side. After the Revolutionary War, when our new nation added the Northwest Territory to the original Thirteen Colonies, Thomas Jefferson urged the Continental Congress to adopt Northwest Ordinances in 1785 and 1787. These comprehensive acts provided for governance of the newly acquired lands. Several provisions written then affect Alaska's relationship to the federal government to this day. First of all, a new state was to be admitted "on an equal footing with the original states in all respects whatever." Second, the ordinances were considered "as articles of compact, between the original states and the people and states in the said territory, and forever remain unalterable, unless by common consent."

*A Statehood Compact is more than a law that can be changed at the whim of Congress.*

These principles have been honored throughout U.S. history. A Statehood Compact is recognized as more than a law that can be changed at the whim of Congress. It is an agreement between the United States of America and the people of a state. Congress even required Alaska's voters to go to the polls to approve both the concept and the terms spelled out in the Alaska Statehood Act. On August 26, 1958, Alaskans overwhelming voted in favor of statehood. On the "terms and conditions of the land grants," Alaskans voted 40,739 in favor to 7,500 against,[28] a resounding 84 per cent approval. This contract, once approved, cannot be altered without the agreement of both parties.

In crafting the Act, Congress not only guaranteed that we would acquire all the attributes of sovereignty granted to all other states under the Constitution, it ensured that we would be able to live up to our responsibilities in practical economic terms. It did this by "making the new State master in fact of most of the natural resources within its boundaries . . ." according to a congressional report at the time.

Regardless of the clear legal and historical precedents, Congress locked up large areas of federal lands in Alaska that could produce the promised royalties. By 1993, 171 million acres of Alaska (roughly the size of the State of Texas) had been withdrawn from mineral development. To remove such a large potential revenue source without compensation to Alaska was a breach of the Compact, and the State of Alaska sought redress and damages.

In the 1970s and 1980s, most Congressmen considered the decision to lock up Alaska a cheap environmental vote. It was much easier than addressing the controversial, local environmental issues facing their own states. The irony to Alaskans was that no state had a better environmental record. Including all of the oil activities on the North Slope, we had fewer miles of roads than the State of Rhode Island and had developed less than one-half of one per cent of Alaska. What we had done, we had done carefully, obeying strict state and federal guidelines. Alaskans wouldn't want it any other way. But we also had to have an economic base.

*It is a truism that land cannot be conveyed without access.*

Knowing that neither the U.S. Congress nor the federal agencies could legally change our Statehood Compact without the approval of the Alaskan people, we filed suit. The most important case defended the Compact itself. On July 22, 1993, we charged the United States with "breaching the Covenant of Good Faith and Fair Dealing by withdrawing more than 100 million acres of federal land from mineral leasing, thereby rendering meaningless the terms of the Statehood Compact that grants the state 90 per cent of mineral revenues from these lands."[29]

Other litigation sought to ensure access to Alaskan state lands because, as far back as English common law, it is a truism that land cannot be conveyed without access. The vast ANILCA withdrawals were so situated that in many areas of Alaska they blocked access to state lands. In addition, we challenged the federal ban on the export of North Slope crude oil with two lawsuits seeking compensation of $2.5 billion. No other state was exclusively prohibited from selling its resources in the world marketplace. As these suits fought their way through the appeals process, Congress and the White House saw the logic of lifting the ban on Alaska oil export and passed legislation to that effect. Our suit had gotten their attention.

We also filed suit to confirm the promises in our Compact regarding Alaska's title to submerged lands beneath our navigable waters and to fight for our right to manage fish and wildlife on all lands in Alaska.

Some members of the legal community made light of the suits, saying, essentially, that Congress can do anything it wants. If it doesn't want to give Alaska resource revenues from federal lands, it doesn't have to. I countered—and I've heard no reasonable response—that if Congress can unilaterally cancel Alaska's ownership of those resource revenues, why can't it take the State's land as well? Of course, it can't, any more than it can reclaim homesteads patented to western settlers 100 years ago. If the federal government takes it, they have to pay for it.

We set up a special section in the Department of Law to work on these cases—it was staffed by a group of dedicated attorneys, including Cheri Jacobus, deputy attorney general, Joanne Grace, Kyle Parker, and Sun Tan, who I later appointed to the bench. As these attorneys prepared the suits, the question arose of how much money we should demand for the violations of the Compact. We had no way of knowing how much money we had lost. The federal government made no attempt to develop our resources, and it is hard to put a value on something that did not happen. How much would Alaska have received from another Prudhoe Bay oil field? Geologists tell us there may be vast oil reserves like those at Prudhoe under the Coastal Plain of the Arctic National Wildlife Refuge. I decided on the figure: $29 billion. As large as that figure may be, it represents less than one-eighth the value of the oil already removed from the North Slope.

To my dismay, after I left office, Alaska lost the $29 billion lawsuit. The attorneys who represented the State have since told me that if a future generation of Alaskans tries again, and adequately frames the issue, we will prevail. My successor in office then dropped the remaining suits. I would have taken them to the U.S. Supreme Court, and then, if need be, to the World Court.

# PART FIVE

# The Future

# 12

# Energy and Freedom

There is an unusual tie-in between energy and the environment, energy and life, energy and poverty, and energy and peace. One of the major challenges we face in the 21st century is for both the developed and the developing nations to work together to meet our common need for energy. That effort, an enormous undertaking, is a top priority for all of us who are concerned about a healthy global environment and a peaceful world.

Show me any area in the world where there is a shortage of energy, and I will show you basic poverty. Where there is extreme poverty, people seldom give the environment a second thought. So for those concerned about caring for the commons—whether it is the rainforests of the Amazon, the vast and beautiful lands of Africa, the world's oceans, or the remote regions of the Arctic—energy must be at the top of the agenda.

All human activity takes energy. When a subsistence farmer goes to town from the countryside, he uses energy, even if he walks. It is hard to fathom today, but nearly all earlier civilizations, races, and tribes enslaved human beings to provide the energy to plant, harvest, build, fight, mine, and supply domestic service. There are still many places on earth where humans provide what the developed world considers to be animal and machine labor, such as pulling a plow, carrying water, lifting boulders, even transporting other human beings. When I was a boy on the farm, the only energy we had outside of our muscles and our horses was the wind that pumped the water for the cattle and the house in which we lived. When the wind didn't blow, we pumped by hand. Energy is just that fundamental. Fire is energy. Water is energy. Food is energy.

Most Americans today require the energy equivalent of hundreds of adult slaves to achieve the standard of living we enjoy. When James Watt invented the steam engine, he was freeing people. Then, Thomas Edison harnessed electricity and, within a few years, inexpensive electricity had become the second Great Emancipator. In most parts of the world, it enabled the human race to lift the yoke of brute labor from weary shoulders. Today's generation has the opportunity to make that great fundamental freedom a reality throughout the rest of the world.

*Show me any area in the world where there is a shortage of energy, and I will show you basic poverty.*

The importance of energy goes even further. Any successful fight against disease, ignorance, and lack of shelter demands energy. As we intensify the effort to eradicate pollution from our lives, we cannot turn against this great freedom fighter that improves the lot of humankind. Energy gives freedom to individuals and independence to nations. How then do we produce the energy our nation needs? How do we help other people around the world obtain the energy they need to elevate themselves and their societies?

Many Americans are angry that we are still oil dependent. In our larger cities, we resent the smog in our skies, and although scientists disagree about the impact of the greenhouse effect on climate change, there is no argument that the world is gradually getting warmer. Critics claim that the oil and auto industries conspire to feed our addiction to oil, undermine alternative energy programs sponsored by government, and fight to prevent affordable electric cars from becoming available to the public.

More than thirty years ago, I became fascinated with finding alternative sources of energy. When I was Interior Secretary, we studied how to tap the mountains of oil shale that exist in the West, and we looked at ways to gasify coal deep beneath the earth's surface. In 1972, as a private citizen, I chaired a national conference on geothermal energy, intrigued because Alaska is part of the Rim of Fire that encircles the Pacific. Our spectacular volcanoes illustrate the vast subterranean power that awaits those who learn to tap it.

In business, I have encouraged Edmund de Rothschild and Peter Ullman in their quest for environmentally safe tidal energy and its potential to support a hydrogen economy. Alaska has some of the highest tides in the world.

My optimism for these and other technologies is long-standing. In a speech at a seminar on future energy production in 1976 in Dubrovnik, Yugoslavia, I told scientists from around the world "You are grappling with forces so powerful they light the sun; so gentle they coax life from a sleeping seed. You are among the great hopes of this generation."

Over the years, a steady stream of inventors and engineers have visited me in Anchorage and invited me to their laboratories around the world to explain their ideas for breakthroughs with solar, wind, nuclear, and tidal power. One explained how heat transfer systems can power ships by taking one degree of heat from the ocean and recharging it with the sun. In the 1980s, I imagined a hybrid car that used electric batteries recharged en route by a small engine powered by clean natural gas.

*As we work on exciting new energy sources, we must provide for immediate needs.*

Hydrogen is thought to be the energy of the future, partly because it is as plentiful as the oceans. Each water molecule ($H_2O$) is two parts hydrogen. In February 2001, Dr. Evgeny Velikhov and his team at the Kurchatov Institute in Moscow showed me their concept for using wind power to generate hydrogen. They suggested that Alaska's Aleutian Islands, the location of some of the world's strongest and most continuous winds, would be an ideal location to produce liquid hydrogen to fuel the fishing fleets in the North Pacific.

For several years, an inventor in Minneapolis kept me in touch with his research on harnessing the ultimate—nuclear fusion, the process that powers the sun. When we finally discover a sun in a test tube, we will hold it in our hands and say, "How obvious. It was there all the time." There will be no limitation on mankind's imagination or accomplishments once fusion is mastered.

As we work on these exciting new energy sources, we must be realistic and provide for immediate needs. Solar and wind energy systems are appealing alternatives to fossil fuels. However, last year, when combined, they met the needs of only .1 per cent of national energy use. Geothermal generated .3 per cent of our energy. Hydroelectric power, which has limited growth potential in this country, produced 3.1 per cent, and biomass (wood waste and alcohol) 3.3 per cent. Nuclear power plants generated 8.1 per cent, and the remainder, or 85.1 per cent, came from fossil fuels—oil, natural gas, and coal.

### U.S. Energy Use by Source in 2000  (in quadrillion BTUs)

| | | |
|---|---|---|
| Solar and wind | .1 | (.1%) |
| Geothermal | .3 | (.3%) |
| Hydroelectric | 3.1 | (3.1%) |
| Biomass (wood waste & alcohol) | 3.3 | (3.3%) |
| Nuclear | 8.0 | (8.1%) |
| Coal | 22.4 | (22.6%) |
| Natural Gas | 23.4 | (23.7%) |
| Petroleum | 38.4 | (38.8%) |
| TOTALS | 99.0 quadrillion BTUs | 100% |

*Source:* U.S. Energy Information Agency, Department of Energy, www.eia.doe.gov, November 17, 2001

Conservation is part of the answer. There is no excuse for wasting energy. It's a moral issue, and all of us can play a part. Some conservationists believe that with better personal and industrial strategies, we could save upward of 10 per cent of the energy we use in this country.

All of these approaches deserve serious attention. But, for our immediate future, we will risk the health, security, and freedom of our people if we fail to provide our country with adequate supplies of fossil fuels. The best sources of oil, natural gas, and coal—in terms of U.S. jobs and balance of trade—are those we produce at home. Best of all, domestic sources, especially those in Alaska, are produced with the finest technology and highest environmental standards. That's why oil and gas from Alaska are vital to the nation.

## ANWR AND THE NATIONAL COMMONS

When George W. Bush ran for president in 2000, he said that the Coastal Plain of the Arctic National Wildlife Refuge (ANWR) should be explored for oil and that development could take place without harming the wildlife or the environment. He saw ANWR as a key to meeting America's energy needs. In raising this issue, he presented to millions of Americans a classic issue of the commons—the national commons.

All Americans own this remote refuge in northeast Alaska, and all Americans should examine the values and priorities regarding its use and its protection. If the 1.5 million-acre Coastal Plain of ANWR, thought to be the most promising oil and gas province in North America, is opened for its energy potential, all Americans must help make that decision. If it is added to the 171 million acres of federal wilderness and restricted conservation units in Alaska, all Americans should be involved in that decision as well. The debate over ANWR contains issues that will impact our quality of life, our value system, and the economic health and independence of our nation.

Bush's statement about the Coastal Plain was not an offhand suggestion. He lived in Fairbanks in the 1970s, working with a company that provided transportation services in interior and northern Alaska. There, he became familiar with the sheer size of Alaska, the wildlife population, the landscape of the Coastal Plain, and the role the trans-Alaska pipeline plays in providing energy resources to the nation. Even prior to his campaign for the White House, he had been vocal about his awareness of ANWR's importance to meeting the energy needs of America.

Vice-President Al Gore, Bush's opponent in the presidential race, also recognized ANWR as a critical issue, illustrating the contrast between himself and Mr. Bush. Gore referred to the Coastal Plain as "the Serengeti of Alaska," referring to the wild animal reserve in Kenya, East Africa. He promised that if elected, the Coastal Plain, like the rest of ANWR, would be placed off-limits to resource development of any kind.

Most Alaskans found Gore's characterization a real stretch, even ludicrous. Except during the seasonal caribou migration, the wildlife on the Arctic Coastal Plain of ANWR is sparse, and the attractiveness of the region is in the eye of the beholder.[1] Few of us would rate the Coastal Plain as one of the crown jewels of Alaska. Far from it. The area is flat and nearly featureless, and it experiences some of the harshest weather conditions in the world. Winds blow with great intensity across the Coastal Plain, and temperatures drop to nearly −70°F. Although the Brooks Range, which is already off-limits to development, can be seen in the distance, there are no mountains on the Coastal Plain. There are no forests, no trees.

For ten months a year, the plain is covered with snow and ice and is devoid of most living things. This changes in late spring when a carpet of lichen and tundra emerges from beneath the snow attracting a migratory caribou herd named for the Porcupine River. During that brief period, from late May to early June, the Porcupine Caribou Herd, one of Alaska's twenty caribou herds, often grazes and calves on the Coastal Plain. The animals take advantage of breezes from the Beaufort Sea that help them cope with a blizzard of mosquitoes. In 2001, the Porcupine Herd didn't calve on the Coastal Plain. It gave birth to its young many miles to the east, across the Canadian border. It calved in Canada the previous year as well. Normally, within one week, the entire pregnant female population of the herd gives birth. Nature's just-in-time delivery protects the newborns from an onslaught of predators, mostly wolves and bears. If the herd is to survive, the young must quickly learn to walk, then run. Remarkably, within two weeks, the wobbly-legged newborns are able to run with the herd. If the snow is knee-deep on ANWR's Coastal Plain, the herd finds a safer place to give birth.

*Most Americans find it difficult to visualize the reality, the richness, and the responsibility of the Arctic.*

Because of this ability to adapt, it is unlikely that exploration and drilling on the Coastal Plain will harm the Porcupine Herd. Most biologists believe that the Herd will react to the presence of human activity much the same way the Central Arctic Herd has adjusted to oil development at Prudhoe Bay. That herd has not only survived but flourished.[2] In 1978, after the pipeline started delivering oil to America's South 48 states, the Central Arctic Caribou Herd numbered 6,000. Since then it has grown to 27,128.[3] It is important to note that in the Arctic, Alaska oil drilling is restricted to the wintertime, and from early fall to early May, the Porcupine Herd is not on the Coastal Plain. It roams south to the Porcupine Mountains and east into Canada.

## A DIFFERENT WORLD

Federal decisions leading up to today's national controversy began when President Dwight Eisenhower established the Arctic National Wildlife Range in 1959, the year Alaska became a state. When Congress passed the Alaska lands act (ANILCA) in 1980, it more than doubled the size of the range and re-designated the area as a wildlife refuge, with both the benefits and restrictions shared by all U.S. refuges. ANWR covers an enormous area. This one unit encompasses nineteen million acres. Four New England states combined—New Hampshire, Vermont, Massachusetts, and Connecticut—comprise twenty million acres.

Congress designated the most beautiful sections of ANWR— eight million acres of it—as federally mandated wilderness. Human activity in federal wilderness is restricted to hiking, backpacking, camping, and rafting. No motorized vehicles are permitted, and no development of any kind is allowed. This wilderness heart of ANWR includes the eastern reaches of the Brooks Range. Journalists, using photographs or footage of these mountains, often give the impression to readers and viewers that the Coastal Plain of ANWR includes these rugged mountains.[4] It doesn't.

In re-designating and expanding ANWR, Congress recognized that the 1.5 million-acre Coastal Plain was a unique situation and deserved intensive study. It has long been known to have great potential for oil and gas resources. As a result, for more than twenty years, scientists from the Department of the Interior have studied this area, and their work has produced optimistic predictions, including oil estimates in the billions of barrels. Most of the scientists involved recommend that exploration be permitted.

But in the meantime, ANWR became a national symbol. Advocates for wilderness preservation launched a massive, nationwide campaign, not unlike the (d)(2) lands battle of a generation earlier.[5]

## A PLACE WE CALL HOME

One voice in the national debate has been largely ignored. Inupiat Eskimos have lived on the North Slope for thousands of years, and they deserve to be heard. George Ahmaogak, Sr., the mayor of the North Slope Borough, an experienced leader and whaling captain, sums up his peoples' views and frustrations this way: "Environmentalists who live thousands of miles away have decided that our backyard is an untouched wilderness, and we should be locked out of it. They make the mistake of separating the land and the wildlife from the people who live here. They forget that ANWR is just their name for a place we call home."

Understandably, the Inupiat people were at first leery of oil development. Now they see it as a key to a much-improved quality of life. "Unlike most Americans, we do not have the option of working in our choice of industries," Mayor Ahmaogak explains. "Well-meaning Americans crusading against the Coastal Plain development would deny us our only opportunity for jobs—jobs providing a comfortable standard of living for the first time in our history."[6] Last summer, a water and sewer system was under construction in Kaktovik, the only village actually located in ANWR. For the first time, Kaktovik homes will have flush toilets.

The Gwich'in people live south of ANWR, several hundred miles from the Coastal Plain, but they, too, have depended on the Porcupine Caribou Herd for food, clothing, and cultural needs. The fears of the several hundred residents of Arctic Village regarding oil development have been amplified by non-Native environmental activists. Financed by the national environmental lobby, Gwich'in elders have traveled throughout the nation speaking against ANWR oil development, creating the false impression that all Native

Alaskans oppose ANWR drilling. The Inupiat leaders who live in ANWR have urged the Gwich'in elders to visit the North Slope to see how oil development can peacefully coexist with the resident caribou population. So far, they haven't accepted their invitation.[7]

## REPLACING SAUDI OIL

Geologists have studied the surface rocks on the Coastal Plain of ANWR ever since the 1968 Prudhoe Bay discovery, fifty-five miles to the west. Their conclusions differ as to where the most oil may exist and just how much may be recoverable, but most agree that the plain could contain the largest remaining onshore oil and gas reservoir in North America—literally billions of barrels of oil.

In 1973, Alaska's State Geologist, Don Hartman, reported that 1800 feet of the Sadlerochit formation are exposed south of Camden Bay, near Marsh Creek Anticline, just across the western border of ANWR. This is the same formation of sandstone, siltstone, and shale that houses Prudhoe Bay oil. Hartman estimated that nearly 14 billion barrels of recoverable oil could be lying in place beneath the plain.[8] Three years later, the U.S. Geological Survey (USGS) identified an area farther east, south of Barter Island where the village of Kaktovik is located, as having "a hydrocarbon resource potential that could approach that of the Prudhoe Bay area."[9]

The most recent study, conducted by the U.S. Geological Survey in 1998, estimated that the Coastal Plain (known as the 1002 area) contains between 5.7 billion to 15.9 billion barrels of recoverable oil.[10] The federal Energy Information Administration (EIA) concluded that Coastal Plain oil in ANWR has a mean or expected potential of 10.3 billion barrels.[11] To compare how much that is, the entire rest of the U.S. has 21 billion barrels of recoverable oil. How valuable is this? The EIA pegs the total value of recoverable oil from the 1002 area at between $125 billion and $350 billion.[12]

All this is speculative. But if you can't speculate, you can't pioneer.

How much would an oil reservoir that size, just a few miles from the trans-Alaska pipeline, mean to America and our energy future? The EIA estimates the Coastal Plain could produce 600,000 to 1,900,000 barrels of oil a day. This new source of Alaskan oil could more than supplant our annual oil imports from Saudi Arabia and ensure that the trans-Alaska oil pipeline would continue to deliver domestically produced energy to American consumers for decades to come.

Opponents of opening the Coastal Plain argue that the bulk of ANWR oil will be exported to Japan. This is legal, but unlikely, in part due to an export ban, which was lifted in 1994. In the nearly twenty-five years of production in the Arctic, more than 93 per cent of Alaska oil has been shipped to U.S. markets.[13] Since April 2000, one hundred per cent of North Slope oil has been shipped to West Coast consumers.

## THE WORLD'S BEST TECHNOLOGY

I have visited many oil-producing regions throughout the world. The production techniques are often primitive and risky, both to the workers and the environment. In contrast, the technology being used in Alaska's Arctic to find and develop oil is the best in the world. The Alaskan people and the oil industry are rightfully proud of the pioneering work that has taken place at the North Slope. Active research and new technology are constantly being pursued. As a result, when and if development takes place on the ANWR Coastal Plain, there will be little traceable disturbance once the oil has been produced. Seismic tests to locate the oil and the actual drilling will take place in the winter, using ice roads that will later melt. Small gravel drilling pads, only six acres in size, will be removed when drilling is complete. Although early efforts sometimes left marks in the tundra, that is not true today. Using much improved methods and machinery, Slope workers take pride in challenging visitors to find any trace of winter work activities after the snow melts.

Before drilling begins, modern prospectors use three-dimensional seismic imaging to determine the nature of the geological structures beneath the earth's surface. Earlier 2–D seismic techniques can be compared to an X–ray, while 3–D is similar to a CAT scan. Engineers can now capture images thousands of feet below the surface on their computers, examine them closely, and turn them around on their screens to study them from all sides. Like a neurologist studying a brain scan, geologists can use their computers to slice through the images of rock and sand structures they have captured electronically to examine their capacity to hold hydrocarbons. As a result, the hit and miss of traditional oil exploration has changed dramatically. Using 3–D seismic, six out of ten exploratory wells in a new province hit oil, and seven to eight out of ten in a mature oil province are successful.

If oil is discovered, the size of the surface area disturbed will be dramatically less than when Prudhoe Bay was developed thirty years ago. Most experts estimate that development activities will directly impact less than 2,000 surface acres on the 1.5 million acre Coastal Plain. Revolutionary new techniques of directional drilling have made this possible. Operating from their small gravel pad, a crew can drill thousands of feet down and then elbow out, running parallel to the surface as far as two miles in any direction to tap into a cone-shaped, subsurface drillable area of more than fifty square miles. To the west of Prudhoe, the Alpine field operated by Phillips Alaska is a prototype for ANWR. Alpine sits on two pads connected by a gravel road that doubles as an airstrip. The total operation encompasses 100 surface acres. Far below, the high-tech drilling methods are tapping a 40,000–acre substructure containing 400 million barrels of oil.

Drill cuttings and drilling muds, formerly brought up and dumped on the surface, are now isolated from the living environment. On the North Slope, these waste materials are ground into slush by a ball mill, then re-injected thousands of feet back below the surface of the earth.

Learning from the mistakes of the *Exxon Valdez*, the Alaska oil tanker fleet is steadily being replaced with double-hull craft, providing the best protection against oil spills in the world. These ships are many times more sophisticated than the tankers that deliver oil from Asia, South America, Africa, and the Middle East. It is ironic that Congressmen from California and Washington, New York and Massachusetts fight against oil development in Alaska, when the most direct danger of oil polluting the environment is on their coastlines, unloading in their ports from what has been known in the trade for years as "the rust bucket fleet."

## INTEGRITY—A SCARCE RESOURCE

Environmental groups use Alaskan issues to raise tens of millions of dollars each year. In 1999, more than 8,000 environmental organizations raised a total of $3.5 billion in the U.S., mostly in small contributions,[14] and much of this money was generated by concerns, real or imagined, about Alaska. *The Sacramento Bee* reported in a three-part series in 2001 that five major groups, including the Sierra Club and Greenpeace, spent more than forty per cent of their budgets on preparing and mailing solicitations, membership retention and overhead. Philanthropic watchdog groups say that at least 60 per cent of an environmental organization's budget should be used for actually helping the environment. What was once a grassroots movement of dedicated volunteers has evolved into something very different. In 1999, the chief executives of nine of the nation's ten largest environmental groups all earned more than $200,000 a year, and one CEO's salary topped $300,000.[15]

*The Bee* documented that the truth is of little concern to those who design the direct mail solicitations sent out by these groups. "What works with direct mail? The answer is crisis. Threats and crisis," said Daniel Beard, the chief operating officer of the Audubon Society. "You reach the point where people get turned off. But I don't want to say direct mail is bad because, frankly, it works."[16] Unfortunately, false threats and imagined crises damage the integrity of the debate about Alaska and the care and use of our national commons.

The Natural Resources Defense Council sent mailings in the spring and summer of 2001 featuring movie star Robert Redford, who serves on their board of directors. Both the cover sheet and an inserted postcard featured a photo of a polar bear family. The appeal called ANWR a threat to "our nation's most important birthing ground for polar bears, caribou and other Arctic wildlife." This implies that Alaska's polar bears and caribou are at risk.

This appeal from a popular movie actor may raise funds, but it is not based on fact. Steve Amstrup of the U.S.G.S. has never starred in a movie, but he has studied polar bears in ANWR and off the Arctic coast for more than twenty years. He observes the bears and their movements with the use of radio collars, keeps denning records, and has even been known to climb into a den to check on a hibernating mother bear and her young. He has found that polar bears normally change their denning sites annually and are extremely mobile, often walking 1,000 miles a year. On Alaska's north coast, dens are widely scattered and distributed at a low density compared to other bear habitat elsewhere in the world. He reports that with careful timing and spacing of drilling locations, "impacts (of oil development) to polar bear denning (in the 1002 area) would be minimal or absent."[17]

The editorial page editors of the *Anchorage Daily News* have followed the oil industry in Alaska closely for more than thirty years and are strong voices for protecting Alaska's beauty and its environment. They wrote the following conclusion in their lead editorial on April 25, 2001: "We believe that drilling can go on in ANWR with safeguards for calving caribou and other wildlife, with a determination to make as light a landing as possible. The benefit for Alaska can be continued prosperity and a stronger state treasury—with minimal damage to the refuge."

"The opposition (to opening ANWR) isn't really economic, humanitarian, or even environmental. It is spiritual," wrote Zev Chafets, in the (New York) *Daily News*.[18] "If all the oil in the refuge could be neatly sucked up with a single straw, the naturalists would still oppose it because (to them) human activity in a pristine wilderness is, in itself, an act of desecration." Few people would actually take such an extremist position just to be against the idea of development of any kind. Besides, people already live in this "pristine wilderness."

I take the opposite view. We have proven that energy can be developed carefully, and energy is the key to the future of the human race.


## FOREIGN OIL—NEITHER CHEAP NOR AVAILABLE

America's ability to obtain the energy it needs is a valid national security issue. Dependence on foreign oil exposes us to energy blackmail and compromises our ability to come to the assistance of our friends and allies in a time of crisis.

Several years prior to the Arab oil embargo of 1973, it was part of my assignment as Interior Secretary to run the oil import program. My job was to determine how much foreign oil should be allowed into the U.S. I insisted that we never let our quota of overseas oil exceed twenty per cent of U.S. consumption. In those days, foreign oil was less expensive than domestically produced oil, especially on the East Coast, so a group of U.S. Senators, led by Senator Edmund Muskie of Maine, came to see me. If the quota were lifted, they argued, it would reduce the cost of gasoline and home heating fuel for their constituents. I refused.

The senators were not pleased and soon appealed directly to President Nixon. As a result, the President formed a group of seven Cabinet officers to examine the issue. He went around the room, asking the opinions of each Cabinet secretary. When he asked for my reasoning, I said, "If we lift this quota, in five years foreign oil will be neither cheap nor available." As I looked around the room, I realized I was outgunned 5 to 2. Only Secretary of Commerce Maurice Stans stood with me. The President, however, agreed with our reasoning and backed our minority position, and the pressure from the Eastern senators was rebuffed. During my remaining tenure in office, foreign oil imports remained below our twenty per cent ceiling.

After I left the Cabinet, the situation changed rapidly with dramatic results. My successors buckled to the pressure and raised the quota, and by 1973 the U.S. had become vulnerable. Domestic oil production continued to decline, and the foreign oil-producing nations made their move, refusing to sell us their oil. The Arab embargo jacked up the price of oil in the U.S. from $3 per barrel to $12 by the end of 1974 and caused seemingly endless lines of motorists as they waited to fill up their automobiles at their local service stations. Inflation skyrocketed and we were taught a ruthless but very real lesson. It has a simple moral. The economics of nations live or die on the availability of energy. Since then, our overseas dependence has grown much worse. Today, the United States imports fifty-eight per cent of the oil we use. Senator Frank Murkowski, senior Republican member on the Senate Energy Committee, predicts that by 2010 our dependence may grow to seventy per cent. There is no magic wand to resolve this enormous problem, but

ANWR is part of the answer as is an all-out commitment to alternate energy solutions. The only sensible approach is to combine a multitude of strategies.[19]

## A NEW ENERGY ECONOMY

None of us who uses oil or gas to drive an automobile, fly in a Jet Liner, or heat or air condition an apartment or home can divorce ourselves from the urgent need to produce these resources. If not in Alaska, where? Shall we let other nations drill, pump, refine, and transport oil, so that America's lands and waters are untouched? In a global environmental system, that approach doesn't cure pollution, it exports it. Exported pollution, from the rape of the jungles of Indonesia to the ever-growing wastelands in the Third World, is the result of monumental selfishness in the more technologically advanced nations, especially the U.S.

Opponents of domestic oil production say by their actions, if not their words, "Let other people's children play in polluted streams and choke on polluted air. Let other nations' wildlife be destroyed. We will import the oil we need from them, regardless of how they desecrate the environment."

We can't have it both ways. If we take a moral stand against the destruction of the environment, we must recognize that we are one world ecologically. The answer is neither to export pollution nor to condone it at home. Our goal as a human race must be to produce energy while using the highest standards. Alaska has a proven record of excellence in this field and, rather than be shut down as an energy producer, should be called on to be a model of how to do it right.

A great new source of Arctic oil, which may await us on the Coastal Plain, need not undermine the efforts to encourage Americans to conserve energy. It need not undercut the push to discover alternate energy sources. In reality, we need to move forward on all fronts. Any credible national energy policy must combine the traditional energy sources that are on line today with national conservation measures and alternative energy development. With that as our flag, our country will have a chance to transition more smoothly into a new energy economy.

# 13

# Hope and a
# Model for the World

**W**hen I arrived in Alaska in 1940, I was startled to discover that people were leaving. I especially remember two brothers who told me that everything that was going to happen in Alaska had already happened. Their frontier was over. But I believed otherwise. Others did, too. Together we won statehood and a land entitlement of 103 million acres. We discovered oil and put together a $10 billion, 800-mile, state-of-the-art pipeline stretching from the North Slope to Valdez. It required new technology and new ways to care for the environment. Using the ownership of our resources, we broke the chains of colonialism by providing our Owner State with a financial engine. With the wealth of our commons, we upgraded our schools, our cities, and many of our smallest villages, and for nearly twenty-five years we have provided at least twenty per cent of the oil produced in the United States. It all worked because, in spite of our personal agendas, we were determined to put Alaska first, and we kept the frontier spirit alive.

Frontiers have nothing to do with a coonskin cap and a rifle. They have to do with limits. And limits are things we set for ourselves. You either believe in them or you do not. Frontiers summon the creativity, the imagination, and inventiveness of the human mind. Few pioneers begin life with much of a bank account. Pioneering starts in the mind. And to be creative, the mind has to be open, and it has to be inspired. The opportunity for the human race is to allow ourselves to have frontiers again.

About twenty-five years ago a group of thinkers formed an organization called the Club of Rome and looked at how the world would sustain itself in the future. They fed all the resource and population data they could find into a computer model and came to the conclusion that the world was running out of everything—oil, gas, trees, fish, wildlife, farmland, and room for the human race. About that time, the University of California Irvine invited me to give a series of lectures challenging those conclusions. As long as we do not run out of imagination, I argued, we will not run out of anything. As I was making my case, a man in the audience scoffed, "Don't you know, we are even running out of cement?" He honestly believed there was a shortage of cement—sand and gravel, ash and limestone. Our resources were not running out, and yet we were readily accepting artificial limits to growth, rooted in our fears and indecision. If we open our minds, we will recognize new frontiers all around us. In reality, we haven't even scratched the surface of the Earth, we've only slid around on the skin of the apple. Our wildest dreams will seem tame when we get to the core.

I am filled with optimism as we begin the 21st Century. The lessons we have learned in Alaska, as we have pioneered our Owner State, hold promise for other areas of the world, the vast majority of which is commonly owned. In Alaska we have designed a model for that future, and I am eager to share our successes. But there is much to do.

*Even one hungry child is too many.*

Pope John Paul II rated the twentieth century as the cruelest in history. Driven by what he called a "culture of death," humankind struggled through World War I, the Great Depression, Nazism, the Holocaust, World War II, the atom bomb, communism, post-Cold War ethnic wars, and late 20th century genocide. The cruelty goes on. The United Nations estimates that there were 17 million refugees in flight or in hiding in 1997. Seven hundred and ninety million people[2] (790,000,000) endure chronic hunger, a staggering number, when even one hungry child is too many. Communism has failed. Socialism limps along, in a few countries, spawning rigid, highly taxed societies. Market economies have proven to be the most effective in unleashing the creativity and the dedication of the individual. Yet capitalism needs diligent oversight, especially in a global economy where the computer revolution has produced innovations that operate close to the speed of light.

In most of the former communist nations, such oversight is not yet in place. Multinational corporations see opportunity in the weakness of fledgling democracies and pander to corrupt officials and those who would abuse working people and the environment. Workers in Poland, disenchanted with the growing gap between rich and poor, even talk about overthrowing their young democracy. The "New World Order" that held such promise in the early 1990s faces serious challenges.

Terrorists attacked the World Trade Center in New York City and the Pentagon as I was finishing the final chapter of this book. This terrible event signaled to all Americans that we can no longer ignore the terrorism, the cultural conflicts, and the economic inequities that have plagued the rest of the world. We must engage ourselves again in global issues, as we did in World War II and afterward with the Marshall Plan. But the next Marshall Plan will require fresh thinking, as we must include strategies for non-industrial nations. It must address the crisis of the commons, as most developing nations are commonly owned or owned by top-down governments.

We must work on two fronts, because the September 11, 2001, attack badly damaged our own economy, an economy already at risk. Prior to the attack, merger mania had already wrecked some of the finest U.S. companies, creating an awesome and troubling consolidation of power while dislocating hundreds of thousands of employees. Many people work too long and too hard, including our youth, our single parents, our newer immigrants and, increasingly, our older citizens. Some are nearly slaves in a free enterprise system, and this slavery can be more insidious than physical slavery. Today's slaves don't know they have been enslaved, especially when high debt chains them to an endless treadmill. Gamely, they struggle to work their way to freedom, stretching themselves to the limit, risking health, relationships, and families.

Why then does my heart lift with optimism as I look to the possibilities of the 21st century? Because I am convinced that we will conquer the abuses of freedom, and we will find a new purpose as we address the seeds of global terrorism and revolution. In doing so, we will move into a new age. Free enterprise will learn that the bottom line must include care of the environment, concern for the working people, improvements to the community, and a commitment to building a better life for all peoples of all cultures and faiths.

The 19th century, as far as America was concerned, was the century of the industrial revolution, agriculture, and westward movement. The 20th century, as far as western civilization was concerned, was the century of technology and electronics. The 21st century, as far as the world is concerned, will be the century of the human. We will no longer work just to make a living. We will work to live a life. We will work on the just and worthy pursuits that ennoble humankind and ourselves.

Even in the dark of the 20th century, we made enormous progress in moving toward the light. We witnessed the near eradication of malaria, polio, and tuberculosis. We saw the green revolution enable formerly hungry nations to feed themselves and export their surplus. We watched transportation evolve from Kitty Hawk to planned trips to Mars. And we can communicate throughout the globe at Internet speed, at virtually no cost. These and thousands of other innovations offer the opportunity to improve both the economic foundation and quality of life as well. And that's just the beginning. Now it is time to discover the untapped capacity of the human brain and its power to heal, to create, and to pioneer. That's what the century of the human will be all about.

People are not the problem. People are the answer. Today, we have six billion people on earth, and the United Nations predicts that world population will stabilize at 11.6 billion sometime in the 23rd century.[3] But I do not fear a world population of 20 or 30 or even 50 billion people. Much of the world is vacant. I have traveled the wide, empty expanse of the 11 time zones in Russia. I know the Arctic well, vast, remote, and sparsely populated. There is no shortage of space on earth, and there is no shortage of protein. There is only a shortage of distribution and a lack of imagination. The earth is inexhaustible, because God made man's mind inexhaustible.

## A FORMULA THAT WORKS

The concept described in this book can be summed up simply. More than ninety per cent of the surface of the earth is owned in common (see inside covers). To prosper, the world needs a new attitude, a new understanding, indeed, a new system to manage that commons. Alaska's Owner State is a model worth considering. We are governed by a democracy that sustains itself by encouraging private enterprise to develop our commonly owned lands and resources for the benefit of all our people. The same system could work throughout the Arctic, Africa, the Middle East, Asia, Russia, and China, and anywhere natural resources are plentiful and owned in common.

Alaska's report card looks quite good, with a stable economy, minimal taxes, a large savings account, and vast opportunities for further resource development and protection of our unique environment. We have a young, well-educated population, an excellent quality of life, and indigenous people are prominent players in our cultural, political, and economic life. In all, our experiment works.

The starting point is to adopt a strong constitution that empowers people to govern and develop their commons democratically. Some cultures around the world may choose to use a model for democracy different from ours. They don't have to adopt the American Way. They should fashion their own system that meets their cultural needs. But we have learned in Alaska that local people should control what they own, and that they need leaders with the ability to manage their commonly owned assets to build an economy and a quality of life that meets the community's needs. A locally elected democratic government can act as conservator and developer at one and the same time, because through democracy everyone's interest is represented and resolved. The best democratic systems are built on constitutions that require the rule of law, integrity in public service, and court systems and law enforcement agencies that demand and reward integrity.

There is nothing socialistic about Alaska. We have no state-owned resource development companies. Our conflict-of-interest laws prevent officials from giving away public resources to insiders, political supporters, or anyone else. Our success depends on the initiative and drive a free enterprise system provides. The government opens the commons for development to generate jobs for our people; to provide the revenue for public projects and services such as roads, schools, scientific study, and to support the arts; and to earn revenues for the government's own upkeep, saving the people from heavy taxation. Alaska is the proof that it can be done.

## PERFECTING THE MODEL

We are still young as a state and have much to learn. We have made mistakes and have not yet mastered all of our challenges. The following are five key issues with which Alaska continues to wrestle, presented here so that others can learn from our experience and our struggle.

**1. Be on guard against monopoly.** Alaska knows a lot about monopoly. In the early part of the 20th century, the Alaska Syndicate, owned by the Guggenheim family, J. P. Morgan, and other titans of industry, exploited our copper at Kennecott and, on departure, sold the railroad they had built for scrap. The Alaska Commercial Company monopolized our fur trade. For three quarters of a century, Seattle fishing interests, using the power of the federal government, controlled our shipping and plundered our salmon streams with fish traps.[4]

More recently, we faced an equally dangerous monopoly in the combination of the major Alaska oil producers at the North Slope. In April 1999, BP/Amoco announced its intentions to buy Atlantic Richfield, including all of its Alaska holdings. If this deal had been consummated, BP/Amoco would have controlled more than seventy per cent of Alaska's North Slope oil and gas and more than seventy per cent of the trans-Alaska pipeline. One company would have determined what happened on the North Slope, using the resources owned by all Alaskans as but one pawn in their global corporate game.

But government power, especially when it is combined with citizen power, can checkmate inordinate corporate power. Monopoly is not inevitable if the leaders and citizens have the courage to confront it. Unfortunately, Alaska's governor, Tony Knowles, actively supported BP/Amoco and put the weight of the state government behind the merger. This outraged the citizens—Democrats, Republicans, Independents, and Greens—including many long-time Alaskans. We formed a group called Backbone and rallied the public and the media.

At our own expense, we flew to Washington, D.C., to explain the Owner State to the Federal Trade Commission. The FTC agreed with our concerns and filed a $1.2 billion antitrust lawsuit, the largest in its history. To avoid the court battle, BP/Amoco divested itself of ARCO Alaska (Atlantic Richfield's Alaska division), selling it to Phillips Petroleum. Competition was preserved in our oil fields, the lifeline of our economy. This brush with monopoly in modern times stands as a clear lesson to Alaskans of today and tomorrow.

**2. Use resource wealth wisely.** The Alaska Permanent Fund made the non-renewable resources of the North Slope into a renewable financial resource that should yield revenue to Alaska forever. It has been returning a healthy twelve per cent. But many Alaskans, especially new arrivals, regard the fund and the annual dividend as their personal property, not as a commons to help advance the entire state. The result was an "I've got mine" attitude that, until now, has made any other use of the fund's earnings impossible. Essentially, by giving it away in little pieces, we may have destroyed the public purpose of a promising renewable resource.

**3. Help officials stay free.** The governor of an Owner State must be more than a politician. He or she must live up to the great obligations that come with great ownership. Candidates running for office, if they are not careful, can become tied to the very interests they will face across the desk when they are elected. Pleasing these interests often runs counter to the sworn duties of the governor and the legislature of an Owner State.

If the governor is concerned about winning a second term, the desire to please powerful supporters may mean he or she is not free to make decisions that are right for the total. A single six-year term would be a partial solution, as would a two-year budget cycle. Public campaign financing would also help. More fundamentally, we must train our future governors, and the people who elect them, to understand what the job entails. Those who understand the Owner State must critique the actions of our governors in terms of how well they advance the care and use of the commons. If a governor is beholden to special interests, the citizens and the media must spotlight those connections for all to see. Academia must study the Owner State and document its performance, much as investment analysts report on corporate outcomes. Every voter should be informed clearly and simply what our assets are worth and what return we are receiving from them.

The legislature, like the governor, must understand its Owner State responsibilities and be able to act in an economic as well as a political arena. It, too, must innovate and advance the state's interests on the commons. To address these obligations, the legislative process needs some overhaul. For instance, the committee system gives veto power to committee chairs, making it much easier to stop bills than to pass them. Veto power held by a dozen committee chairs creates numerous opportunities for economic interests to subvert the process inconspicuously, and it makes it difficult to pass legislation to develop or protect the state's resources.

**4. Public servants deserve respect.** The civil servants in the executive branch make important Owner State decisions every day, often continuing in their jobs from one administration to the next. Upon their capabilities, integrity, and attitude depend the ability of any governor and legislature to carry out their responsibilities. Unfortunately, the American stereotype of civil service, or bureaucracy, stigmatizes the very people we depend upon for our success. Instead of being upheld as public servants who devote their careers to the public good, our people often view government employees with contempt. We drive down their morale so that good people get out and others simply mark time until they earn a generous retirement package. Rarely are their successes publicly rewarded.

It doesn't have to be this way. Those who served in the British civil service of the 19th and early 20th centuries, for example, stood in high esteem with their fellow countrymen. They administered a global empire, and their former colonies remain among the best run of the world's developing nations. It did not take high pay to achieve those results. It took the respect and appreciation of the public and the politicians.

The Owner State staff especially needs support. In Alaska, they are found mostly in the Natural Resources department, Community and Economic Development, Environmental Conservation, and sections of Law and Revenue. They need more people and better training than similar departments in other states in the U.S. Their job is to manage, care for, and develop 103 million acres of land and some 34,000 miles of coastline with about 1,600 employees, less than 10 per cent of the state government's total workforce.[5] In addition to having enough staff, these departments need adequate financial resources. We do not even know what natural resources we own in Alaska, because we have not spent the money to find out. Unless we understand the ocean ecosystem, for example, we will have no idea how much food the seas and rivers can produce and how best to enhance and harvest the resource. That sort of research is staff intensive and expensive, but ignorance is more costly. Ignorance leads to bad decisions that destroy the commons or leave them fallow.

*Conservative legislatures often gut the agencies that make development possible.*

It is not surprising that corporate interests use their considerable political weight to lobby for reduced state budgets. As budgets are cut, their taxes are reduced. Without a competent and courageous Owner State staff, industry has no one to look over its shoulder; even more important, without the staff to back him or her up, the governor sits across the negotiating table from the industry at a significant disadvantage. A telltale sign is when conservative legislators, who normally favor resource development, gut the agencies that make development possible in the name of more efficient government. Alaska's Department of Environmental Conservation (DEC) is a common target, but in my experience the DEC, when properly led, does not stop development. Rather, it enables development to go forward by analyzing possible impacts and preparing for them. Fire that staff, and permits will never be issued, or a proposed project will ignite an environmental backlash that buries future proposals.

Civil servants have a challenging job reviewing resource development projects, determining which make sense, and saying "yes" to the good ones. In the Owner State, these officials must learn the risk-taking skills and decisionmaking that are commonplace in business. It is not easy. Unlike the business executive, there is no direct financial reward for a civil servant who does his or her homework and makes a good decision. For example, not many Alaskans know the names of Tom Marshall and Roscoe Bell, the bureaucrats who persuaded Governor Bill Egan to acquire the land where we later discovered the Prudhoe Bay oil field. Marshall and Bell did not get rich from that decision, but Alaska did. The state's leaders must begin to recognize and reward those who do good work and find a way to shield them from punishment for honest mistakes.

**5. Maintain a sense of history.** After we struck oil on the North Slope, a new wave of residents arrived in Alaska. Some brought a different set of values with them. These newcomers often were attracted either by high-paying jobs or by a strong environmental ethic. Few had any sense of Alaska history, and most lacked understanding of the original idea behind our state. As recently as 1980, no politician would have dared to suggest Alaska give up its 90/10 split of federal oil revenues, as guaranteed in the Statehood Act. Ten years later, in the 1990 governor's race, both major party candidates did so. The public simply did not know or remember what the Statehood Compact meant or realize that billions of dollars were at stake.

## CAN ENVIRONMENTALISTS LEARN TO CARE FOR THE TOTAL?

Early environmentalists were among the first to recognize the challenges facing the commons. Naturalist John Muir eloquently championed the cause of preserving the natural wonders of the American West and Alaska. Rachel Carson told the story of the impact of pollution on the biological commons in her book *The Silent Spring* and changed the thinking of her generation. A movement was born. As battles were fought to clean up neighborhoods and communities, it became obvious that changes in laws and policies had to be applied on a regional level, a state level, a national level, and even on an international and world level. You cannot clean up part of a stream. All rivers eventually flow into a common sea. Everyone breathes the same air. We in Alaska cannot protect the millions of magnificent migratory birds that nest here in the summer if their winter habitat in the South 48 is poisoned, drained, or paved. As Secretary of the Interior, I helped to devise some of the early national environmental strategies and standards that remain on the books today. I have worked side by side with those who addressed these issues on a global scale, yet I cannot agree with those who fight for a single issue to the detriment of the larger community.

*You cannot clean up part of a stream. All rivers eventually flow into a common sea.*

This conflict was dramatically illustrated at the Earth Summit in Rio de Janeiro, Brazil, in June of 1992. Canadian Maurice Strong served as Secretary General of the global environmental summit, as he had in Stockholm twenty years before. The Rio event attracted 178 nations; 148 heads of state attended, the largest gathering of national leaders in the history of the world. And, once again, Strong asked me to participate. I was the only U.S. Governor to attend, credentialed as a delegate, and I was asked to help set the tone for the conference with a presentation at the Global Forum on the eve of the official opening.

Rio de Janeiro was an ideal location for the Summit. The symbolism was hard to ignore. On many days, a canopy of smog blocked the view of the 90-foot statue of Christ the Redeemer standing with arms outstretched on Corcovado, a granite mountain high above the spectacular city. Some of the world's most beautiful beaches—including Copacabana and Ipanema—border the city itself. But next to these idyllic playgrounds, bumper-to-bumper traffic bellowed an angry chorus that rose above the beat of the surf. Hillsides covered with shantytowns called *favellas* formed the backdrop to the city's tall buildings. One *favella* is said to be home for 300,000 men, women, and children. In Rio, the United Nations found the perfect setting to dramatize the issues facing the Earth—environment, development, pollution, and poverty.

I spoke as part of a panel that included Secretary Strong and Klaus Nobel, the son of the founder of the Nobel Prize. The event was in downtown Rio in Flamengo Park, the meeting place for 400 nongovernmental organizations (NGOs) from around the world who had gathered to debate environmental issues from many points of view. Reminiscent of Stockholm, Strong showed up at our panel discussion at the last minute, but this time by helicopter, not Volkswagen. In his opening remarks he recalled "Whale Night at the Hog Farm" south of Stockholm: "Of all the advice I have received from world leaders, none I value more than what I have received from Governor Hickel."

In my comments, I challenged the world conservation community, including myself, to keep people, especially people in poverty, as part of the environmental equation. "We will not conquer pollution, until we conquer poverty." Calling on the environmental movement to avoid the anti-growth trap, I said, "This conference must become the turning point where the protestors of progress become the protestors of poverty."

> *We will not conquer pollution until we conquer poverty.*

I also appealed to the U.N. to address the scandalous abuse of the commons in the waters of the North Pacific. "Just as the whale was a symbol in Stockholm, I call on the nations of the world meeting in Rio to protect our fisheries from the waste that comes from greed. The worst environmental disaster of the 1980s was not the wreck of the *Exxon Valdez*. It was the rape of the great fisheries in the North Pacific. Three hundred million pounds of edible fish are caught accidentally and discarded overboard—dead—every year. It is hard to imagine, when people in our world are starving."

Rio was a turning point. You could not participate with those thousands of delegates from all corners of the world and not become aware of the bigger picture. One environmental observer wrote upon her return to the U.S.: "In Rio, I had to re-think everything . . . . It's not just about the environment. It's also about equity. We have got to care about people, too." To win the public trust, all of us who consider ourselves part of the conservation community must address the total environment. Without healthy economies, we won't have healthy environments.

## CAN BUSINESS THINK BEYOND THE BOTTOM LINE?

Business must also find a new and broader mission. At one time in this country, some business leaders illustrated how to function with a social conscience. They took it for granted that they owed a debt, not just to their bankers and their stockholders, but also to the community at large. Their goals were fourfold:

- to provide a return on investment,
- to provide jobs,
- to provide service to the community,
- to help the unfortunate.

The ambitions of these capitalists went far beyond the bottom line. They took pride in the number of people they employed, a sharp contrast to what we have seen recently when thousands of employees are laid off to make stock prices soar.

In 1831, Frenchman Alexis de Toqueville toured America and subsequently published astute observations about this strange, new country of free people. He noted that, unlike in Europe, businessmen here voluntarily joined together to help others, from building roads for the community to constructing "poor houses" for the destitute. This tradition of community service continues to be the theme of every Chamber of Commerce, trade group, and service club in the nation. It remained as a mainstay of American life throughout the 20th century and a clear example of how wrong Karl Marx could be. Today, however, such dedication to community seems to be viewed as weakness and unimportant, with little connection to the values of the corporate world. But a public conscience in big business can return. In spite of the prevailing cynicism, and in the light of the world struggle with terrorism, America must change. It has changed for the better before and can once again reclaim that earlier commitment to the community. In fact, the public should insist on it.

## A PROPOSAL FOR THE 21ST CENTURY

It's time to move beyond talking about building a new world and literally build it. Historically, national leaders have used war as an economic strategy. War puts people to work and gives nations a unified purpose. But we must think beyond war. And we must visualize what the next Marshall Plan will look like. Wars are just big projects. Why not big projects? Well-designed, appropriate infrastructure is a long-lasting, worthwhile investment. The price of freedom does not have to be blood. It can be sweat.

The idea is not new. It is as old as the pyramids of Egypt and the aqueducts of Rome. In the 1980s, Masaki Nakajima, leader of Japan's Mitsubishi Research Institute, proposed a Global Infrastructure Fund and challenged world leaders to tackle large projects together. The purpose was to rally nations behind projects that could improve the quality of life for millions of needy people. Buckminster Fuller, inventor of the geodesic dome, subscribed to a similar strategy. He dreamed of a global energy network, linking the industrial and developing worlds with an energy grid. Two billion people live without electricity today, including many in the Islamic world. He observed that existing electrical generators, unused during nighttime hours in the North, could be tapped—at virtually the speed of light—to provide poverty-fighting power to the South.

*The price of freedom does not have to be blood. It can be sweat.*

The transportation of fresh water is another exciting opportunity. As Governor of Alaska in the early 1990s, I urged the private sector to build a pipeline to carry fresh water from Alaska to parched and thirsty California. Fresh water is one of the truly vast, untapped resources of the Arctic commons, where seven of the world's longest rivers run north into the Arctic seas. My concept was to transport water from the mouths of our great rivers running it through 20-foot diameter pipelines placed underwater on the continental shelf. We estimated we could deliver billions of gallons of Alaska water a day for just one dollar per day per Californian. Several Los Angeles City Councilmen became enthusiastic about the idea and commissioned Bechtel engineers to study it, but no private sector group has yet come forward to finance and build it. Someone eventually will. Within decades, fresh water will be the most prized resource on earth.[6] Californians already pay three times as much for a quart of Evian bottled water as they do for a quart of gasoline.

Why not help to build a better world through alternative surface transportation? For twenty years, I have discussed with Russian engineers a tunnel beneath the Bering Sea, making possible a rail trip from New York to Paris, crossing the width of the U.S. and Alaska and connecting with the trans-Siberian railway, circling more than halfway round the world. Such a rail system would carry with it a wealth of ideas, of commerce, of wonder and understanding. Meanwhile, the Northern Forum is working on an equally exciting concept that requires very little new construction—to make Russia's Northern Sea Route a common carrier for the world's goods. Using ice-armored freighters that can sail year round through the ice over the top of the world, resources and goods from the Pacific Northwest could arrive in Rotterdam eight days sooner than if they sailed through the Panama Canal. Japanese cargo could arrive even faster.

Centuries ago, monarchs and religious leaders demonstrated that the creation of great public works had two purposes. They provided basic infrastructure needs, and they built loyalty and public spirit. While constructing the cathedrals of Europe, the craftsmen and laborers, some of whom were noblemen, discovered that putting the stones in place was a religious experience in itself. The workers on the trans-Alaska pipeline, a modern wonder of its own, knew they were playing a part in something important. Each one owned a small piece of history.

As we venture forward in this new century, let's agree on some big projects and build them. Let's carry Buckminster Fuller's torch and link up the world's excess electrical generating capacity to benefit those most in need. Let's take water to the dry and dusty South from the water-rich North. Let's construct the Bering Tunnel and join the world's continents. Let's harvest the wealth of northern resources, especially our storehouse of energy. As we tackle these projects, we will learn that the days of pioneering have just begun.

## YOU HAVE TO BELIEVE

I received my education in a small Kansas schoolhouse and grew up to believe anything was possible. One day in 1936, a professor from the University of Kansas paid a visit to our classroom. I was sixteen at the time. "You young people in this room," he told us, "will live to see a man walk on the moon." I was elated. Claflin, Kansas, was a small, German-American town of 800, and that sky belonged to God. But I believed that professor. Thirty-three years later, as a member of the Cabinet, I sat in the bleachers at Cape Canaveral when Neil Armstrong and his colleagues blasted off for the moon. As we watched that incredible lift-off, I remembered that professor and what he had said.

We are not here on this earth just to be users. We were made in the image of a Creator, and we are here to create. In the early 1980s, NASA asked me to join a team that spent several years planning the first human settlements on the moon. Later, I was invited to join fifty engineers and thinkers from around the world gathered in La Jolla, California, to talk about the future of space exploration. After considerable discussion, I asked the question, "How many of you in this room believe we will go to Mars?" Only one engineer, a German, held up his hand, and he did so reluctantly. I said, "The program is dead, because we don't believe. You have got to believe if you are going to make this work." I heard later that that exchange was a turning point in the Mars exploration program. On the 20th anniversary of the first lunar landing, President Bush unveiled a plan to complete the space station, return to the moon, and explore Mars. It's all about attitude.

That same approach can change the world as we know it, because space is the ultimate commons. In space, asteroids as big as Rhode Island are estimated to be seventy per cent copper. I can see future pioneers corralling those asteroids and guiding them down into unpeopled areas in the Antarctic or the Arctic. Other scientists believe they can use beam technology to harness energy from the sun as it is reflected from the moon. It's a risky concept, but just imagining the concept can lead to safer ways to tap into the sun's limitless energy. Risk should not deter us from exploration. Lewis and Clark faced life and death challenges throughout their expedition to the Pacific Ocean. That didn't stop them. Overcoming those challenges is what made them great.

## THE DAY OF THE ARCTIC HAS COME

The world Arctic, the last region on earth to attract the world's interest, has been the first to pioneer the principles of the Owner

State. It is a surprising place to be a model for the care of the world's commons. To many who live and work in temperate climates, down there, looking up, the high latitudes are cold, remote, and as mysterious as the moon. But those of us who live here look at the Arctic differently. To understand sustainable living in the Arctic you need sustained thinking in the Arctic. We don't look up. We don't look down. We look around. To us the Arctic is home. It is heritage. It is our here and now and our hereafter.

At the Earth Summit in 1992, the world had not yet discovered the Arctic. There were no significant Arctic issues on the voluminous agenda. But representatives of many of the regions of the Northern Forum attended the Rio meeting, and we gathered together one evening to plan our future. At the time, there were fourteen governors who were members of the Forum. Today there are twenty-seven, representing regions, states, and provinces in Russia, Norway, Sweden, Finland, Japan, Korea, China, Mongolia, Canada, and Alaska. Staff members from several of these regions, based at the Forum Secretariat in Anchorage, have helped to coordinate Arctic-wide studies addressing an eight-point agenda, including circumpolar pollution monitoring, exchange of Arctic development technology, and circumpolar infrastructure.

In May of 1994, the Northern Forum organized the first-ever Circumpolar Expedition, a symbolic event, illustrating that the day of the Arctic has come. A Reeve Aleutian 727 aircraft, carrying eighty-one representatives from all eight Arctic nations, took off from Anchorage and circled the world in six days, landing in fourteen Arctic cities and touching down in all Arctic nations. In Bødo, Norway, King Harold greeted the adventurers. President Mikhail Nikolayev in Russia's Sahka Republic (Yakutia) welcomed the group in Tiksi, his most northern city, located where the Lena River flows north into the Arctic Ocean. "This Expedition is of the same importance as the opening of the Northern Sea Route 100 years ago," Nikolayev declared. "During this period, we have been separated artificially by national borders and differences of ideology. Let your silvery jet, like the dove of peace, be a symbol of our united work for peace, concord and cooperation in the Arctic."[7]

The strategy of like regions of the world working together is not limited to the North. United Nations Secretary General Boutros Boutros-Ghali received me in his office in 1994, and we talked about the Northern Forum and the regional approach we were taking to issues facing the northern hemisphere com-mons. He was intrigued. He agreed that coun-tries and regions with similar problems and conditions work most effectively together and predicted that that approach would be a future trend in the United Nations. He asked if I would consider setting up a "Southern Forum."

*Ideas change the world, and every great idea has its time.*

The suggestion surprised me. As the sitting governor of Alaska and chairman of the Northern Forum, I had enough to do, and I don't know much about southern hemisphere issues. But the Secretary General had a good idea. Like the Far North, much of the southern hemisphere is commonly owned. Most southern hemisphere coun-tries have colonial economies and depend on the export of natural resources, including large-volume crops.

After leaving office as governor, I set out to advance these con-cepts of regional cooperation and the Owner State. This work led to the establishment of the Institute of the North at Alaska Pacific University. It is the home for scholars and associates studying the commons of the world and working to support the initiative of the Northern Forum throughout the Arctic. This book is one product of that initiative.

Ideas change the world, and every great idea has its time. At first, they may flicker like the flame of a match, but once they start to catch they spread rapidly. My hope is that a century from now, the idea that the commons should be managed for the benefit of the total will be an accepted part of life, as undeniably accepted as freedom, democracy, and human rights will be by then. The stakes could not be higher, and the rewards to the entire human race and to our planet could not be greater.

# Table I

## DATES OF HISTORICAL IMPORTANCE IN THE CREATION OF ALASKA'S OWNER STATE

1867    Treaty of Cession between the U.S. and Russia. Alaska becomes a U.S. military district with no civilian government.

1880    The U.S. Census estimates the population of the Alaska Territory as 33,426. Alaska Natives constitute all but 430 in the entire population.

1884    The First Alaska Organic Act creates a "District" based on the Oregon Code, naming a governor with little authority, judges, and no legislature.

1898    Gold is discovered on the beaches of Nome.

1912    The Second Alaska Organic Act establishes a territorial legislature and limited self-government. Alaskan women win the right to vote. Alaska is the only territory or state without local control of its fisheries.

1914    Congress passes The Alaska Railroad Act to open up the land and to fight monopolies such as The Alaska Syndicate, owned by J. P. Morgan, the Guggenheim family, and others. The railroad was completed in 1923.

1920    The Mineral Leasing Act changes the rules in the public estate and creates America's underground commons. Key subsurface minerals remain in perpetual federal ownership.

1920    Maritime Law of 1920 (Jones Act) restricts Alaska's cargo and shipping by requiring that all ships sailing between Alaska and the South 48 must be American built.

1924    White Fisheries Act of 1924 maintains control of Alaska fisheries by Outside interests.

1924     Native Americans, including Alaska Natives, win citizenship, includ-
         ing the right to vote, to own land, and to claim mineral rights.

1924     Teapot Dome Scandal is revealed.

1941     Pearl Harbor invasion.

1942     Japanese attack Dutch Harbor and occupy Kiska and Attu islands. The
         Alaska Highway is built in nine months (1,420 miles). U.S. troops
         stream into Alaska, peaking at 153,000 in 1943.

1943     Americans retake Attu in the second-costliest battle of World War II's
         Pacific Theater.

1951     Alaska Statehood Bill passes the U.S. House, granting only 3 million
         acres to Alaska cities and 20 million acres to the University of Alaska.

1952     After an intense struggle in the Senate, the Statehood bill is re-com-
         mitted (defeated) by one vote.

1955–6   Alaska Constitutional Convention writes model Constitution.

1957     Oil is discovered on the Kenai Peninsula by Richfield Oil Company.

1958     The birth of the Owner State. Alaska Statehood Act passes Congress,
         and offers Compact with Alaska. The Alaskan voters approve the terms,
         including 103 million acres and 90 per cent of revenues from resource
         development on federal land.

1960     Alaska elects first governor, William Egan, who selects 1.3 million acres
         on the North Slope as part of Alaska's statehood entitlement.

1964     Earthquake of 9.2 on the Richter scale rocks south central Alaska for 5
         minutes.

1966     Wally Hickel is elected governor and commits to open the Arctic and
         establish an economic base so that Alaska can stand on its own.

1967     Governor Hickel leases additional North Slope acreage to Atlantic
         Richfield.

1968     Oil is discovered on the North Slope. It's the largest oil field in Amer-
         ica, and one of the largest in the world.

1968     Federal Field Committee recommends settling of Native land claims
         and designation of "national interest lands."

1968     Senator Bob Bartlett dies suddenly, and Hickel appoints Ted Stevens.

1969     President Richard Nixon appoints Governor Hickel as U.S. Secretary
         of the Interior. State sells additional North Slope leases for $900 mil-
         lion.

1971     President Nixon signs the Alaska Native Claims Settlement Act.

1973    Vice President Spiro Agnew breaks a tie vote in the Senate, leading to the approval of the construction of the trans-Alaska oil pipeline.

1976    Amendment to the Alaska Constitution creates the Alaska Permanent Fund.

1976    The Magnuson-Stevens Fisheries Act claims 200 miles of U.S. jurisdiction in offshore waters, and begins protection of Alaska's fisheries.

1977    First oil flows through the trans-Alaska pipeline.

1980    President Carter signs the Alaska National Interest Lands Conservation Act.

1989    Oil tanker *Exxon Valdez* spills 11 million gallons into Prince William Sound.

1991    Governor Hickel is re-elected as an Independent and negotiates a $1 billion Exxon settlement for restoration and enhancement of Prince William Sound.

1992–3   Community Development Quotas and Individual Fishing Quotas are approved. These management systems transform halibut and bottom fishing in Alaska.

1993    The State files lawsuits against the federal government for reneging on the Statehood Compact. Hickel wins $4 billion in back taxes from the oil industry.

1994    Oil spill in Komi, Russia, is three times larger than Exxon Valdez disaster. Alaskans assist their neighbors.

2000    U.S. Census estimates the population of Alaska to be 626,932. Alaska Natives make up 15 per cent of population.

2001    Thirteen billionth barrel of oil arrives in Valdez from the North Slope, and President George W. Bush includes ANWR oil development in his national energy plan.

2001    September 11 terrorist attack on America adds urgency to Alaska's special role in oil independence for the U.S. Alaska presents itself as a model for local resource management and caring for the commons.

---

*Source:* Malcolm Roberts, Institute of the North

# Table II

## THE ALASKA OWNER STATE MODEL

Alaska's state lands and resources are owned by the state in trust for the people. The State is governed by a democracy that sustains itself by encouraging private enterprise to develop commonly owned resources for the benefit of the people. Here are the fundamental components of an Owner State:

**Local Control**: The people who live on the commons control them through a constitutional democracy. Democracy requires participation, and participation fosters responsibility.

**The Obligation of Ownership**: Both the leaders and citizens are responsible for caring for the commons. They must ensure that the wealth of the commons is used for the benefit of all citizens.

**The Governor**: The Constitution mandates a strong, accountable governor with the authority to manage the land and its resources.

**The Legislature** is expected to act in the economic as well as in the political arena, thinking as owners do, using resource revenues to provide basic services, enhance people's lives, and build infrastructure to strengthen the economy.

**The Judiciary** is built on a strong foundation of law that inspires integrity in the legal system and respect among the people.

**Free Enterprise** is harnessed in the service of the public. The incentives of the free market system develop the wealth of the commons and put the people to work. When the private sector fails to live up to its responsibilities on behalf of the people or the commons, the governor must have the tools to encourage it to do so.

**Value added**: Breaking with traditional colonial economies, Alaska has been most successful when it has added value to its natural resources before export.

**Exploitation**: Both leaders and citizens must beware of those who exploit under the guise of development and those who acquire state lands or leases in order *not* to develop them. They must resist distant governments, businesses, and interest groups that seek to control their lands, lock them up, block access, or monopolize their resources.

**The Environment**: Leaders and citizens are expected to care about the total environment—people, people's needs, and nature. Nonrenewable resources are to be developed with keen sensitivity to the environment. Living resources are to be harvested only at the level of sustained yield.

**Public Service**: Owner State departments need adequate staffing and funding. Land managers must understand the marketplace and use its forces for the public good.

**The People** must be involved and decide if their leadership is doing the job, and, if not, vote them out. To be truly successful, they must be inspired by a unifying vision.

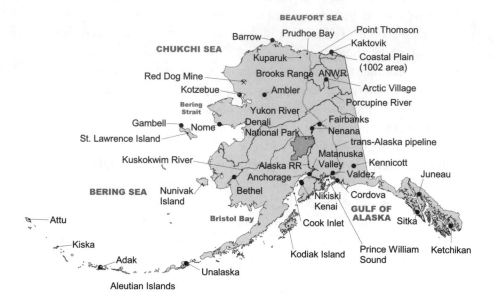

**Figure 1 Map of Alaska with Place Names**

*Source:* Roger Pearson, Institute of the North, 2002

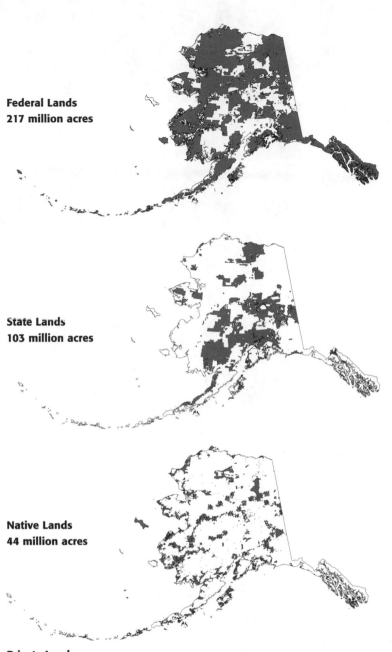

**Federal Lands**
**217 million acres**

**State Lands**
**103 million acres**

**Native Lands**
**44 million acres**

**Private Lands**
**1 million acres**

**Figure 2  Who Owns Alaska?**
*Source:* The Alaska Department of Natural Resources

# Notes

## Chapter 2: Assault on the Commons

1. Associated Press, "Spill Unstanched, Alaskans Report," *Anchorage Daily News*, November 4, 1994.

2. Letter from A. W. Dunham, Executive Vice-president, Conoco Inc., to Gov. Walter J. Hickel, November 14, 1994.

3. Sam Howe Verhovek, "Ruptured Pipeline Spreading Hot Oil In Russia's Arctic," *The New York Times*, October 25, 1994. Lee Hockstader, "Moscow's Reflexive Secrecy Resurfaces in Oil Spill Response," *The Washington Post*, October 28, 1994.

4. Margaret Shapiro, "N. Russian Thaw Shows 'Monster' Scope of Spill," *The Washington Post*, May 23, 1995. Brian Killen, "Russian Oil-Spill Cleanup Nears Completion," *The Washington Post*, September 19, 1995.

5. Garrett Hardin, "The Tragedy of the Commons," *Science* 102, 1968.

6. Ibid., p. 4 of 13.

7. Elinor Ostrom, "Rudiments of a Theory of the Origins, Survival, and Performance of Common-Property Institutions," in Daniel Bromley, Ed., *Making the Commons Work: Theory, Practice, and Policy*. San Francisco, CA: ICS Press.

8. Robert I. Rotberg, "Zaire's Zero Hour," *The Christian Science Monitor*, April 11, 1997, p. 18:1.

9. Thomas Kamm, "Nigeria Executions Raise Sanction Threat," *The Wall Street Journal*, November 13, 1995, p. A-10.

## Chapter 3: Alaska Fights for Its Land

1. These meetings predated the better known "Spit and Argue Club," a similar group which I chose not to join.

2. James Muhn and Hanson R. Stuart, *Opportunity and Challenge; The Story of BLM*. Washington D.C.: Department of the Interior, Bureau of Land Management, 1988. Many of the dates and statistics on the history of U.S. land law throughout the chapter come from this publication.

3. Other laws, with other terms and larger land allocations, privatized public land for other purposes—including the Desert Land Act of 1877 and the Timber and Stone Law of 1878.

4. One trick was to pay men a small fee to file for timberlands under the Timber and Stone Law of 1878. These hired hands would then transfer the land to a logging company so it could control huge acreage. Lary M. Dilsaver and William C. Tweed, *Challenge of the Big Trees; A Resource History of Sequoia and Kings Canyon National Parks*. Three Rivers, CA: Sequoia Natural History Association, 1990.

5. Ron Chernow, *Titan: The Life of John D. Rockefeller, Sr.* New York: Random House, 1998, pp. 74–75.

6. Department of the Interior, *Legislative History of the Mineral Leasing Act of February 25, 1920 (41 Stat. 437) and Amendments Thereof, With Annotations*. Washington, D.C.: Department of the Interior, Bureau of Land Management, 1961. Most of the analysis of the Mineral Leasing Act is based on this typescript document.

7. In Alaska, a coal find on the Bering River was nearing development, and Roosevelt's order came as a bitter setback. For years afterward, Alaskans were forced to import coal rather than use the readily available supplies frozen by Roosevelt. The Bering River withdrawal, included in the Chugach National Forest in 1908, led to a complex political scandal and Pinchot's ultimate resignation. See Lone E. Janson, *The Copper Spike*. Anchorage: Alaska Northwest Publishing, 1975, pp. 109–110; and Claus-M. Naske, *Alaska, A History of the 49th State*. Norman, OK: University of Oklahoma Press, 2nd ed., 1987, p. 93.

8. Ronald W. Tank, *Legal Aspects of Geology*. New York and London: The Plenum Press, 1983, p. 307.

9. M. R. Werner and John Starr, *Teapot Dome*. New York: The Viking Press, 1959, p. 86.

10. Claus-M. Naske, *A History of Alaska Statehood*. Lanham, Maryland, and London: University Press of America, 1985, pp. 165–166.

11. Editorial, "Both a Defeat and a Victory," *The Anchorage Times*, February 28, 1952, p. 2.

12. Walter Hickel, "Hickel Takes Editorial Apart, Tells Inside of Defeat of Bill S50," *Anchorage Daily News*, March 4, 1952.

13. Editorial, "Hickel's Heckles," *The Anchorage Times*, March 5, 1952.

14. Walter Hickel, "Hickel Heckles Again," *Anchorage Daily News*, March 7, 1952.

15. The final land grant of 103 million acres included the 100 million acres I told Senator Taft we needed plus 3 million acres already allocated for communities in the Tongass National Forest.

## Chapter 4: Winning Local Control

1. Ernest Gruening, *The Battle for Alaska Statehood*. College, AK: University of Alaska Press, 1969. The speech is reprinted in whole.

2. Claus-M. Naske, *A History of Alaska Statehood*. Lanham, Maryland: University Press of America, 1985.

3. Much of the history and analysis of the fishing industry in this book comes from Richard A. Cooley, *Politics and Conservation; The Decline of the Alaska Salmon*. New York: Harper and Row, 1963.

4. Cooley, p. 18.

5. David M. Dean, *Breaking Trail: Hudson Stuck of Texas and Alaska*. Athens: University of Ohio Press, 1988, pp. 276–290.

6. Naske, p. 122.

7. U.S. Congress, *An Act For The Protection of the Fisheries of Alaska, and for Other Purposes*, Public Law 204, 68th Congress, 1st Session, 1924 (43 Stat. 464).

8. These words led to a great debate in Alaska in the 1990s over whether rural subsistence users of fish and game deserved a priority in times of scarcity, a priority I endorse.

9. Gerald E. Bowkett, *Reaching For A Star*. Fairbanks: Epicenter Press, 1989, p. 56.

10. Gruening, p. 88.

11. Bowkett, pp. 18–19, 97.

12. Naske, citing *The Daily Alaska Empire*, April 3, 1953.

13. Naske.

14. Details on Lehleitner are found in Naske; Gruening; and Bowkett.

15. Naske.

**Chapter 5: The Creation of an Owner State**

1. The setting for the convention and many details from: Victor Fischer, *Alaska's Constitutional Convention; National Municipal League State Constitutional Convention Studies Number Nine*. Fairbanks: University of Alaska Press, 1975; Gerald E. Bowkett, *Reaching For A Star*. Fairbanks: Epicenter Press, 1989; researcher interviews with Thomas Stewart, August 8, 1999, and Vic Fischer, August 1999.

2. Stewart conveyed his memories to researcher Charles Wohlforth, August 8, 1999.

3. Public Administration Service, *Constitutional Studies*. Juneau: Alaska Statehood Committee, November 8, 1955.

4. PAS, Vol. 1, Part III, p. 3.

5. Ernest R. Bartley interview with researcher Charles Wohlforth, September 7, 1999.

6. PAS, Vol. 1, Part III, p. 30.

7. Bartley interview, September 7, 1999.

8. Fischer, pp. 26 and 130.

9. Bartlett speech transcript, p. 4.

10. Gordon S. Harrison, *Alaska's Constitution; A Citizen's Guide*, 3rd ed. Juneau: Alaska Legislative Research Agency, 1992, pp. 149–150.

11. Fischer, p. 132.

12. Vincent Ostrom, "Report on Clarifying the Meaning of Article VIII: Natural Resources As Adopted by the Alaska Constitutional Convention, in 1956, With Addenda," Bloomington, Indiana: Workshop in Political Theory and Policy Analysis, Indiana University, February 25, 1994, pp. 4–5. Additional details from interview with Ostrom by researcher Charles Wohlforth on September 9, 1999.

13. The initial draft document is found in Ostrom, p. 39.

14. Harrison, pp. 149–166.

15. Fischer, pp. 134–137.

16. Ultimately, the legislature and governor set up a Board of Fish and a Board of Game, with members appointed by the governor. These bodies allocate fish and game resources, while the professional Department of Fish and Game, under the governor's direction, handles scientific decisions on conserving the resources. For the most part, this arrangement has worked well to insulate state biologists from political pressures.

17. Fischer, p. 107, citing *Fairbanks Daily News-Miner*, December 5, 1955.

18. In my book *Who Owns America?*, I argued that the simplest way of keeping the process honest is to finance campaigns with public funds, a cost that would amount to a few dollars per person while avoiding resource plunder that could cost the public billions. I feel the same today. I came up with that proposal more than a year before the 1972 Watergate scandal, after I saw the influence of campaign money in Washington, D.C., during my term as Secretary of the Interior.

19. Dick Burton later served as Commissioner of Public Safety both with Governor Jay Hammond and in my second term.

20. Burton interview with researcher Charles Wohlforth, September 30, 1999.

21. A letter from Laura Olson, Legislative Assistant to Senator Ernest Gruening, to Frank Murkowski, Jan. 9, 1968, describes the Treasury proposal. *Alaska State Archives.*

22. Details of the reasons behind the policy changes and talks are summarized in a Feb. 7, 1968, news release from the Governor's office, dateline Tokyo. *Alaska State Archives.*

23. Some details drawn from Jack Roderick, *Crude Dreams; A Personal History of Oil & Politics In Alaska.* Fairbanks/Seattle: Epicenter Press, 1997.

24. Tragically, he died a few years later in a boating accident.

25. Roderick.

26. Democrat Mike Gravel defeated Elmer Rasmuson in the general election.

27. C. Robert Zelnick, "That Senate Vacancy; How Stevens Got the Nod," *Anchorage Daily News*, December 24, 1968, p. 4.

**Chapter 6: Opening the Arctic Frontier**

1. Alaska Division of Oil and Gas.

2. Daniel Yergin, *The Prize; The Epic Quest for Oil, Money and Power.* New York: Simon & Schuster, 1991, p. 571.

3. Roderick.

4. Roderick.

5. Letter, Egan to Udall, August 7, 1963; found in Gene Rutledge, *Prudhoe Bay—Discovery!* Anchorage: Wolfe Business Services, 1987, pp. I 13–14.

6. Roderick.

7. Letter, Egan to Udall, January 3, 1964; in Rutledge, pp. I 14–16.

8. Rutledge, *Prudhoe Bay—Discovery to Recovery!* Anchorage: Wolfe Business Systems, 1998, pp. II–1.

9. Malcolm Roberts, North Slope Pioneer *John C. "Tennessee" Miller,* unpublished manuscript, Chapter 11, p. 27.

10. Roderick, pp. 204–205.

11. Speech to AFN, October 21, 1966. Hickel papers.

12. Rutledge, *Prudhoe Bay—Discovery to Recovery!,* pp. II 2–4.

13. *The Tundra Times,* Editorial—Cooperation a Must, December 30, 1966.

14. *The Anchorage Times,* from Associated Press, "State To Test Native Claims; Hickel Asks Preparation of Law Suit; North Slope Sale On For Next Week Without Protests," January 17, 1967, p. 1.

15. Rutledge, *Prudhoe Bay—Discovery to Recovery!* Anchorage: Wolfe Business Systems, 1998, pp. II–1.

16. After oil was discovered, the people of the region formed a local government, the North Slope Borough, and raised immense revenues from property taxes on the oil fields.

17. Yergin, p. 571.

18. Roderick, p. 213.

19. Bergt later was founder of Interior Airways and chairman of Western Airlines.

20. Lael Morgan, "All He Wants for Christmas: A North Slope Oil Strike," *Fairbanks Daily News-Miner,* May 3, 1967.

21. Drilling was stopped the next day and resumed November 18. Before Christmas, Jamison confided that they had hit 400 feet of sand, and I knew we would have some oil.

22. See Chapter 12 for an in-depth description of ANWR.

23. Alaska Department of Natural Resources, Division of Oil and Gas.

24. Roderick, pp. 224–235.

25. Naske, Claus-M., *Alaska, A History of the 49th State.* Norman, OK: University of Oklahoma Press, 2nd ed., 1987, p. 250.

26. Naske, pp. 94–97.

27. Evangeline Atwood, *Frontier Politics: Alaska's James Wickersham.* Portland: Binford & Mort, 1979.

28. The Alaska Railroad was sold to the state in 1984.

29. Editorial, *Fairbanks Daily News-Miner,* "A Time for Action in North," August 2, 1967.

30. *The New York Times*, "Study Due on Northern Spur for Alaska Rail Line," August 6, 1967; *The Anchorage Times*, "Lindbergh To Serve On North Commission," March 21, 1968.

31. Mike Dalton, "North Members See Arctic," *Fairbanks Daily News-Miner*, July 31, 1967.

32. Naske.

33. Tom Brennan, ". . . Ice Road," *The Anchorage Times*, November 16, 1968, p. 1.

34. Press release, Office of Governor Walter J. Hickel, December 24, 1968. Hickel papers.

35. The legislature later named the haul road the Dalton Highway.

36. Naske.

37. Alaska Department of Natural Resources, Division of Oil and Gas, *Historical and Projected Oil and Gas Consumption*. Anchorage, May 1999.

38. Roderick, p. 416. The true cost is a matter of dispute.

39. Interview by Mike Wallace, CBS *News 60 Minutes*, November 24, 1969. Hickel archives.

40. See Chapter 8.

41. Roderick pp. 295–296.

42. Letter, Hickel to Gravel, July 25, 1969. Hickel papers.

43. Memos from William Pecora, Director, U.S. Geological Survey, and from Robert S. Byrd, Acting Deputy Assistant Commissioner for Operations, Federal Water Pollution Control Administration, to Assistant Secretary for Fish and Wildlife and Parks, both dated June 27, 1969. Hickel papers.

44. Memo, Russell Train to Hickel, July 3, 1969. Hickel papers.

45. Letter, Train to Hickel, June 30, 1969, covering unsigned meeting minutes memo from the Office of the Secretary of Transportation, June 24, 1969. Hickel papers.

46. Arthur H. Lachenbruch, *Some estimates of the thermal effects of a heated pipeline on permafrost*, undated draft summary. Hickel papers.

47. Years later, Senator Stevens praised the Menlo Park group. With their expertise, he was able to assure Congress that he had reviewed all of the complaints. "That's why we were able to get the pipeline through. It set the stage for Congressional action." Quoted from Roderick, pp. 381–382.

48. Naske, pp. 253–255.

49. Letter, Josef Holbert, press secretary to the Interior Secretary, to Bill

Snedden, Publisher, the *Fairbanks Daily News-Miner*, August 12, 1970. Hickel papers.

50. Holbert to Snedden letter, August 12, 1970.

51. Roderick, pp. 335–343.

### Chapter 7: Caring for the Commons

1. The one other offshore production incident took place the following year in the Gulf of Mexico. Chevron ignored the new regulations, specifically the requirement to have storm chokes on its rigs, leading to a spill during a major storm. With Attorney General John Mitchell's help, we took Chevron to a grand jury in New Orleans, winning indictments on 500 counts. The fine was a record high of $1 million.

2. Immediately following the conference, Strong attended the International Whaling Commission meeting in London and convinced them to adopt a version of the Stockholm resolution.

### Chapter 8: The First Peoples' Commons

1. Charles Wohlforth, "Bowhead Whale Population Up, Study Reveals," *Anchorage Daily News*, April 2, 1990. A census in 2001 of Bowheads in the waters off the North Slope estimated a total of 8,200 animals, matching the highest count ever, *Anchorage Daily News*, June 8, 2001.

2. In the Yup'ik language of St. Lawrence Island, they are called *angyaqs*.

3. Ann Chandonnet, *The Alaska Almanac, 18th ed*. Seattle: Alaska Northwest Books, 1994.

4. Speech to AFN, October 21, 1966. Hickel papers.

5. Robert D. Arnold, et al., *Alaska Native Land Claims*. Anchorage: The Alaska Native Foundation, 1976, p. 119.

6. Hickel, *Native Land Claims, An Address to the People*, February 7, 1967; Hickel papers.

7. Arnold, p. 119.

8. Arnold, p. 119.

9. This provision was not included in the 1971 Alaska Native Claims Settlement Act, but Congress did write it into the Alaska National Interest Lands Conservation Act (ANILCA), which passed in 1980.

10. Remarks before the Indian Affairs Sub-Committee of the House Interior and Insular Affairs Committee by Governor Walter J. Hickel, July 11, 1968. Hickel papers.

11. Don Mitchell, *Sold American; The Story of Alaska Natives and Their Land; The Army to Statehood.* Hanover: University Press of New England, 1997, p. 383. Arnold, p. 140.

12. See Chapter 6.

13. In 1969, Native groups agreed to waive their claims along the pipeline corridor in exchange for jobs and contracts with the oil industry.

14. Arnold, pp. 138–140.

15. Arnold, pp. 144–147.

16. Arnold, p. 411.

17. "The Top 49ers" are picked on the basis of annual gross revenues by the *Alaska Business Monthly.* See October 2000, p. 43.

18. Section 7(i) of ANCSA. The 13th Regional Corporation, consisting of Alaska Natives living outside of Alaska, does not benefit from this provision.

19. "Between Two Worlds," A *Juneau Empire* Special Report, 1998, p. 32.

20. Ibid., p. 36.

21. Ibid.

22. David I. Schwartz, Ed., *Atomic Audit: The Costs and Consequences of U.S. Nuclear Weapons Since 1940.* Washington, D.C.: Brookings Institution Press, 1998.

23. Interior Department Briefing Paper, "Political Future of the Trust Territory," March 20, 1969. Hickel papers.

24. Ron Walker was later appointed Director of the National Park Service.

25. Press conference transcript in May 15, 1969, "Highlights" newsletter of the Office of the High Commissioner, Trust Territory of the Pacific Islands, and Saipan. Hickel papers.

26. *60 Minutes* reported this in a segment called "Who Gives a Damn?" Kissinger denied he made the comment, but I was there and heard him say it.

27. Howard Willens, interview with researcher Charles Wohlforth, May 13, 1999.

## Chapter 9: Setbacks to the Dream

1. The Rockefeller Brothers, for example, contributed both funding and consulting expertise to the Alaska Coalition. Interview by researcher Malcolm Roberts with Chuck Clusen, Director of the Alaska Coalition, April 2001.

2. Robert D. Arnold et al., *Alaska Native Land Claims*. Anchorage: The Alaska Native Foundation, 1976. Arnold indicates that the environmentalists' strategy was to fight against a "quick Native Claims settlement."

3. David Hickok et al., *Alaska Natives and the Land*, p. 537.

4. John McPhee, *Coming into the Country*. New York: Farrar, Straus and Giroux, 1976.

5. Clause-M. Naske, *Alaska, A History of the 49th State*. Norman, OK: University of Oklahoma Press, 2nd ed., 1987, pp. 224–240.

6. Ron Strickland, *Alaskans: Life on the Last Frontier, Divvying Up Alaska*. Stackpole Books, 1992, pp. 96–101. Also see Robert Cahn, *The Fight to Save Alaska*. Audubon, 1982, p. 10.

7. George F. Willis, *Do Things Right the First Time: The National Park Service and the Alaska National Interest Lands Conservation Act of 1980*. U.S. Department of the Interior, National Park Service, 1985.

8. Dr. David Hickok and Mark Ganapole (Hickok), interview with Malcolm Roberts, February 14, 2001.

9. Walter Parker, interview with Malcolm Roberts, February 2001.

10. The Bureau of Land Management offered to field a team but was rebuffed by the Secretary's office. See George Schmidt, BLM Input to the (2) Lands Debate, (d) (2), *Part 2*, Alaska Miners Association, J. P. Tangen, Ed., December 2000, p. 54.

11. This mandate was changed dramatically with the passage of the Federal Land Protection Management Act of 1976 (FLPMA).

12. "Between Worlds," A *Juneau Empire* Special Report, Morris Communications, 1999, p. 3.

13. *D (2), Part 2, op. cit.* p. 55.

14. Roderick Nash, *Wilderness and the American Mind*. New Haven/London: Yale University Press, 3rd ed., 1982, p. 299.

15. *The Washington Post*, May 4, 1978.

16. Walter J. Hickel, *Freedom and the Land*, speech to Citizens for the Management of Alaska's Lands, November 23, 1977.

17. Walter J. Hickel, Speech to Eagle River Kiwanis, December 7, 1977.

18. Ron Birch, interview, March 28, 2000.

19. Cecil Andrus, *Politics Western Style*. Seattle: Sasquatch Books, 1998.

20. Now the location of KeyBank, at the corner of 5th and F Streets.

21. Founding Board Members of Commonwealth North were Governor William A. Egan, Governor Walter J. Hickel, Max Hodel, Helen Fischer,

Morris Thompson, William Sheffield, Robert Hartig, Millett Keller, Carl Brady, Sr., Larry Carr, Henry Hedberg, Loren Lounsbury, Dr. Glenn Olds, Glenn Simpson, William J. Tobin, and Executive Director Malcolm Roberts.

22. *The Anchorage Times,* June 18, 1980, p. B-1.

23. Jimmy Carter, *Keeping Faith, Memoirs of a President.* New York: Bantam Books, 1982, p. 583. Statement by the President upon the signing of ANILCA.

24. In the summer of 2000, former President Carter and Secretary Andrus returned to Alaska to celebrate the 20th anniversary of ANILCA. Speaking on a panel, Carter said he'd been encouraged by members of Ronald Reagan's transition team to finish work on ANILCA before completing his term. Afterward, I asked two leaders of that team well familiar with Western issues—former Senator Paul Laxalt and Reagan Domestic Policy Advisor Martin Anderson—if they knew of such a communication. Both said they didn't. William Casey, a leader of the Reagan campaign, had met with me prior to the election on this issue. I recommended a delay, but he had declined to get the campaign involved before the election. President Carter did not answer a request for further details.

25. The abandonment of sound forest management in Alaska and the betrayal of the workers and their families who depended on the Tongass deserves a book of its own.

26. Commonwealth North, January 2001.

## Chapter 10: The Challenges of Wealth

1. Philip Revzin, "'The Dutch Disease'; Holland's Gas Money Has Brought Affluence and Economic Woes," *The Wall Street Journal,* Monday, December 5, 1977.

2. Interview with Thomas R. Stauffer by researcher Charles Wohlforth, October 7, 1999.

3. Thomas R. Stauffer, *Oil Rich: Spend or Save; How Oil Countries Have Handled Their Windfall,* in *The Trustee Papers; Wealth Management; A Comparison of the Alaska Permanent Fund and Other Oil-Generated Savings Accounts Around the World.* Juneau: Alaska Permanent Fund, April 1988.

4. John Whitehead, "Principles and Interests: The Conference Called by History," Alaska Humanities Forum, Anchorage, 1997, pp. 7–8.

5. Editorial, the *Fairbanks Daily News-Miner,* April 26, 1976, cited in Smith.

6. Ably staffed by Malone's assistant Jim Rhode.

7. State of Alaska, Legislative Finance Division, February 2000. Note: this fourfold increase discounts for both inflation and population growth.

8. Jay Hammond, *Tales of Alaska's Bush Rat Governor*. Fairbanks/Seattle: Epicenter Press, 1994, p. 250.

9. Letter from Katherine Nordale to Permanent Fund Committee on November 17, 1977, quoted in Sheila Helgath and Sarah A. Bibb, *The Alaska Permanent Fund: Legislative History, Intent, and Operations*. Juneau: Alaska State Senate Rural Research Agency, January 1986.

10. Ibid.

11. Bartlett's 1955 speech to the Constitutional Convention, p. 4.

12. Clifford John Groh, *The Permanent Fund Dividend Story*, unpublished manuscript, 1982.

13. John Lindback, "Senate OKs Fund Deposit; $1.1 Billion Put in State Savings," *Anchorage Daily News*, May 9, 1986.

14. Peter J. Smith, "The Alberta Heritage Savings Trust Fund and the Alaska Permanent Fund: A Ten-Year Perspective," in *The Trustee Papers; Wealth Management; A Comparison of the Alaska Permanent Fund and Other Oil-Generated Savings Accounts Around the World*. Juneau: Alaska Permanent Fund, April 1988, p. 27.

15. Oliver Scott Goldsmith, "The Economic Cost of a Rent Induced Business Cycle: The Alaska Petrodollar Boom," *ISER Fiscal Policy Working Paper #3*, presented at Annual Meeting of the Western Regional Science Association, Monterey, California, February 26, 1991.

16. Goldsmith, p. 29.

17. University of Alaska Anchorage, Institute of Social and Economic Research, *Alaska Review of Social and Economic Conditions*, February 1988, Vol. XXV, No. 1.

18. University of Alaska, Anchorage, Institute of Social and Economic Research, *Alaska Review of Social and Economic Conditions*, December 1987, Vol. XXIV, No. 2.

19. Goldsmith, p. 26.

20. Hammond, p. 264.

21. G. Michael Harmon, Associated Press, "Newly found ballots heat up controversy," *Anchorage Daily News*, September 25, 1978.

22. *Anchorage Daily News*, "Postmarks on ballots questioned; Hickel raps absentee votes," September 29, 1978.

23. When I was elected governor in 1990, I disposed of my interest in Yukon Pacific to avoid the perception of a conflict of interest.

24. The speech in its entirety is found in *The Wit and Wisdom of Wally Hickel*, compiled and edited by Malcolm B. Roberts. Anchorage: Searchers Press, 1994, pp. 48–55.

### Chapter 11: Reclaiming the Dream

1. E. Michael Myers, "Spill deal pumped up, put down," *The Anchorage Times*, March 14, 1991. Figures are from the Oil Spill Public Information Center.

2. Ernest Piper, *The Exxon Valdez oil spill: final report, state of Alaska response*. Anchorage: Alaska Department of Environmental Conservation, 1993, pp. 17–19.

3. Statement by Walter J. Hickel, September 19, 1990. Hickel papers.

4. Kim Fararo, "Hickel's independent agenda worries oil chiefs," *Anchorage Daily News*, November 9, 1990.

5. Hickel papers.

6. Piper, p. 167.

7. Charles Wohlforth, "State outlines after-spill Sound," *Anchorage Daily News*, November 30, 1990.

8. Piper, pp. 167–168.

9. Wohlforth.

10. David Postman, "Hickel's idea, secrecy mark spill dealing," *Anchorage Daily News*, March 14, 1991.

11. Postman.

12. Postman, "Oil spill talks continue," *Anchorage Daily News*, January 30, 1991. Allanna Sullivan, "Exxon Receives Offer from U.S., Alaska to Settle Suits Linked to Valdez Oil Spill," *The Wall Street Journal*, February 7, 1991.

13. Postman, January 30 and March 14.

14. Jay Croft and David Futch, "It's a deal: $1.1 billion," *The Anchorage Times*, March 13, 1991.

15. Piper, p. 170.

16. Yosemite has a total of 760,000 acres.

17. *Exxon Valdez* Oil Spill Trustee Council, *1998 Status Report*, Anchorage, 1998.

18. When Congress reauthorized the act, years later, it renamed it the Magnuson-Stevens Act, recognizing the pivotal role of Senator Stevens in its creation.

19. Interview with Clem Tillion by researcher Charles Wohlforth, November 9, 1999.

20. Tom Kizzia, "Hickel rewriting fisheries rulebook; Kodiak fishermen don't like year round plan," *Anchorage Daily News*, January 5, 1991.

21. Wesley Loy, "Fishery Quota Passed; Council Doles Out Halibut, Black Cod," *Anchorage Daily News*, December 9, 1991.

22. Tillion interview.

23. Richard A. Fineberg, "Comment: Only Minutes From Rescue, HB541 Drowned in Special Interests," *Anchorage Daily News*, June 3, 1990.

24. Matt Kohlman, Associated Press, "Hickel Oks higher interest rates on back oil taxes," *Anchorage Daily News*, June 11, 1991.

25. Scott Sutherland, director of government relations, Ducks Unlimited, April 2001.

26. Walter J. Hickel, "Oxyfuels: One Size Does Not Fit All," delivered at *Oil & Gas Journal*'s International Oxygenates Conference, October 3, 1995. Hickel Papers.

27. Hickel, ibid., p. 6.

28. Naske, Claus-M., *A History of Alaska Statehood*. Lanham, Maryland, and London: University Press of America, 1985, p. 272.

29. Office of the Governor, *Alaska First, A Special Briefing by Walter J. Hickel Governor*, October, 1994, p. 13.

## Chapter 12: Energy and Freedom

1. Jeffrey Bartholet of *Newsweek* reported that in three June days and nights on the Coastal Plain he spotted twenty caribou, one peregrine falcon, some plovers, ground squirrels, and "the elusive arctic wooly bear caterpillar," August 13, 2001, p. 22. His experience was not unique.

2. Matthew A. Cronin et al., *Arctic*, Volume 51, No. 2, June 1998, pp. 85–93.

3. Ibid.

4. See *Newsweek* article, August 13, 2001. A six-page article on ANWR features a double-page photo of the Brooks Range and no photos of the mountainless plain.

5. See Chapter 9.

6. Letter from Mayor George Ahmaogak, Sr., March 2001.

7. E. A. Lenart, unpublished report, "Central Arctic Caribou Field Work Summary for 2000," Fairbanks: Alaska Dept. of Fish and Game. See *Wildlife Society Bulletin 2001*, 29(2):764.

8. D. C. Hartman, *Geology and Mineral Evaluation of the Arctic National Wildlife Range, Northeast Alaska*, 1973.

9. C. G. Mull, and B. A. Kososki, *Hydrocarbon potential of the Arctic National Wildlife Range Alaska*, U.S.G.S., Department of Interior, 1976.

10. U.S.G.S., *The Oil and Gas Resource Potential of the Arctic National Wildlife Refuge 1002 Area, Alaska*, Open File Report 98–34, 1999.

11. Energy Information Administration, Office of Oil and Gas, U.S. *Department of Energy*, Potential Oil Production from the Coastal Plain of the ANWR: Updated Assessment, May 2000.

12. Ibid., p. viii.

13. www.anwr.org

14. *Anchorage Daily News*, July 1, 2001, p. A-8.

15. Tom Knudson, *The Sacramento Bee*, "Environment Inc.," reprinted in *Anchorage Daily News*, July 1, 2001.

16. Ibid., p. A 11.

17. Steven C. Amstrup, *Distribution of Polar Bear Maternal Dens on Land in Northern Alaska, Spring 1982 through Spring 2001*, U.S.G.S. Biological Resource Division Alaska Biological Science Center Polar Bear Research Project, June 8, 2001.

18. Reprinted in "The Voice of the Times," *Anchorage Daily News*, June 13, 2001.

19. The U.S. House of Representatives passed President Bush's energy bill in August 2001, including a provision to permit drilling on the Coastal Plain. At this writing, the issue is before the U.S. Senate.

## Chapter 13: Hope and a Model for the World

1. U.N. High Commissioner for Refugees, *The State of the World's Refugees*. Oxford University Press, 1997.

2. U.N. Food and Agriculture Organization, *Report on Worldwide Hunger, 1999*, as quoted in *Anchorage Daily News*, October 15, 1999, p. A-11.

3. Maurice Strong, *Where on Earth Are We Going?* Toronto, Canada: Alfred A. Knopf, 2000, p. 40.

4. See Chapter 4.

5. That small number includes summer workers fighting forest fires and cleaning up campgrounds, restaurant inspectors, septic tank regulators, and many other employees who are not managers.

6. The International Water Management Association estimates that by 2025, two billion people will face "absolute water scarcity."

7. Nikolayev, Mikhail, *The Northern Forum*. Yakutsk, Russia: Republic of Sahka, 2000.

# Index

# About ICS

Founded in 1974, the Institute for Contemporary studies (ICS) is a nonprofit, nonpartisan, policy research institute.

To fulfill its mission to promote self-governing and entrepreneurial ways of life, ICS sponsors a variety of programs and publications on key issues including education, entrepreneurship, the environment, leadership, and social policy.

Through its imprint, ICS Press, the Institute publishes innovative and readable books that further the understanding of these issues among scholars, policymakers, and the wider community of citizens. ICS Press books include the writing of eight Nobel laureates and influence the setting of the nation's policy agenda.

ICS programs seek to encourage the entrepreneurial spirit not only in the U.S. but also around the world. They include the Institute for Self-Governance (ISG) and the International Center for Self-Governance (ICSG).